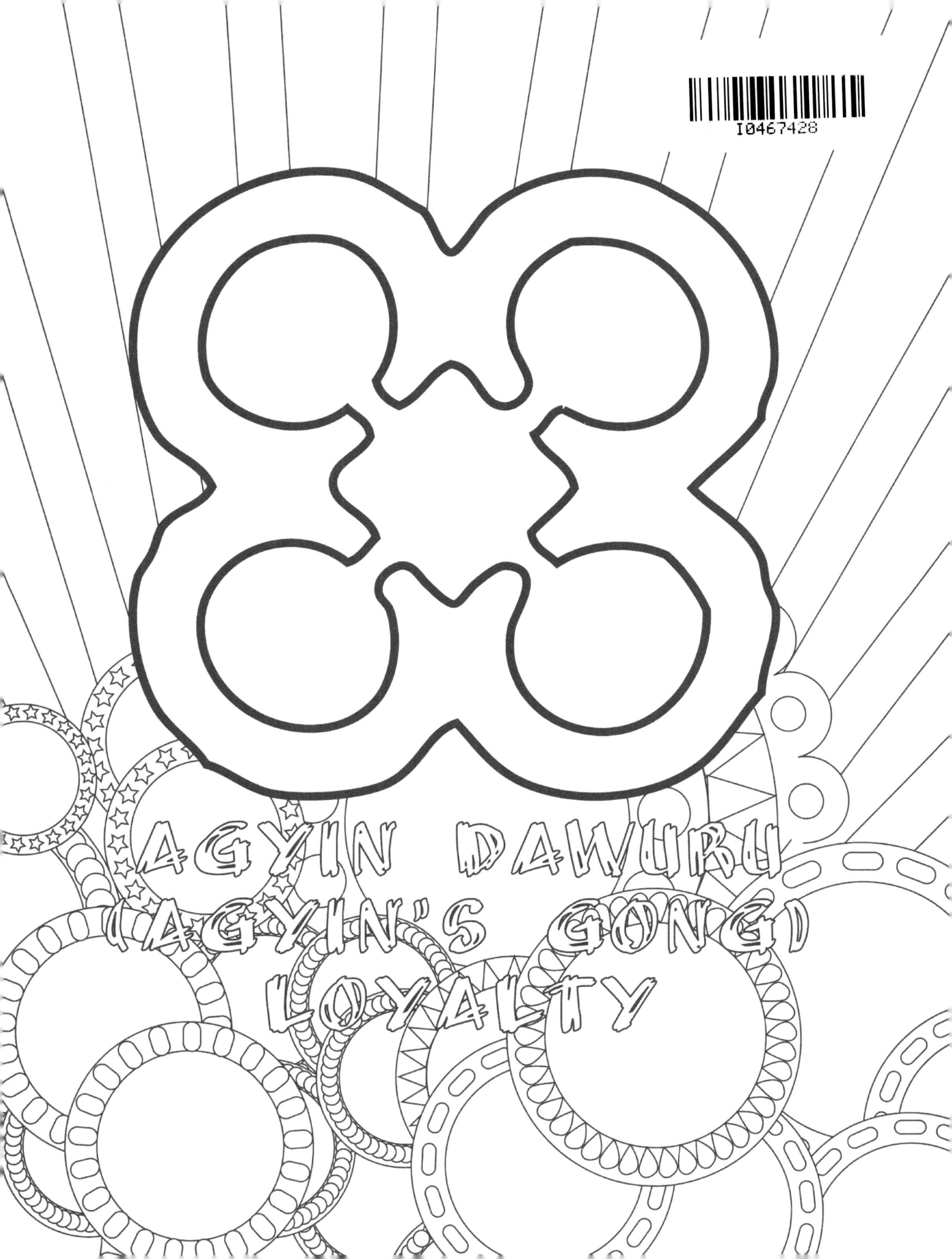

AGYIN DAWURU
(AGYIN'S GONG)
LOYALTY

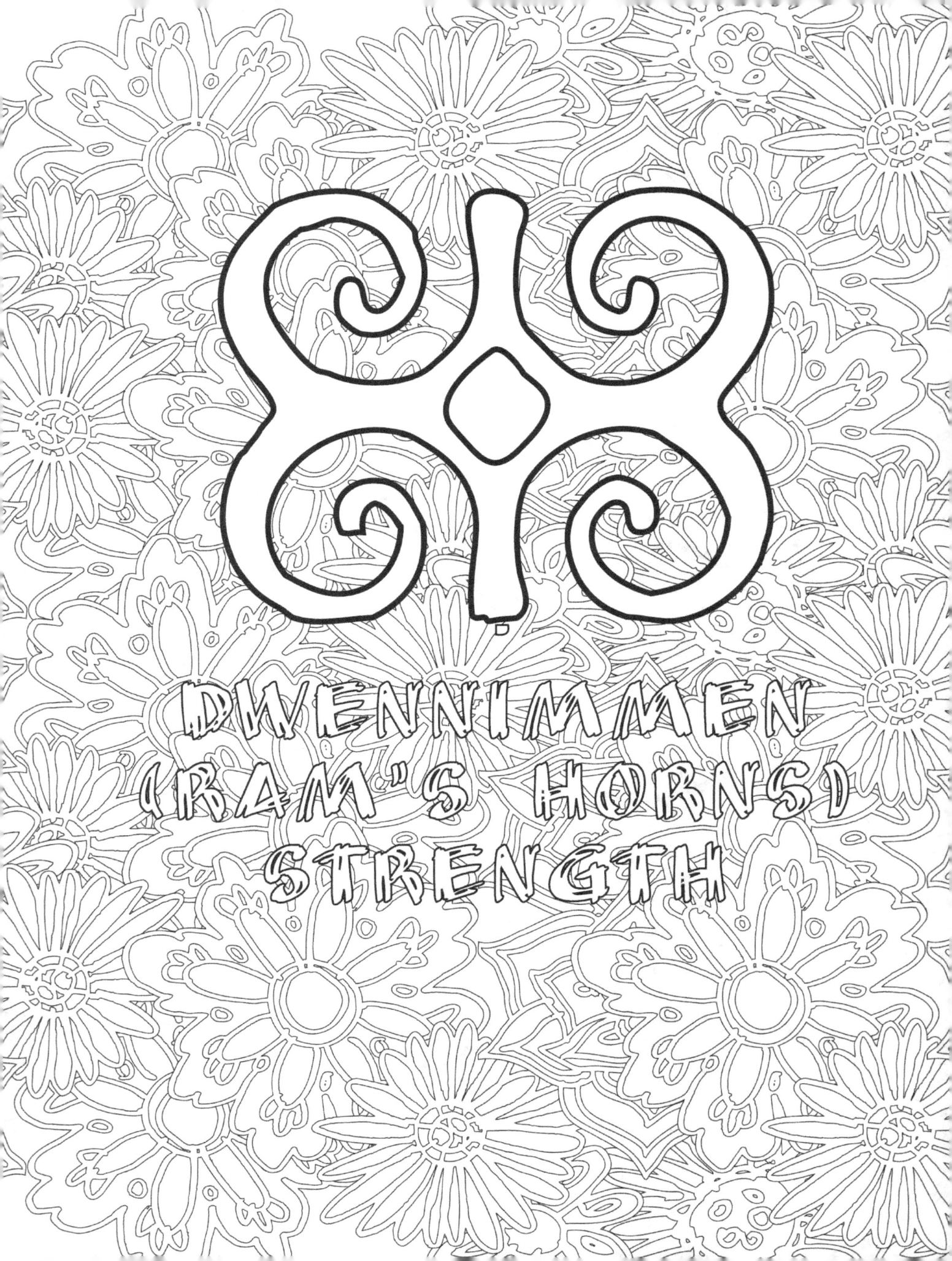

DWENNIMMEN
(RAM'S HORNS)
STRENGTH

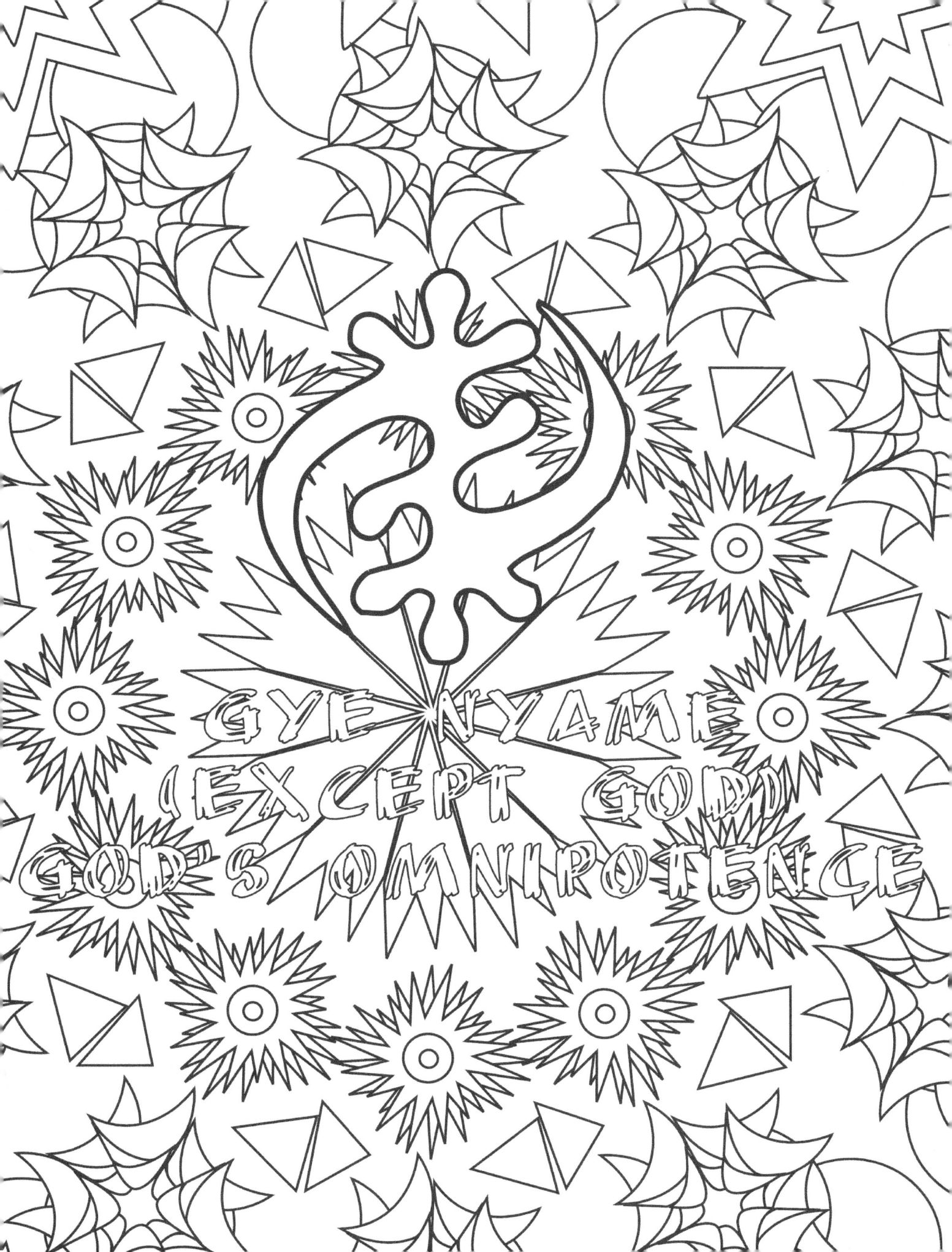

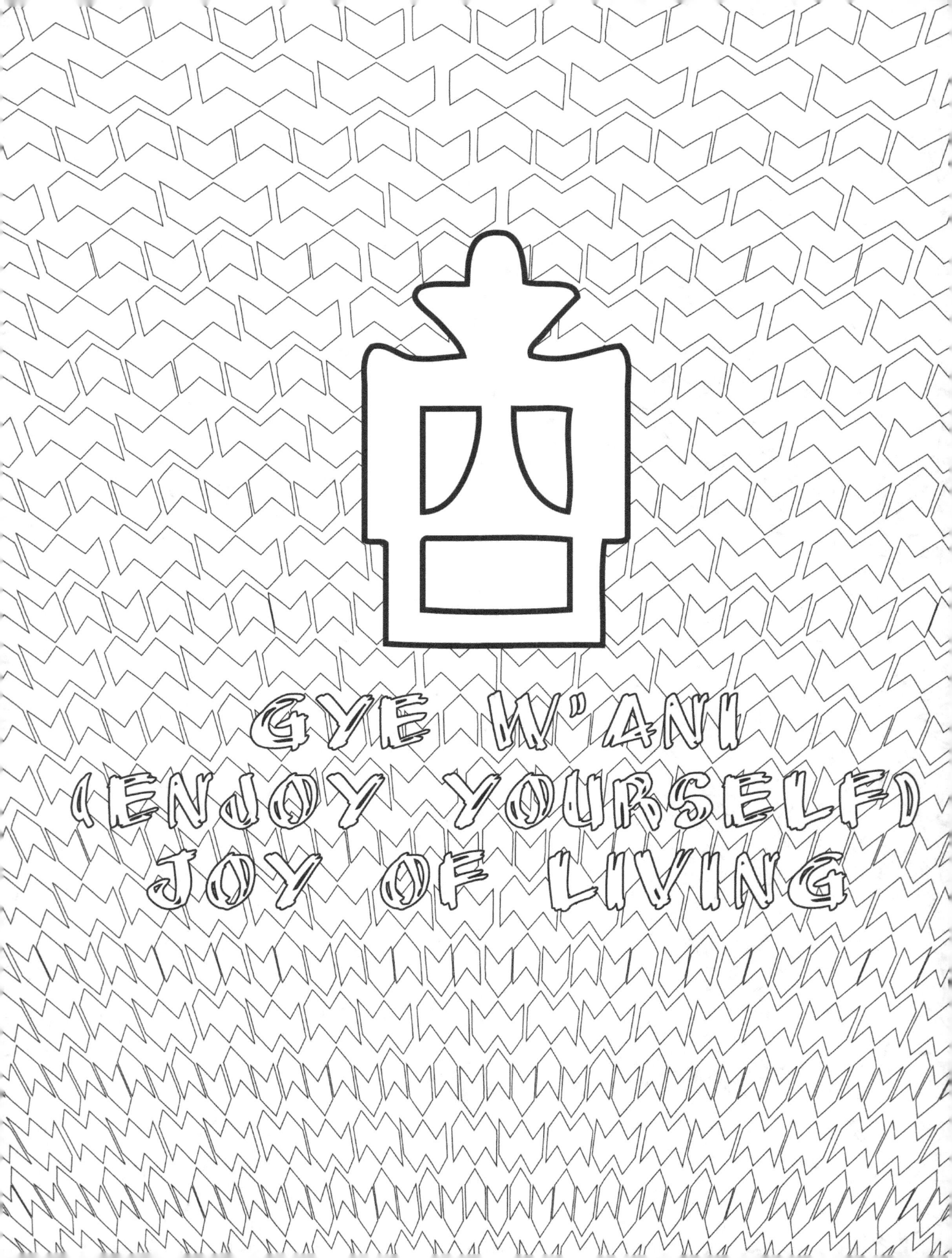

GYE W'ANI
(ENJOY YOURSELF)
JOY OF LIVING

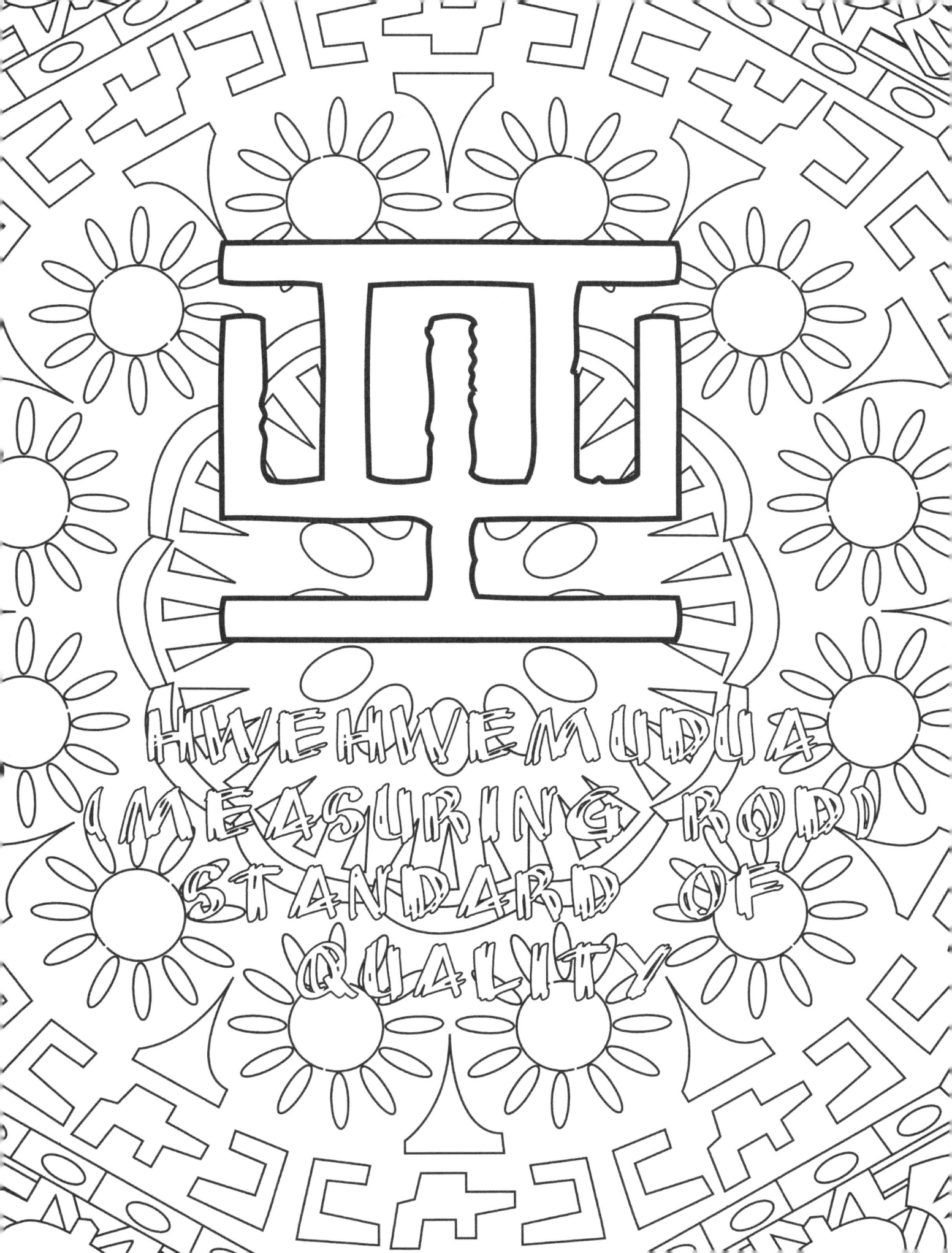

HWEHWEMUDUA
(MEASURING ROD)
STANDARD OF
QUALITY

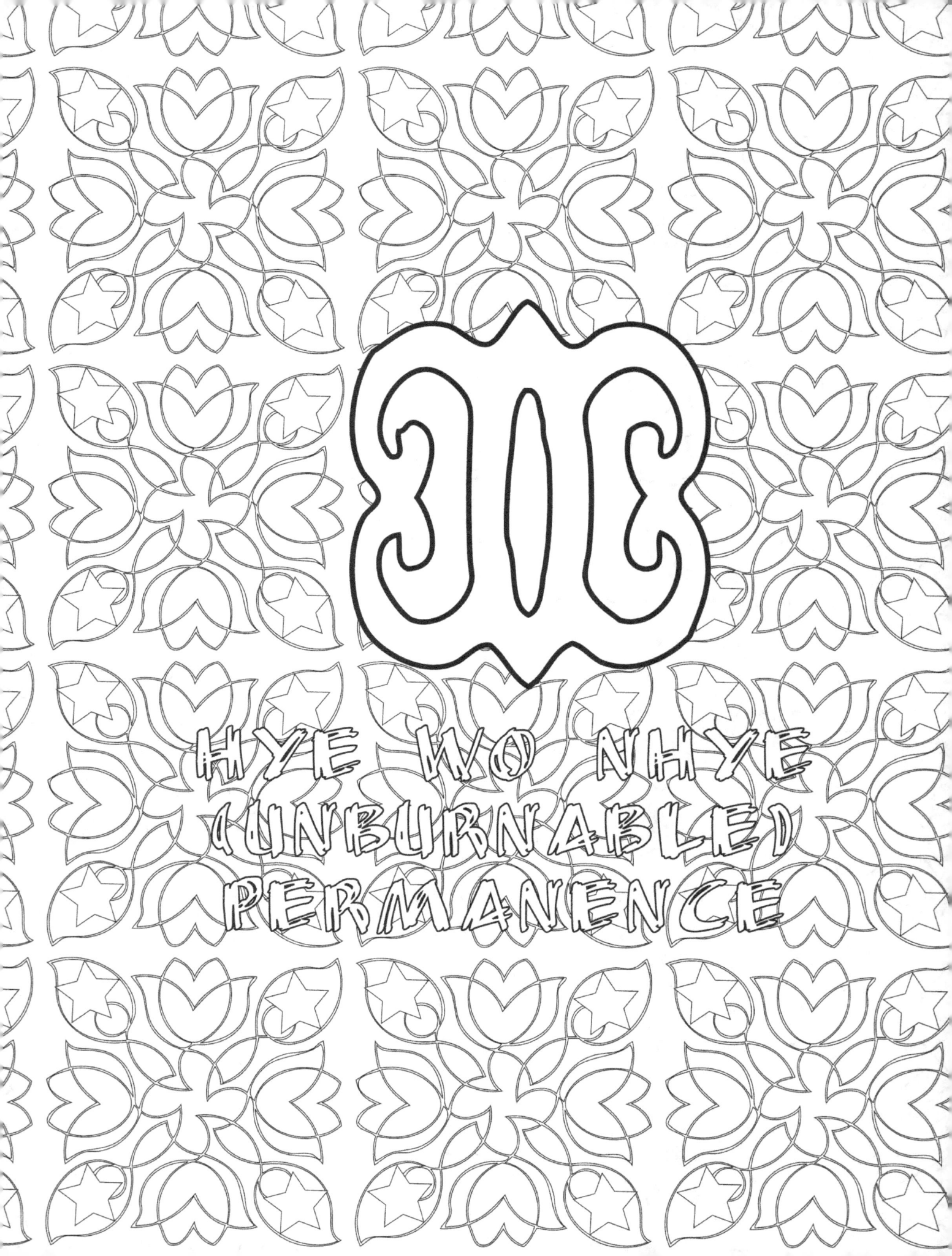

HYE WO NHYE
(UNBURNABLE)
PERMANENCE

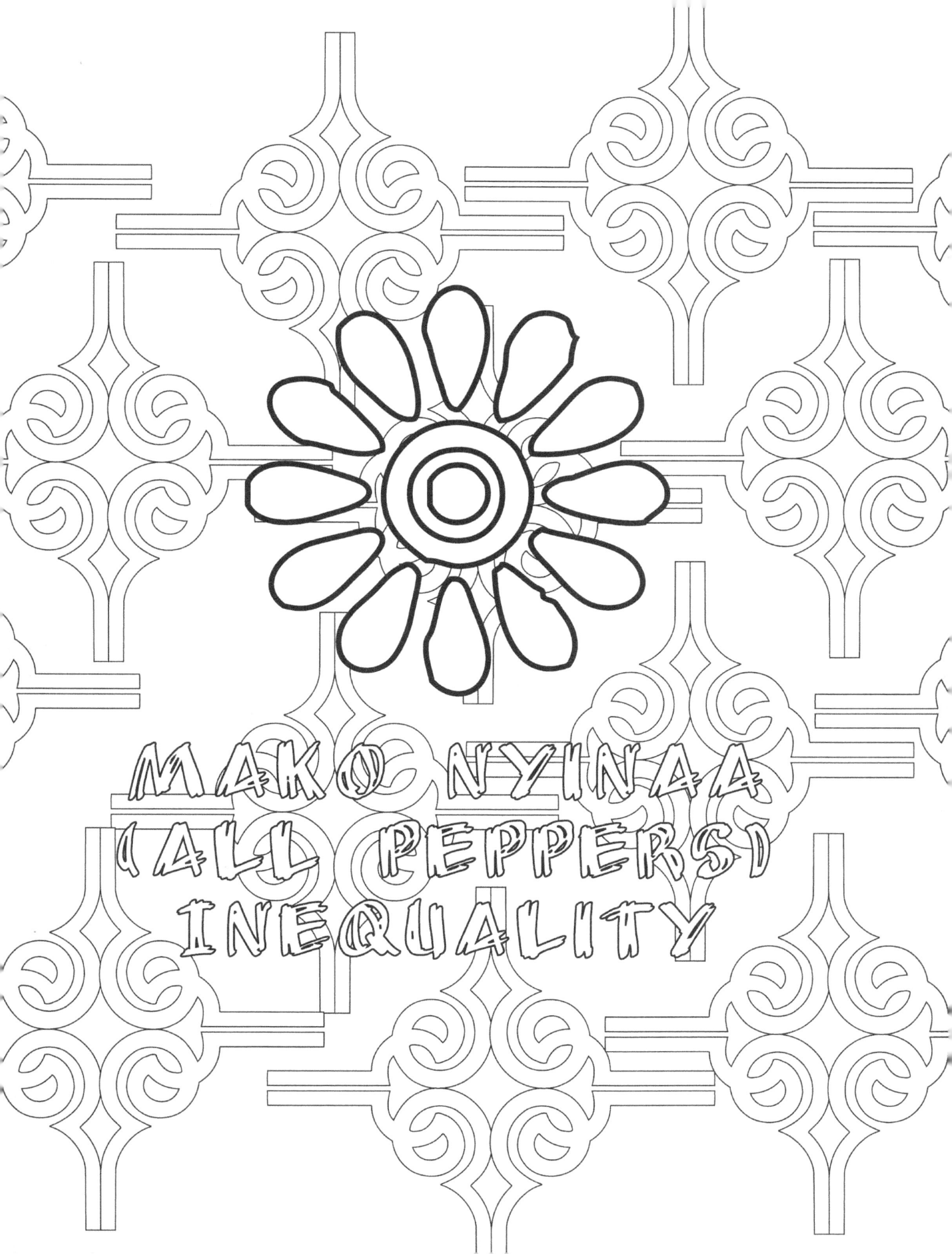

MAKO NYINAA
(ALL PEPPERS)
INEQUALITY

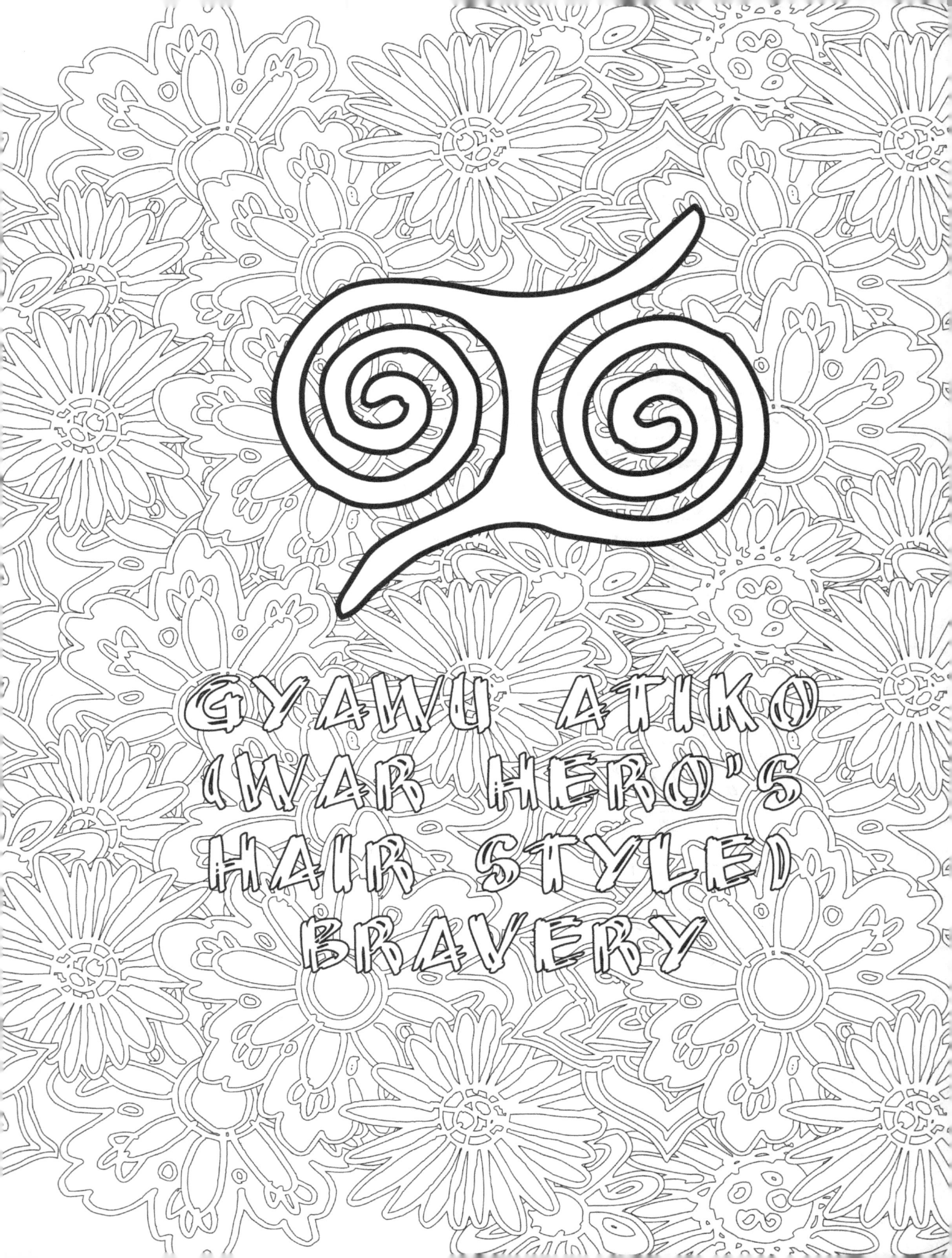

GYAWU ATIKO
("WAR HERO'S
HAIR STYLE)
BRAVERY

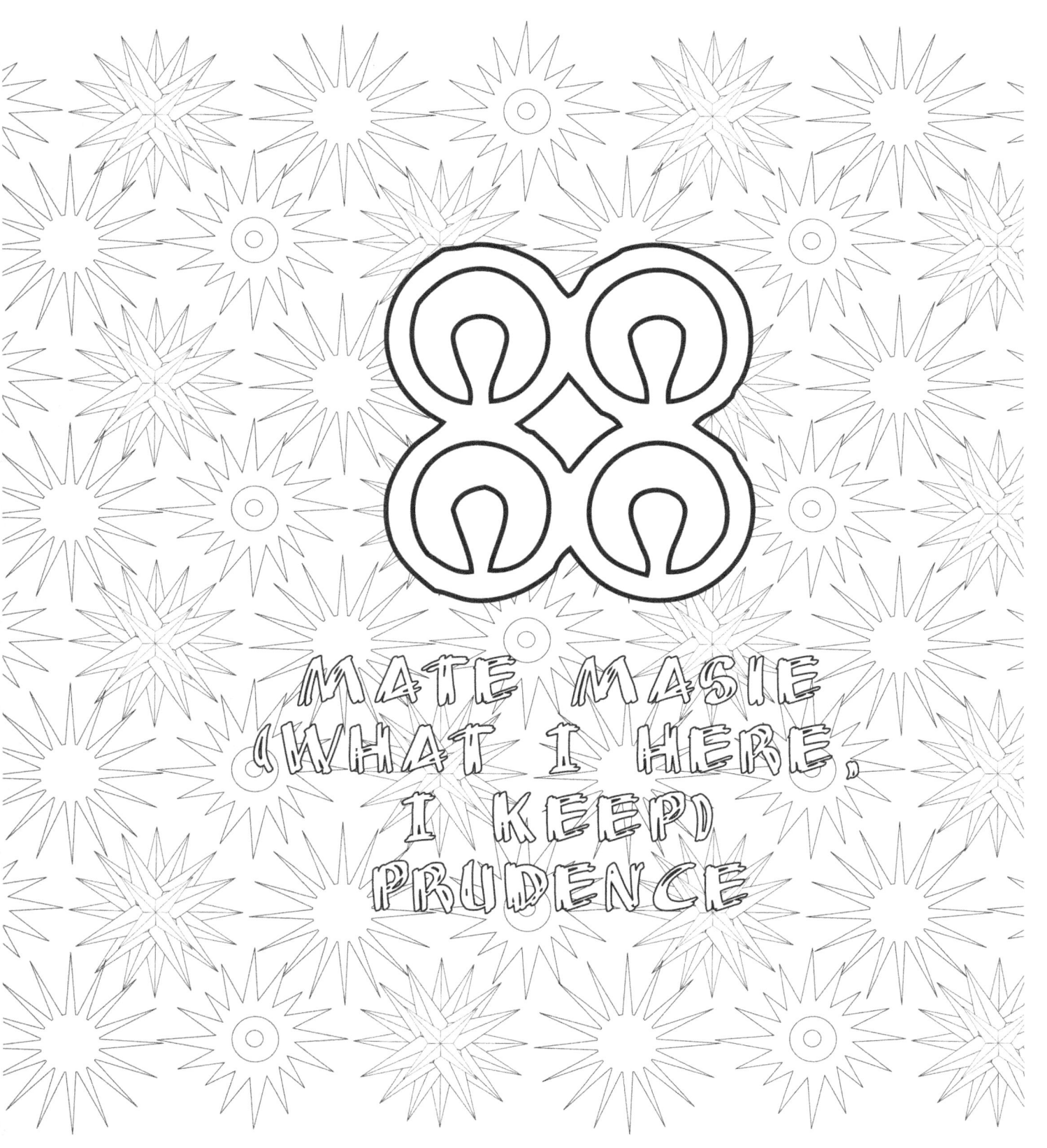

MATE MASIE
(WHAT I HERE,
I KEEP)
PRUDENCE

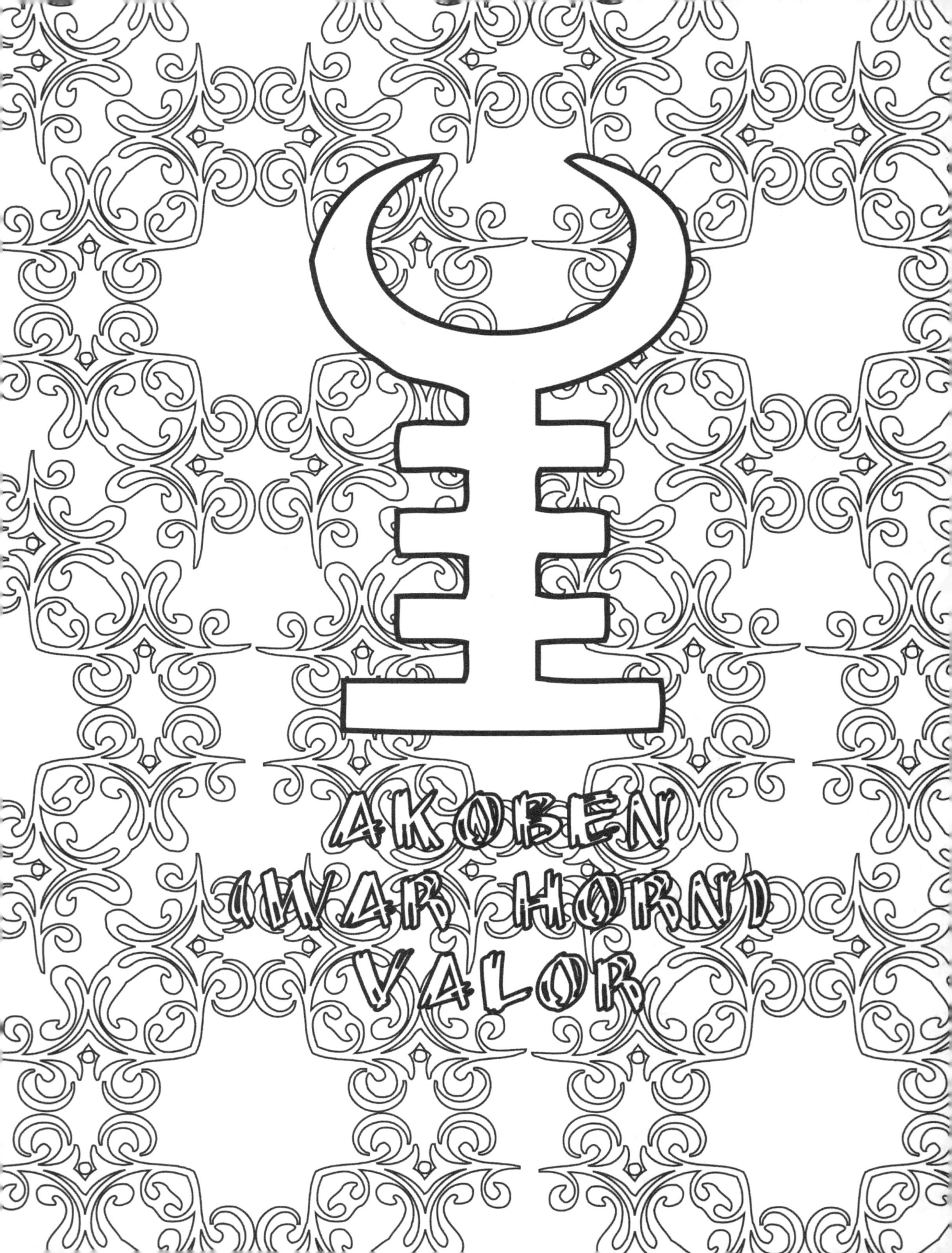

AKOBEN
(WAR HORN)
VALOR

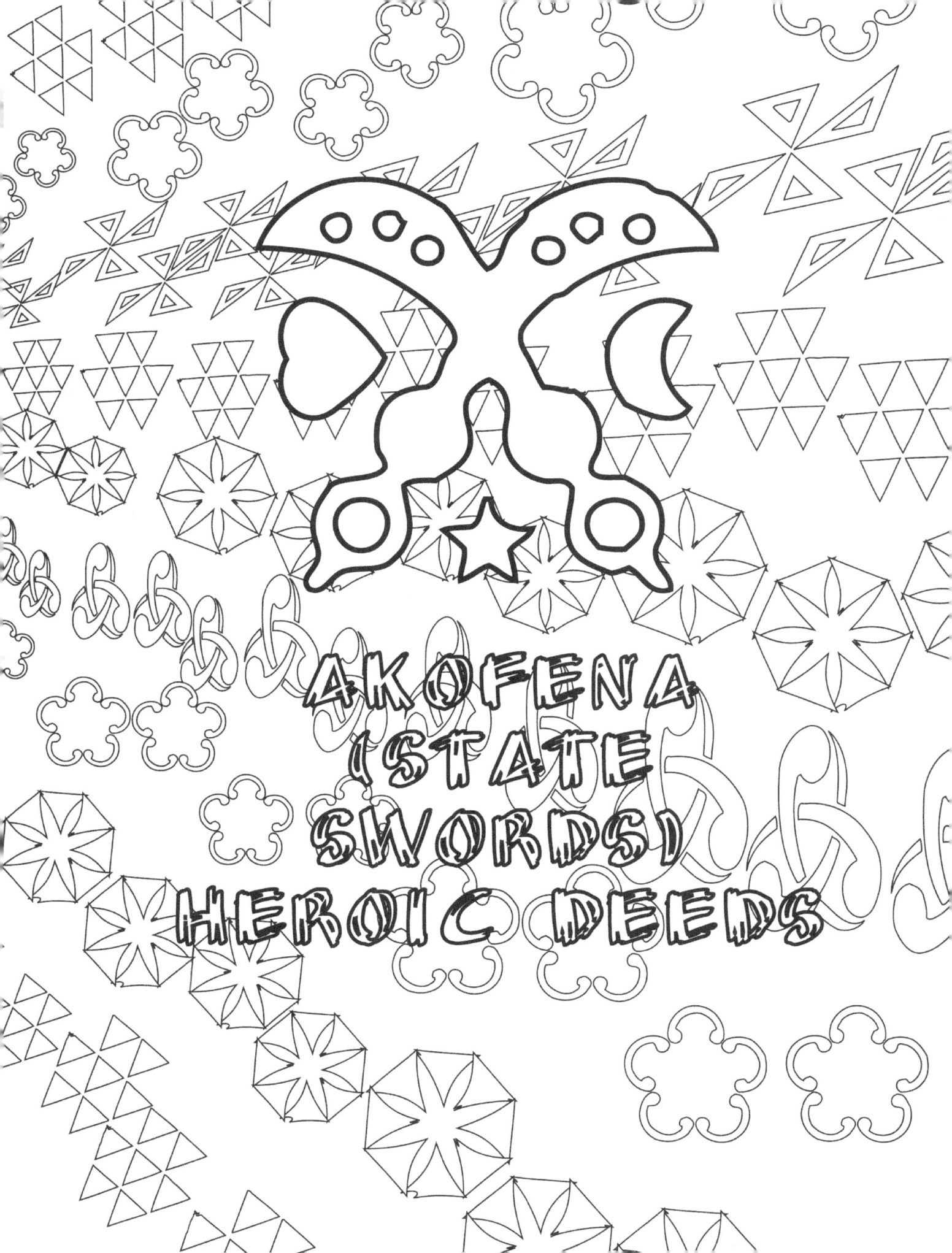

AKOFENA
(STATE
SWORDS)
HEROIC DEEDS

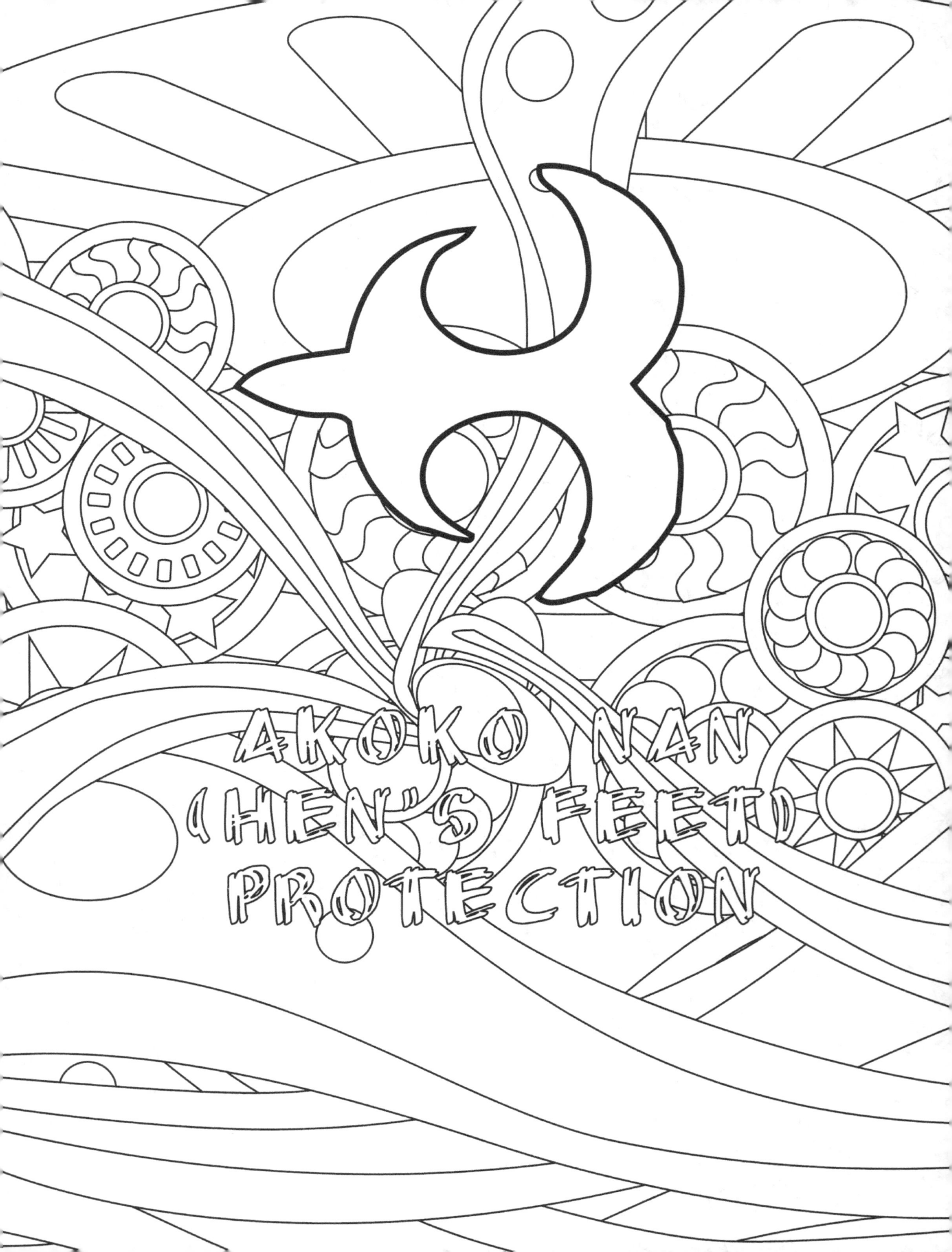

AKOKO NAN
("HEN'S FEET")
PROTECTION

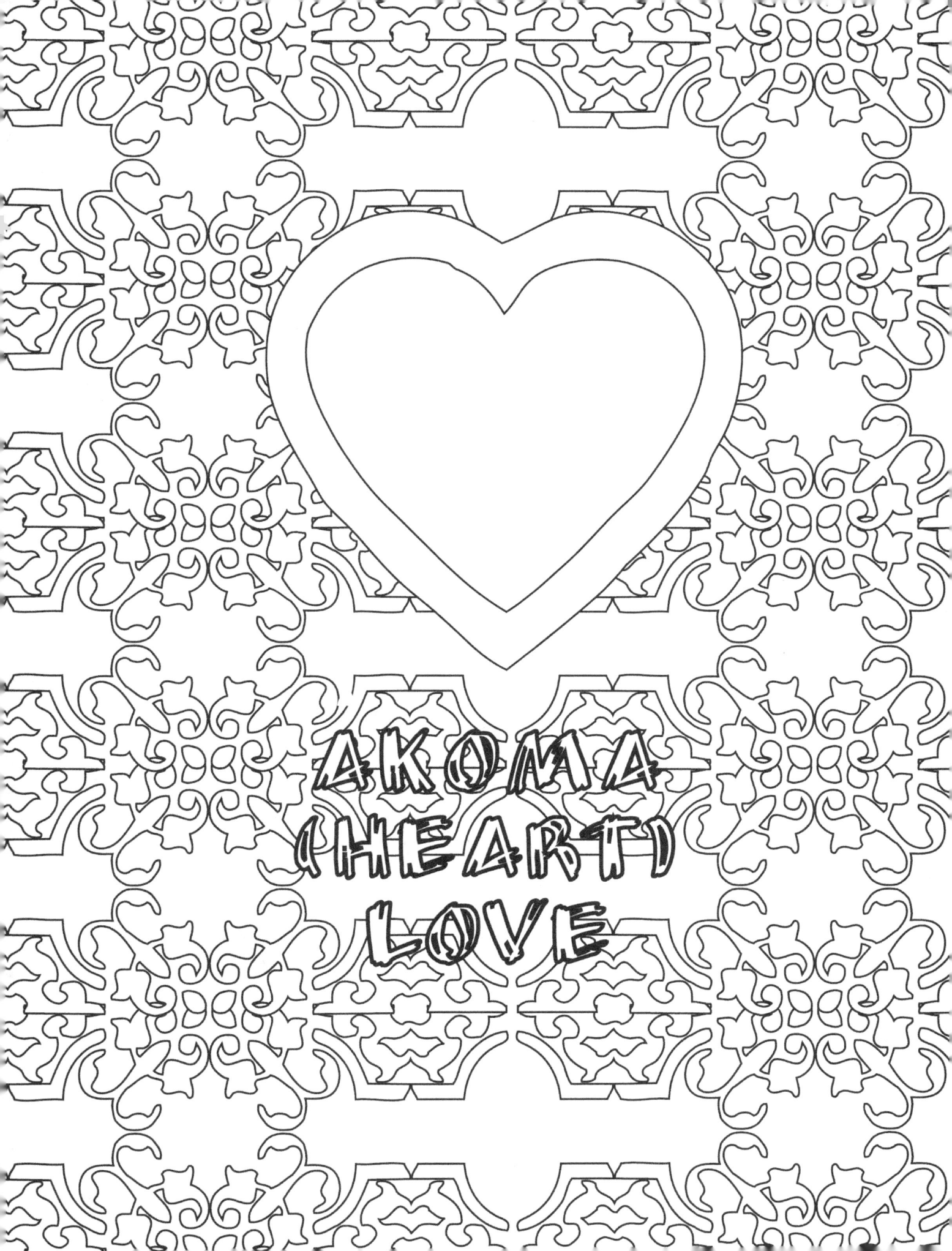

AKOMA
(HEART)
LOVE

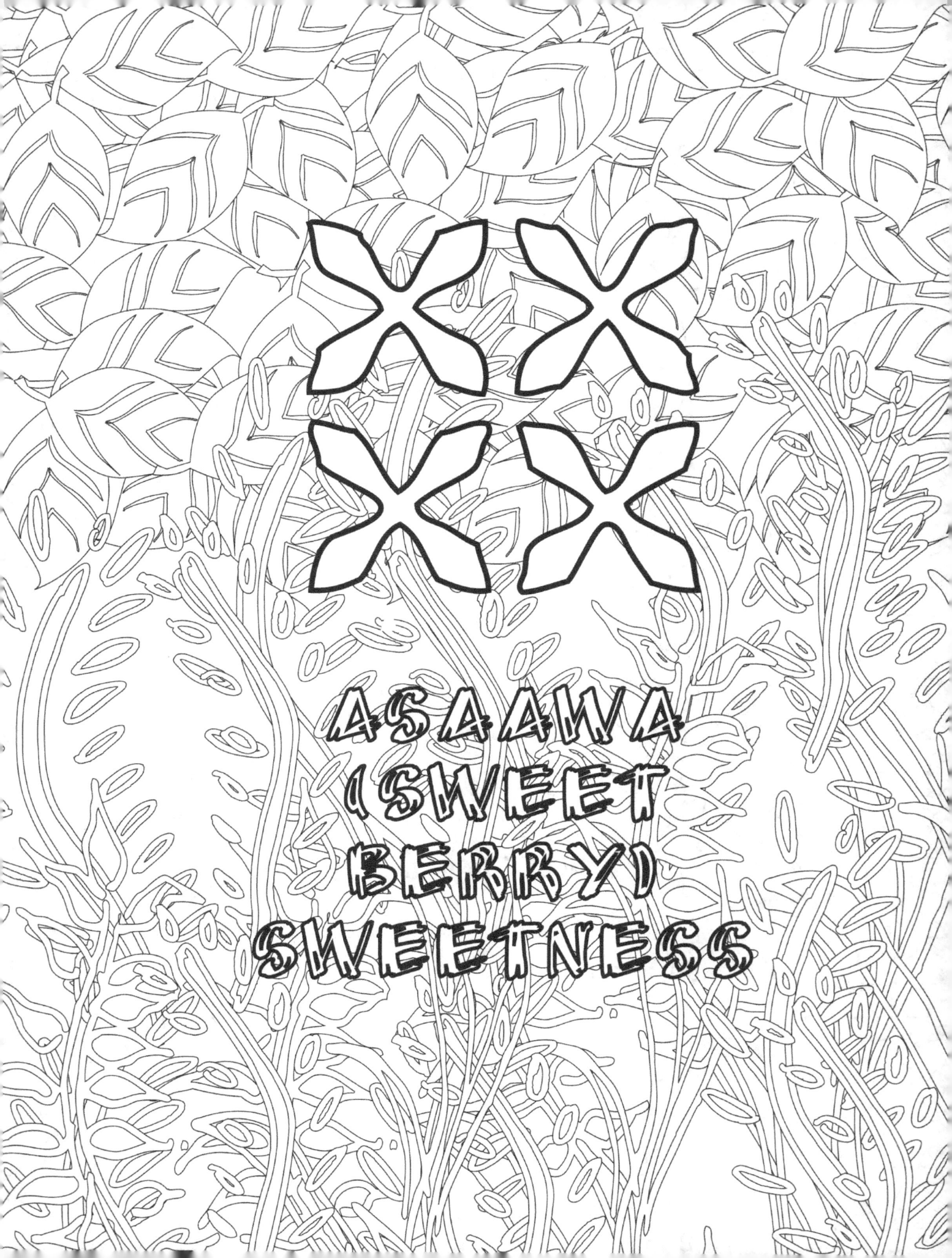

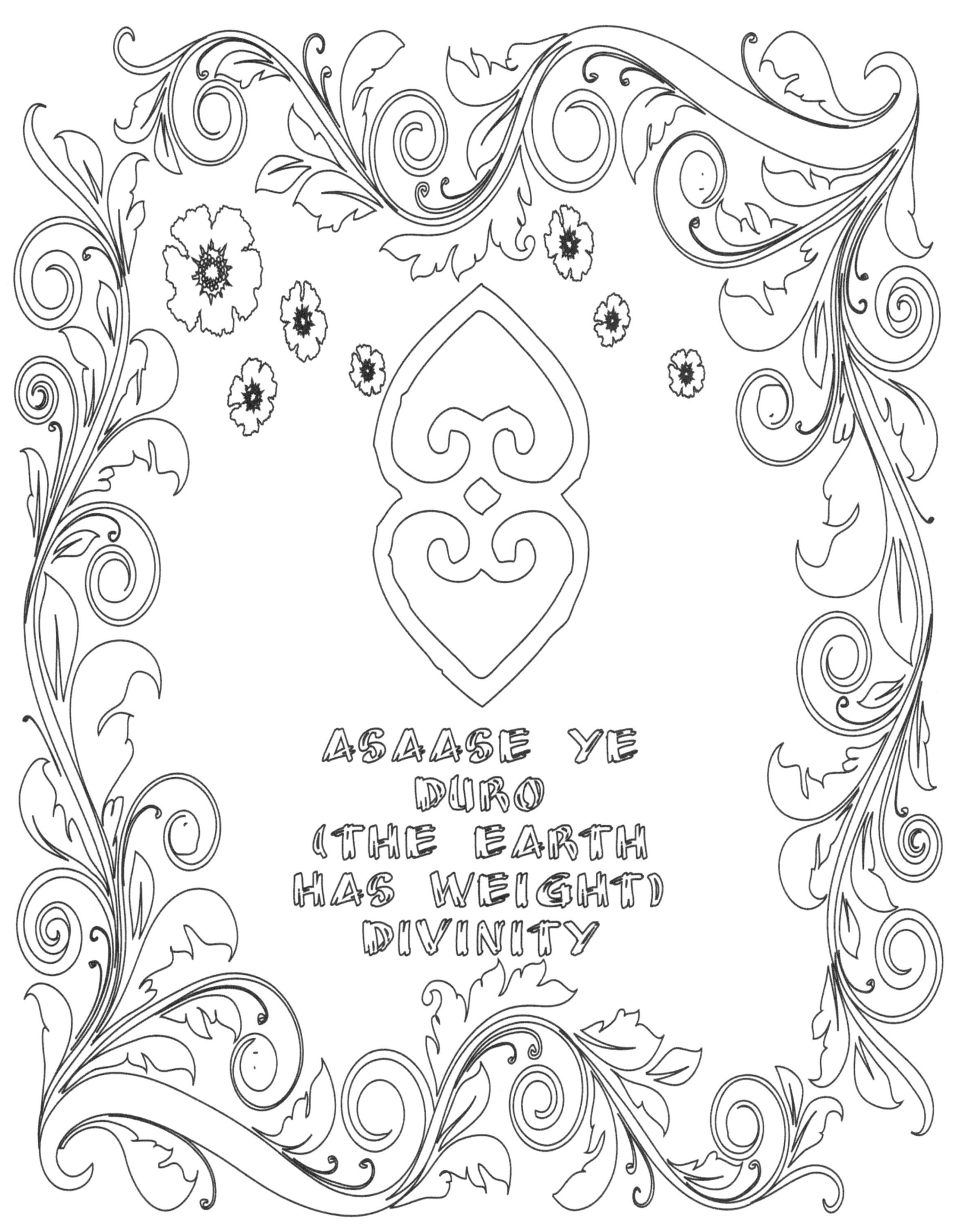

ASAASE YE
DURO
(THE EARTH
HAS WEIGHT)
DIVINITY

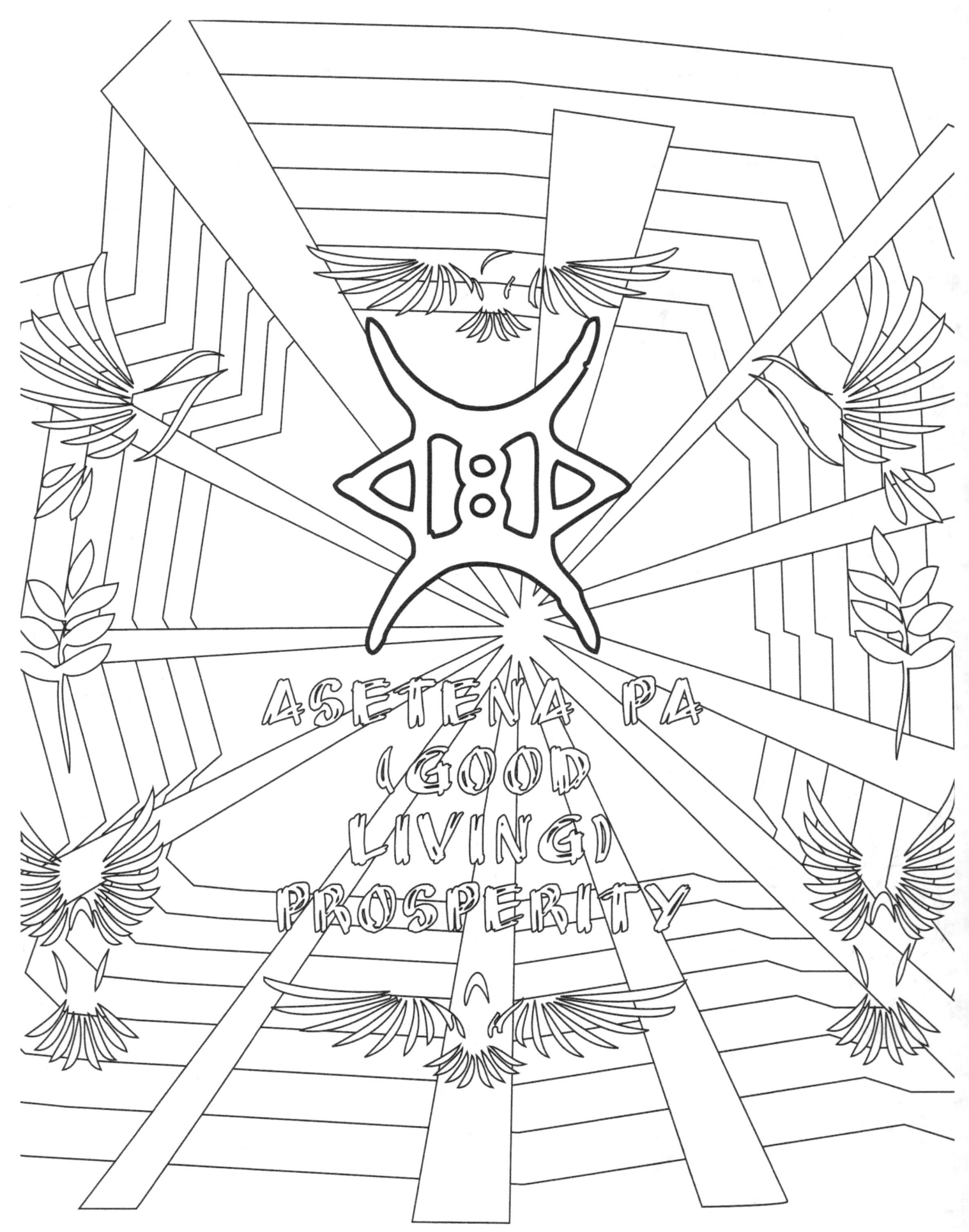

ASETENA PA
(GOOD
LIVING)
PROSPERITY

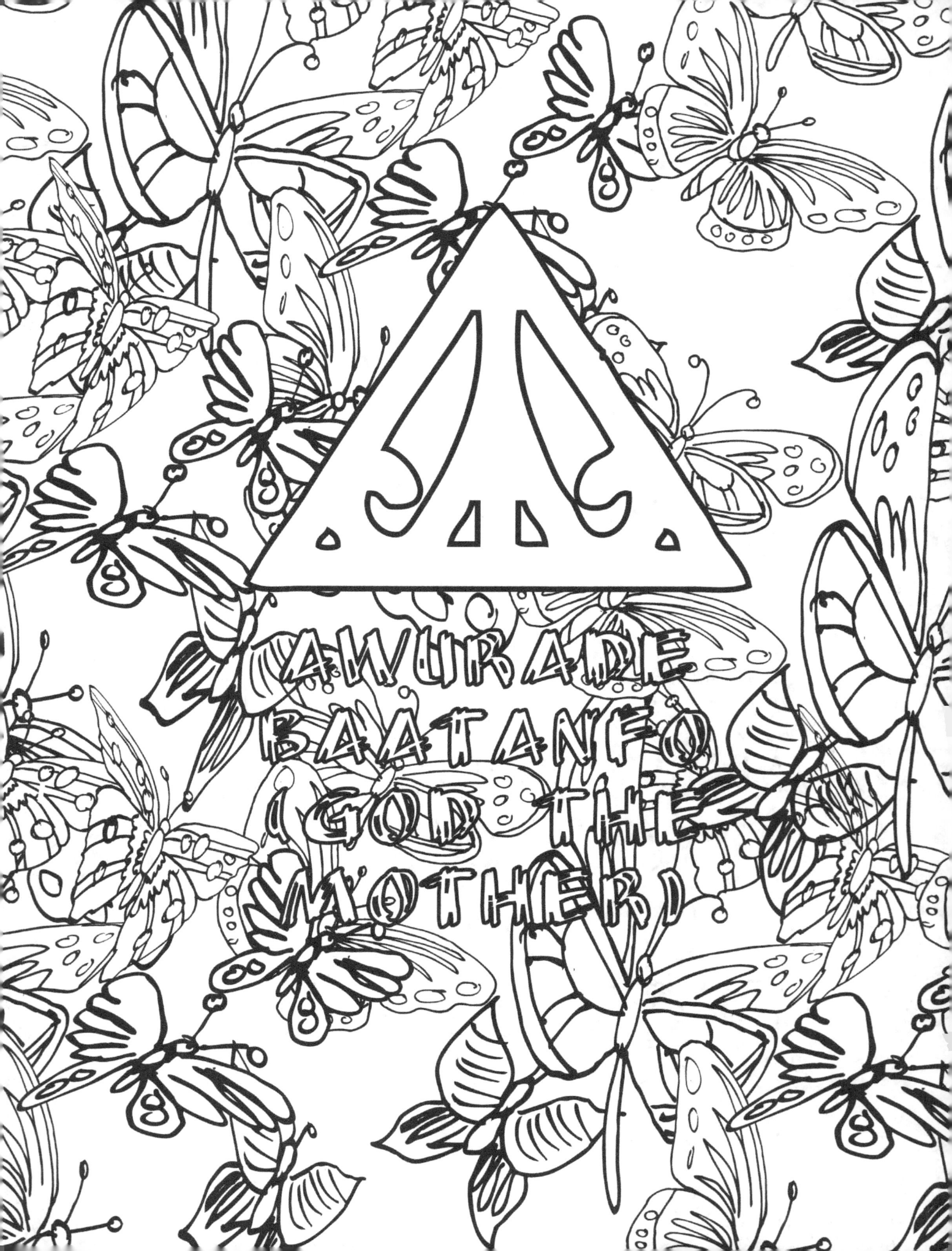

AWURADE BAATANFO (GOD THE MOTHER)

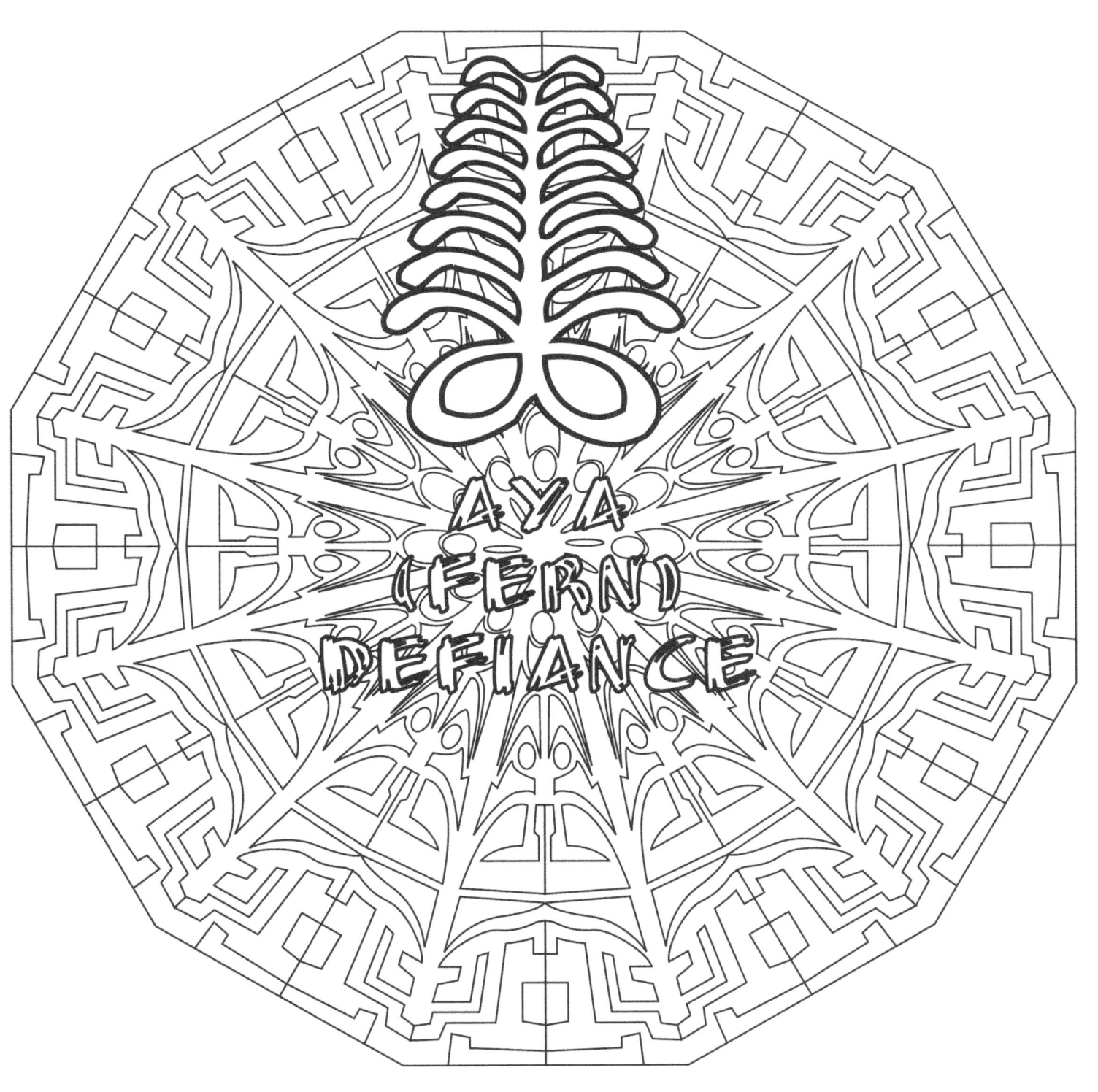

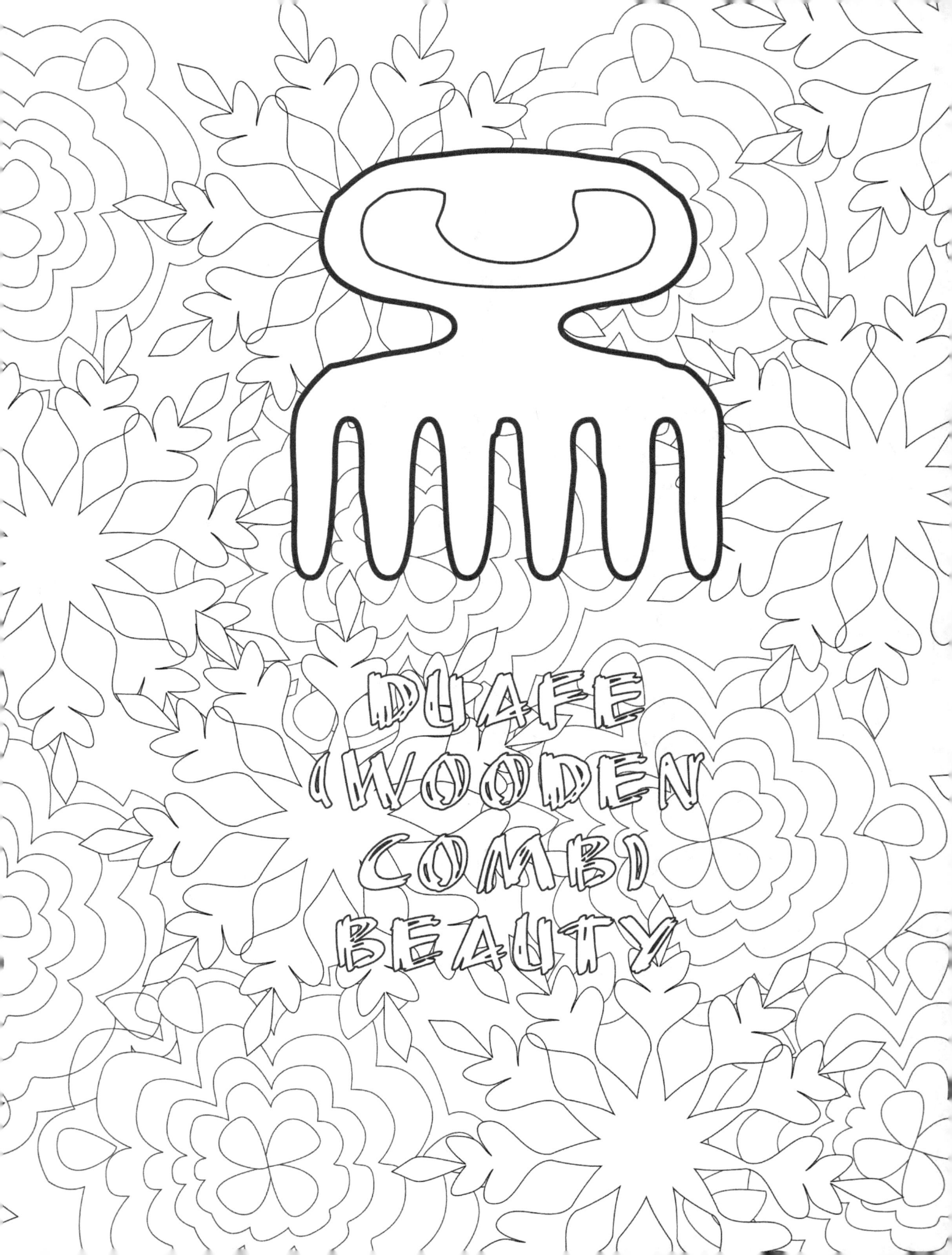

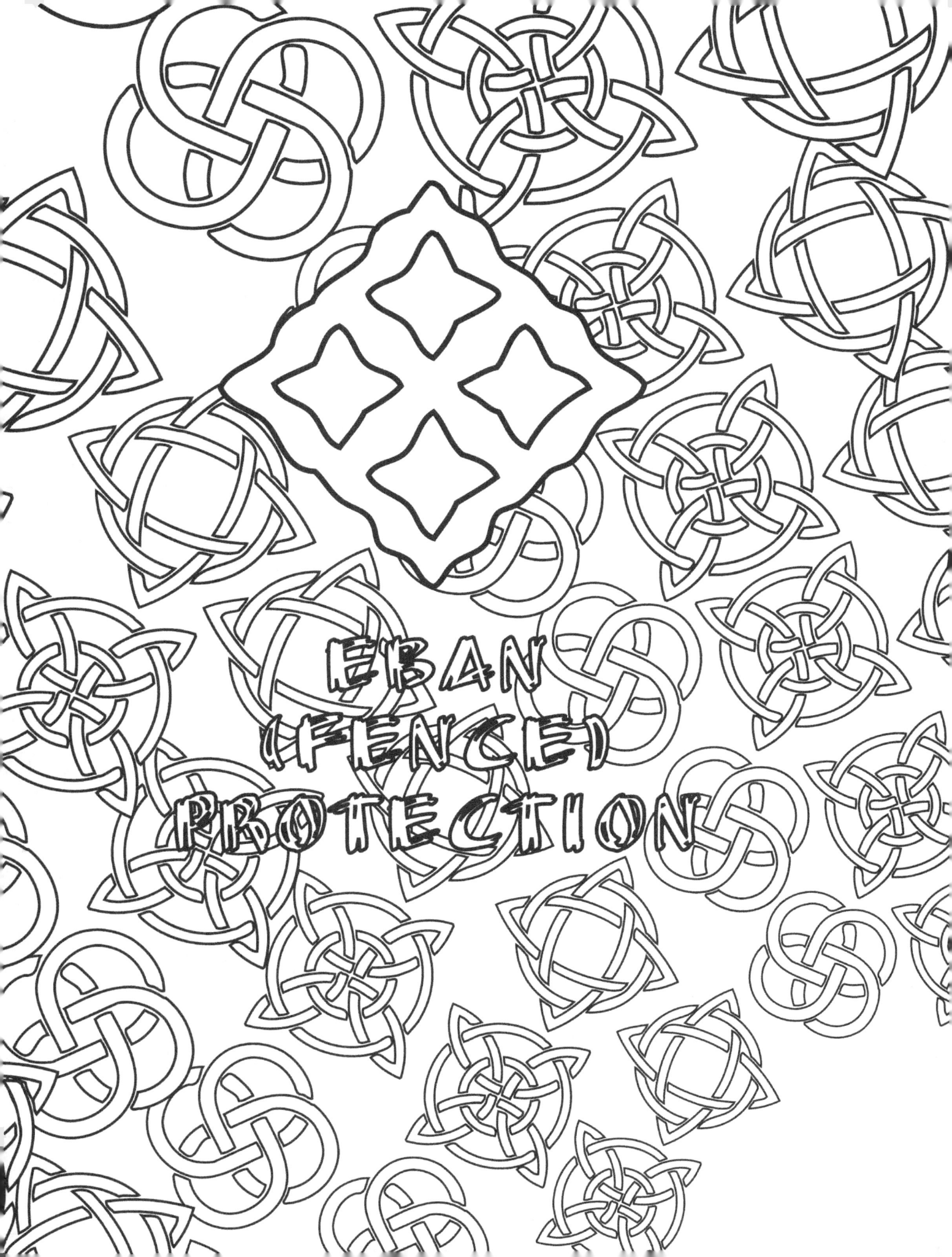

EBAN
(FENCE)
PROTECTION

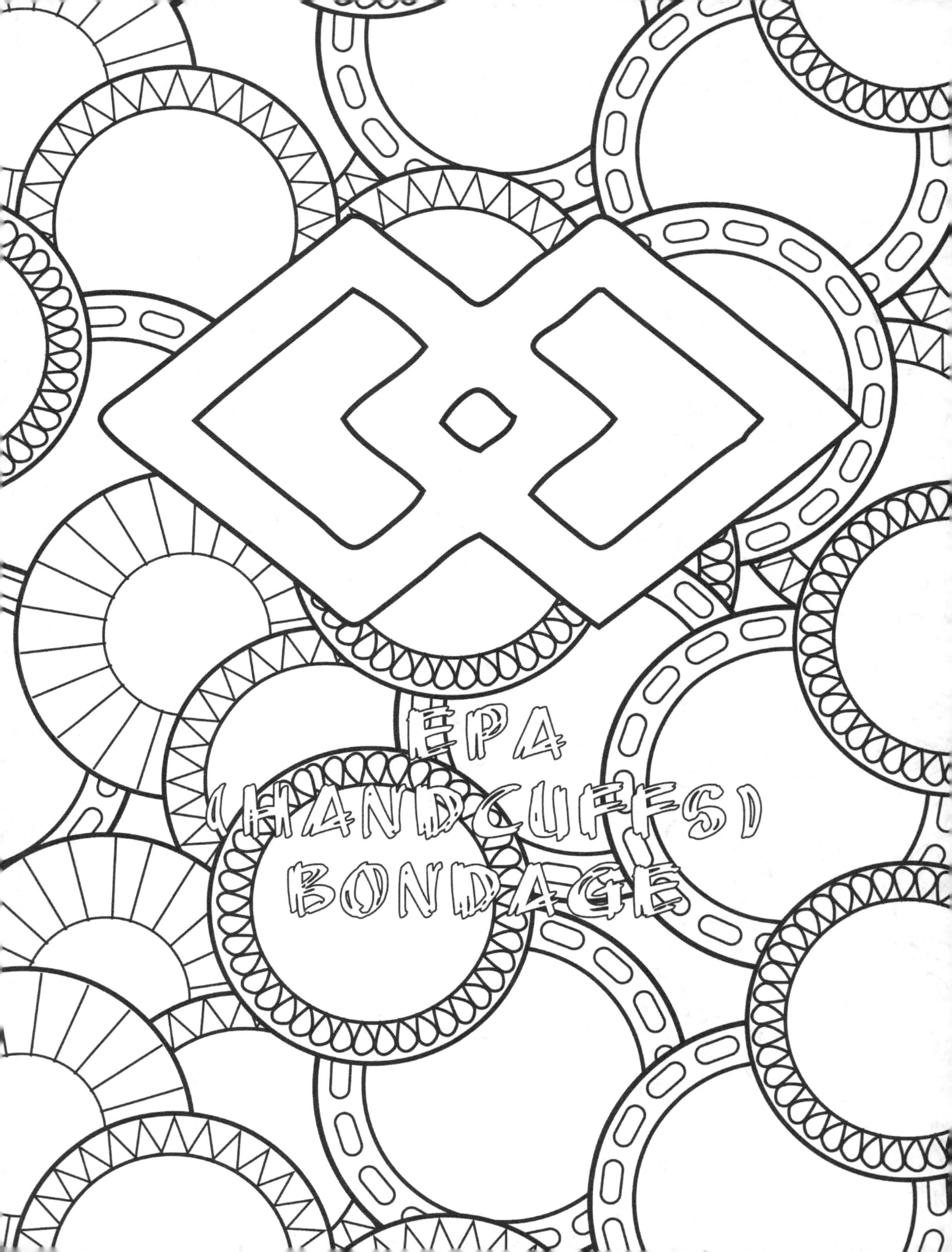

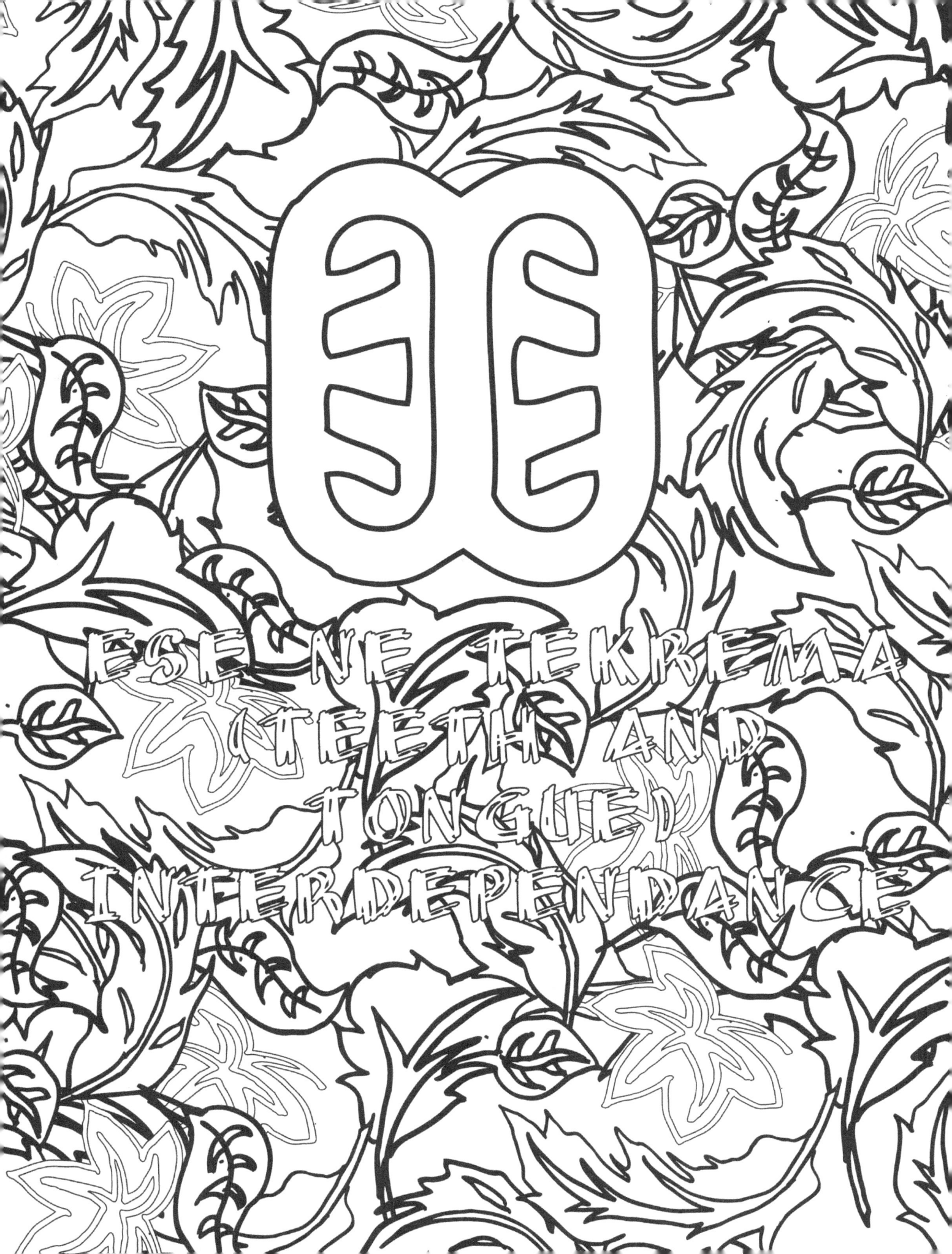

ESE NE TEKREMA
(TEETH AND
TONGUE)
INTERDEPENDANCE

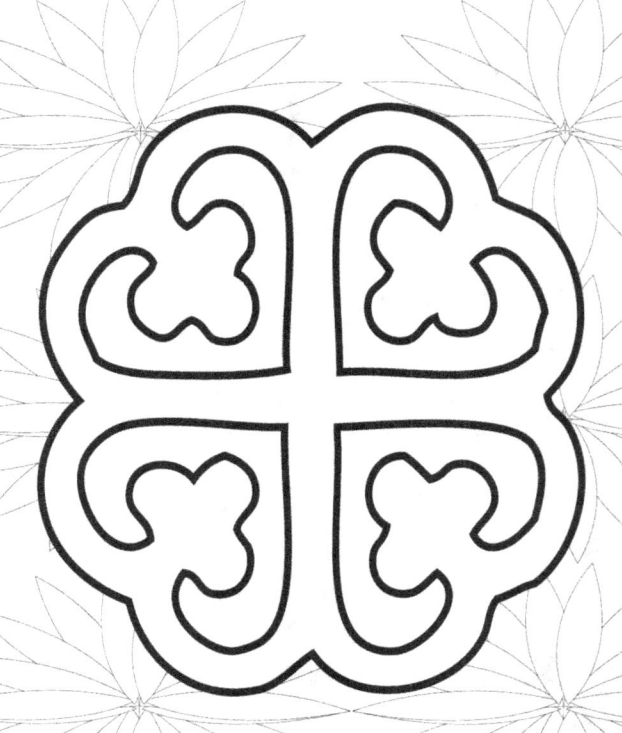

NYAME DUA
(GOD'S ALTER)
GOD'S PROTECTION

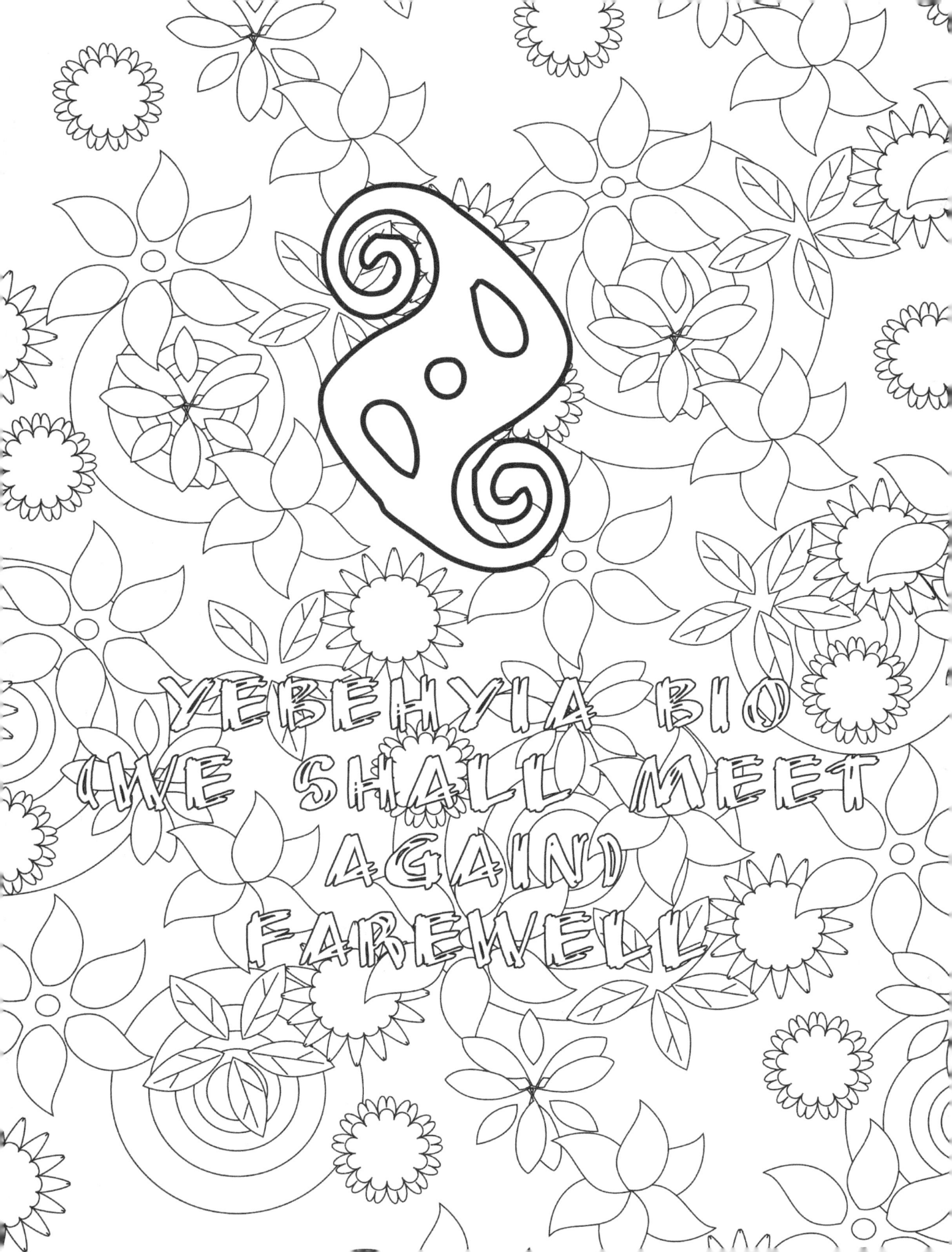

YEBEHYIA BIO
(WE SHALL MEET
AGAIN)
FAREWELL

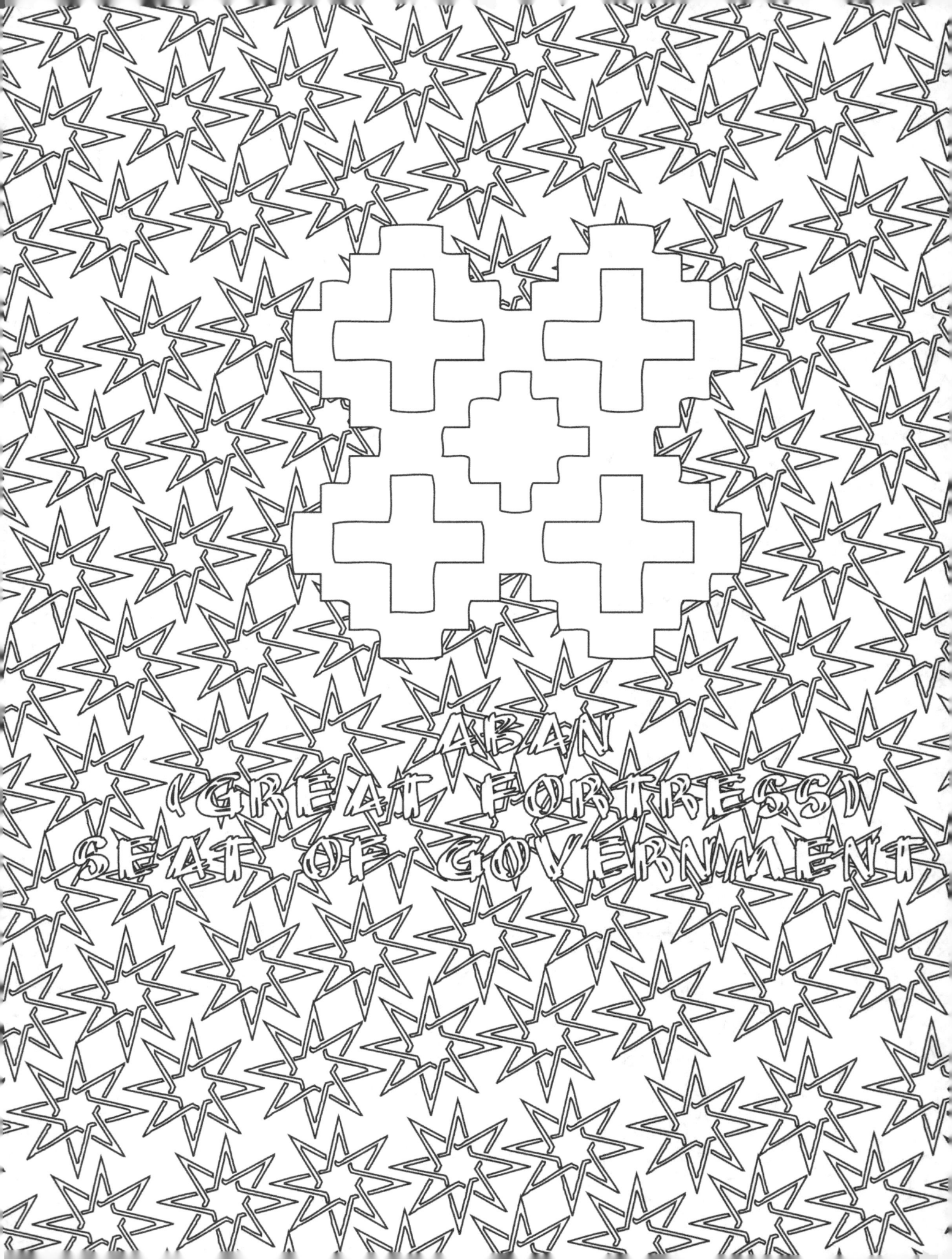

ABAN
(GREAT FORTRESS)
SEAT OF GOVERNMENT

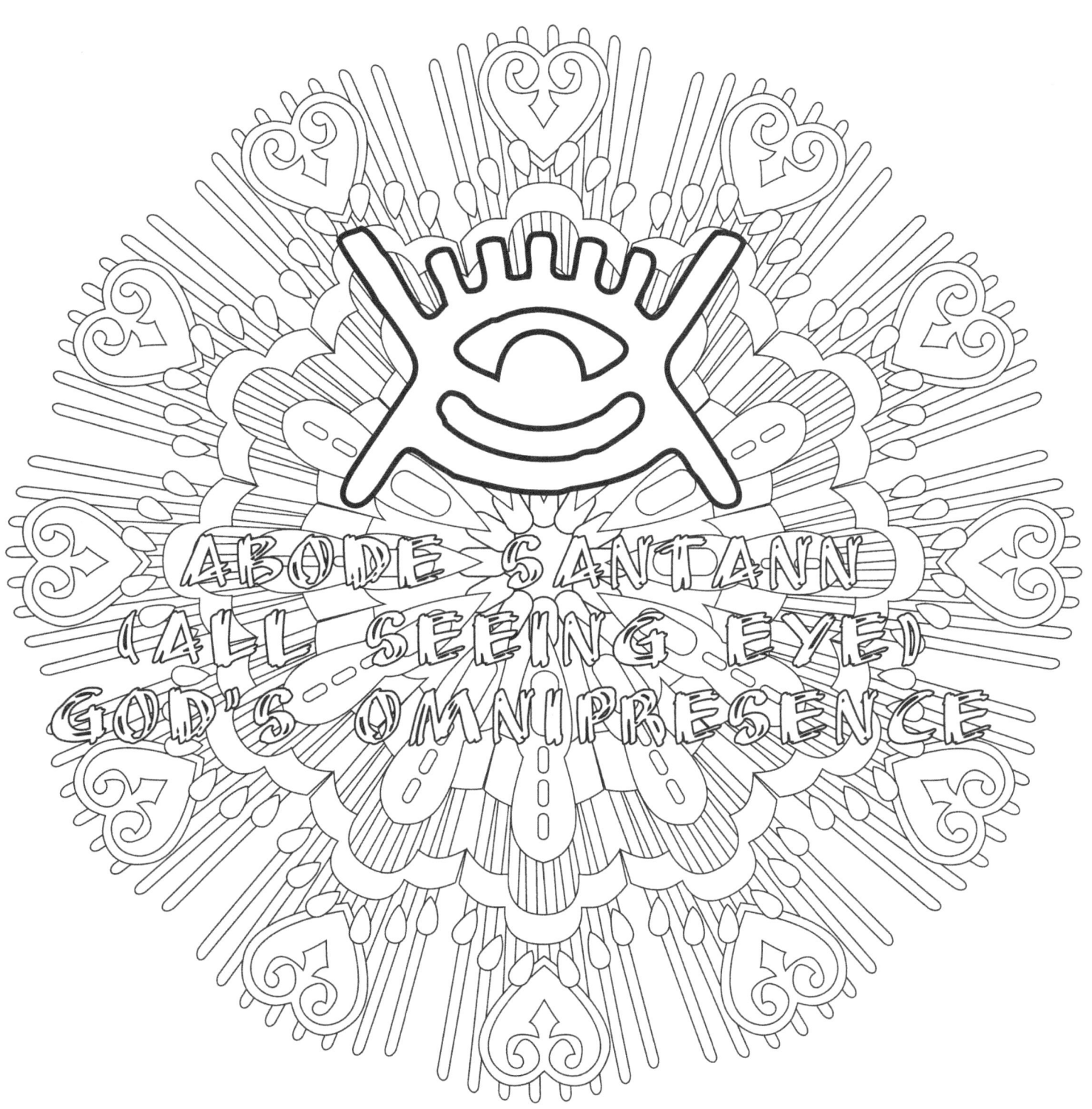

ABODE SANTANN
(ALL SEEING EYE)
GOD'S OMNIPRESENCE

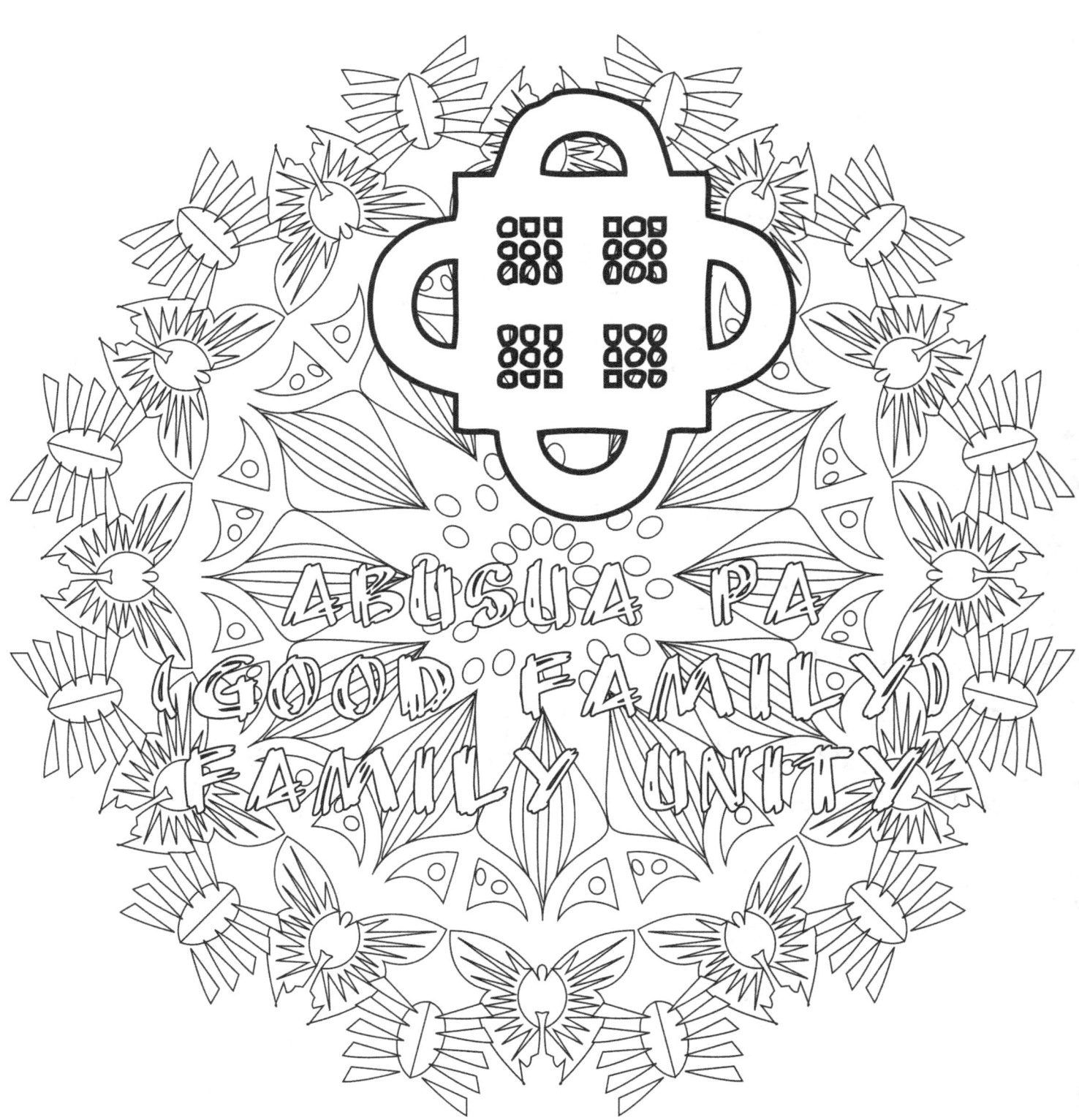

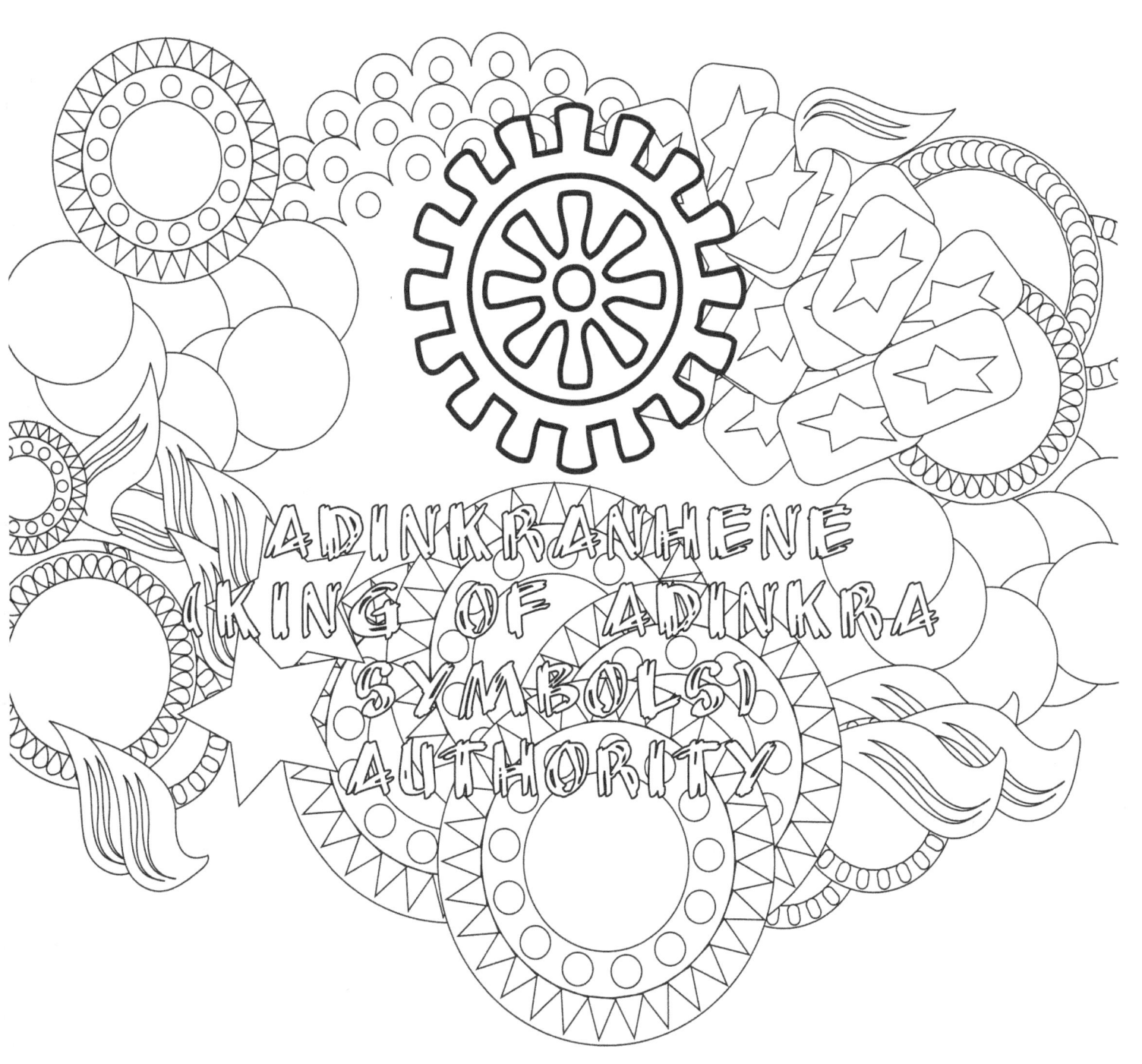

ADINKRANHENE
(KING OF ADINKRA
SYMBOLS)
AUTHORITY

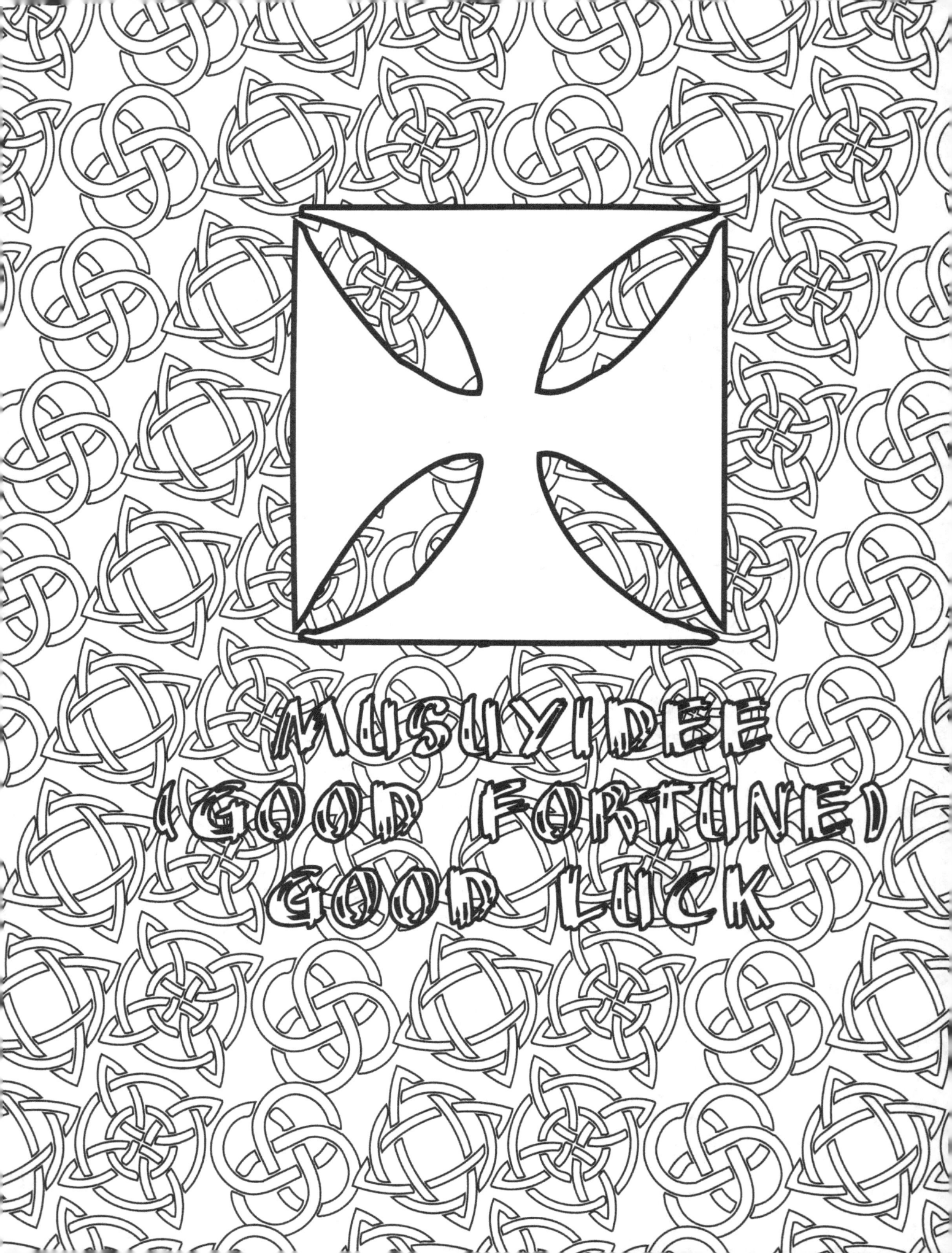

MUSUYIDEE
(GOOD FORTUNE)
GOOD LUCK

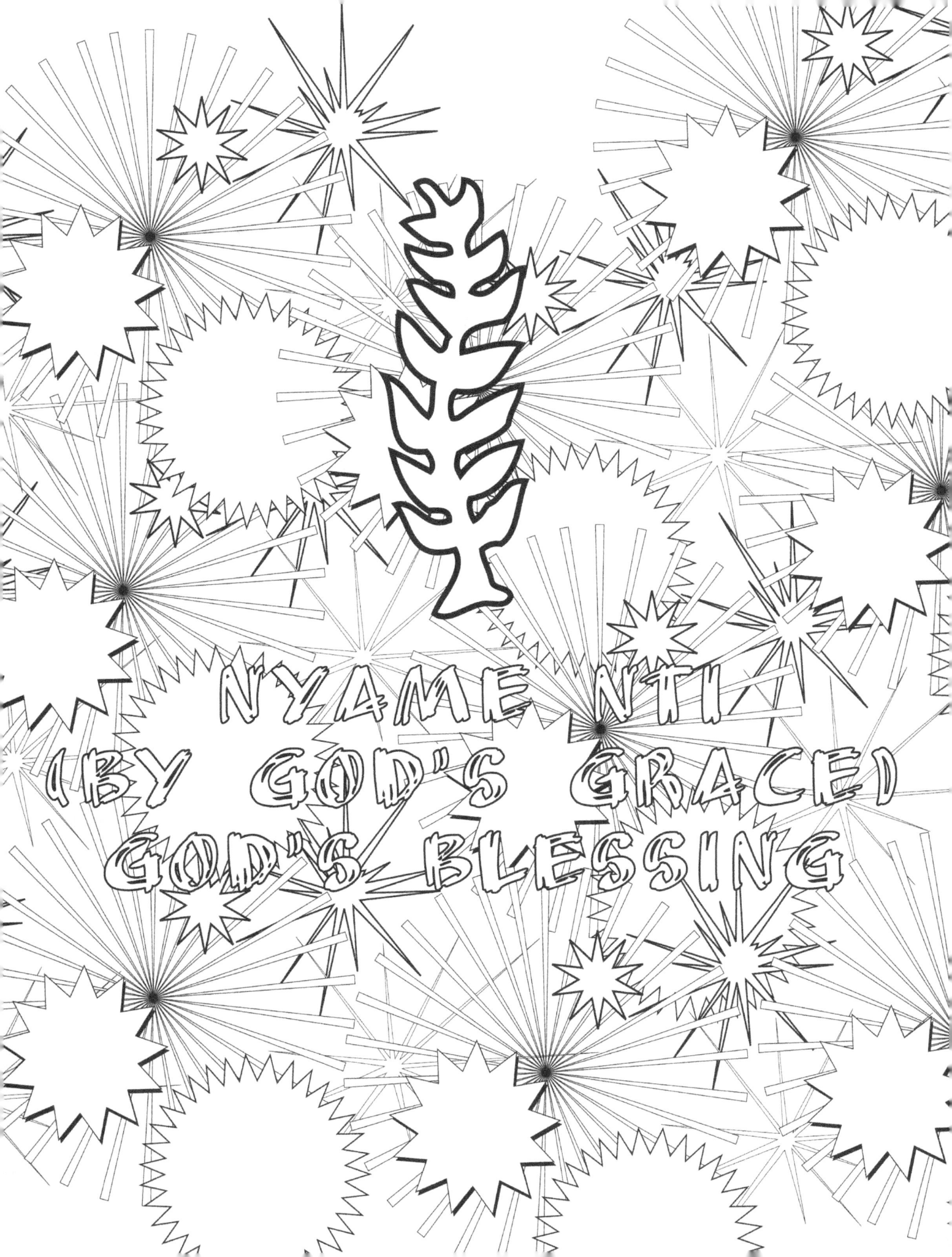

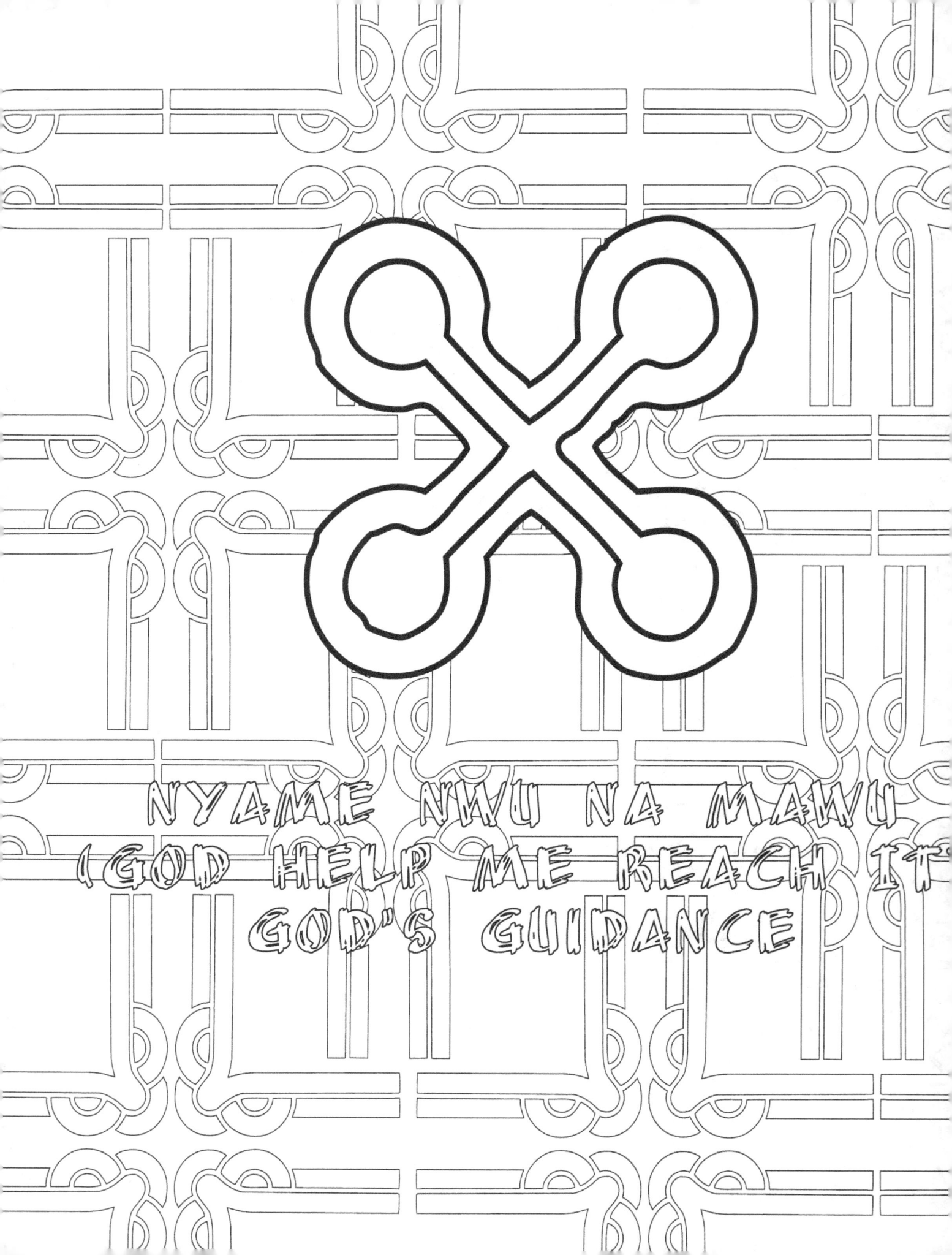

NYAME NWU NA MAWU
(GOD HELP ME REACH IT
GOD'S GUIDANCE

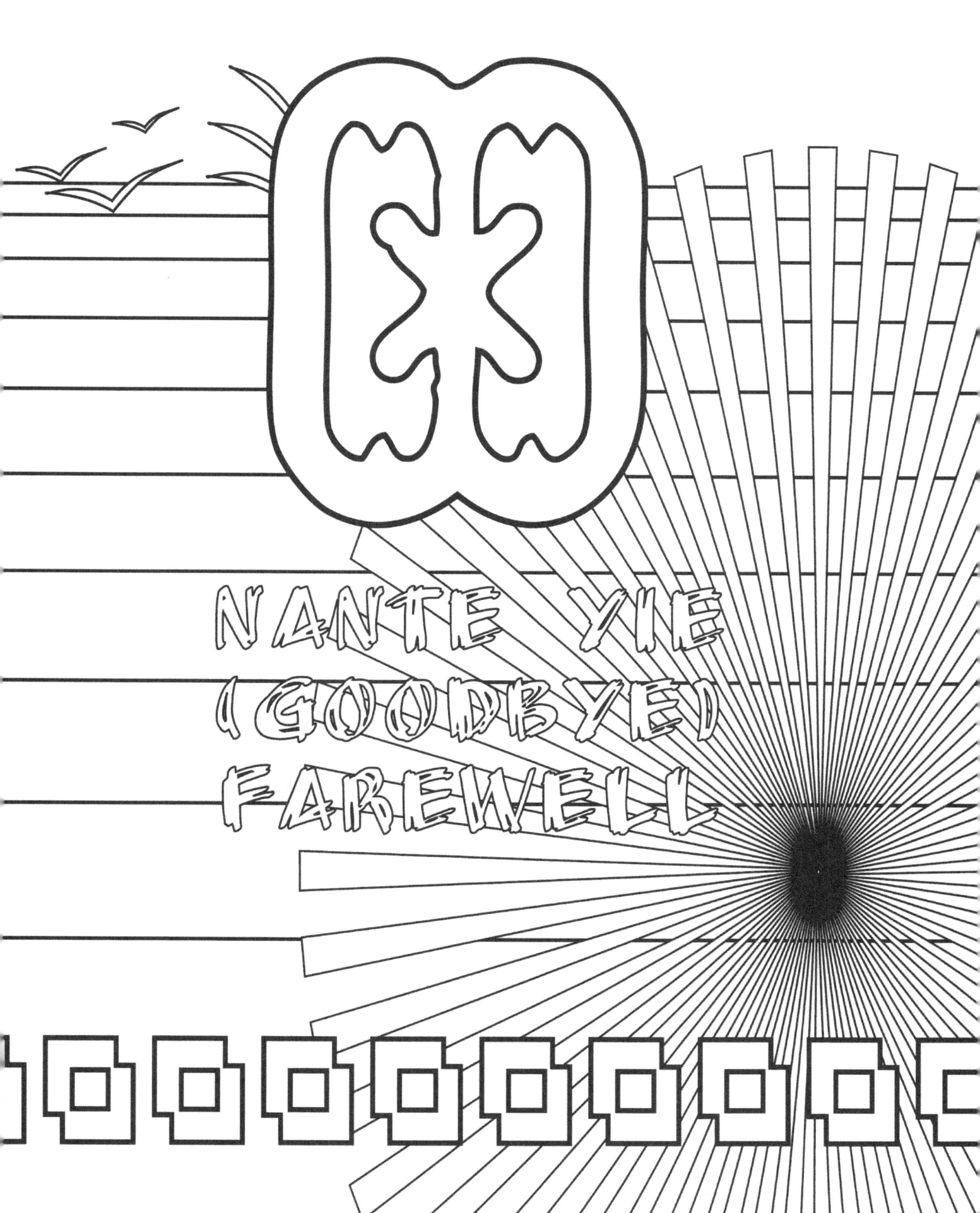

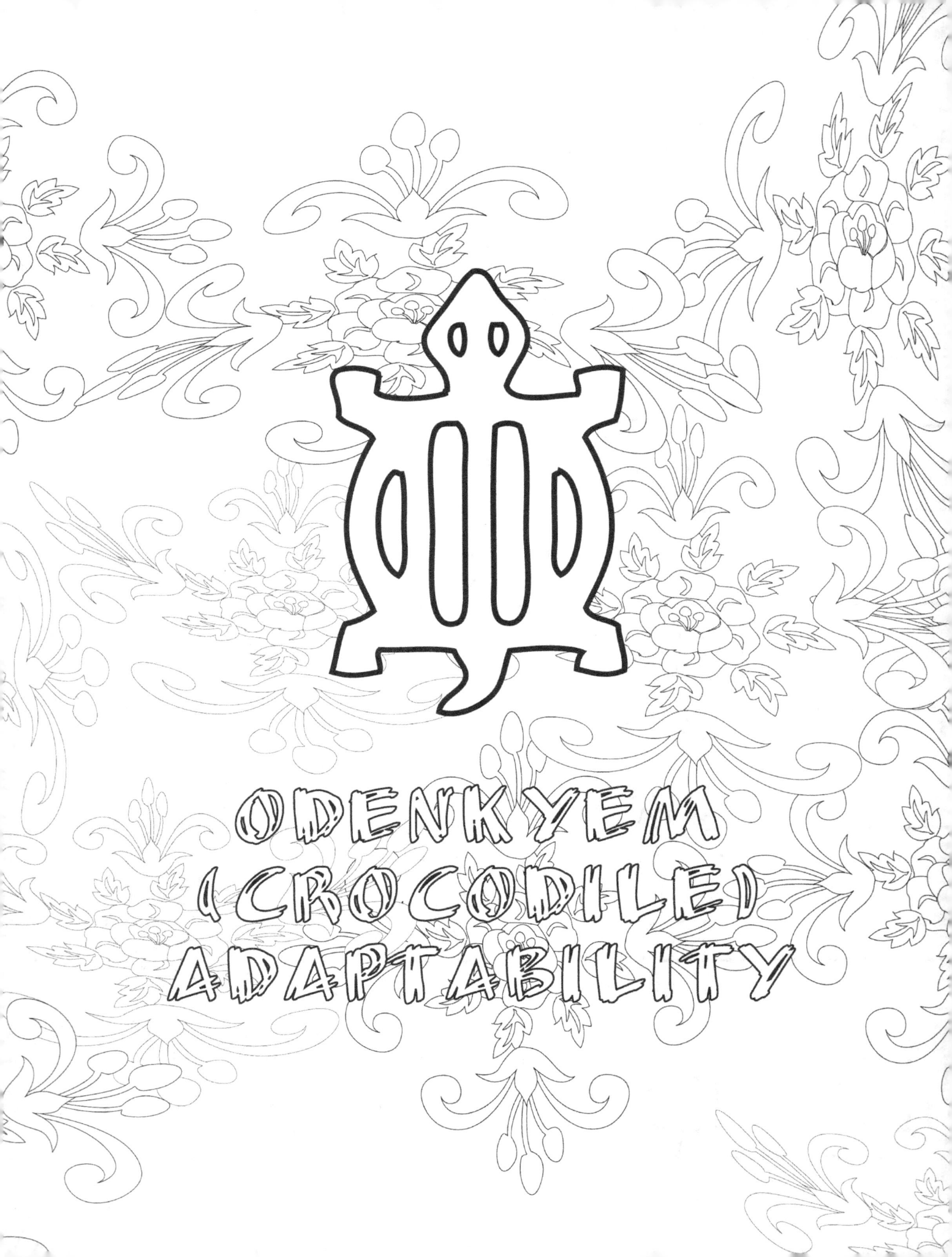

ODENKYEM
(CROCODILE)
ADAPTABILITY

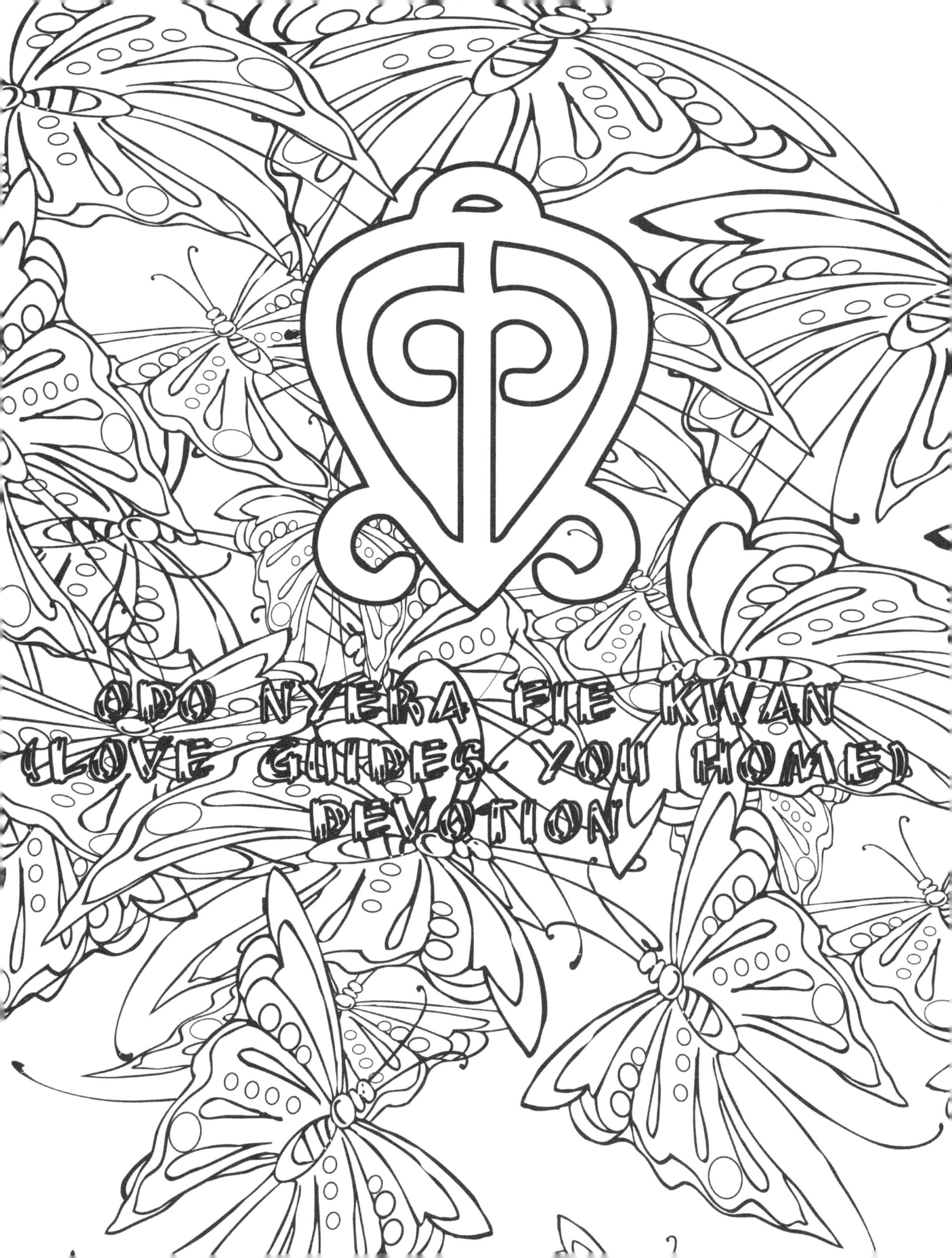

ODO NYERA FIE KWAN
(LOVE GUIDES YOU HOME)
DEVOTION

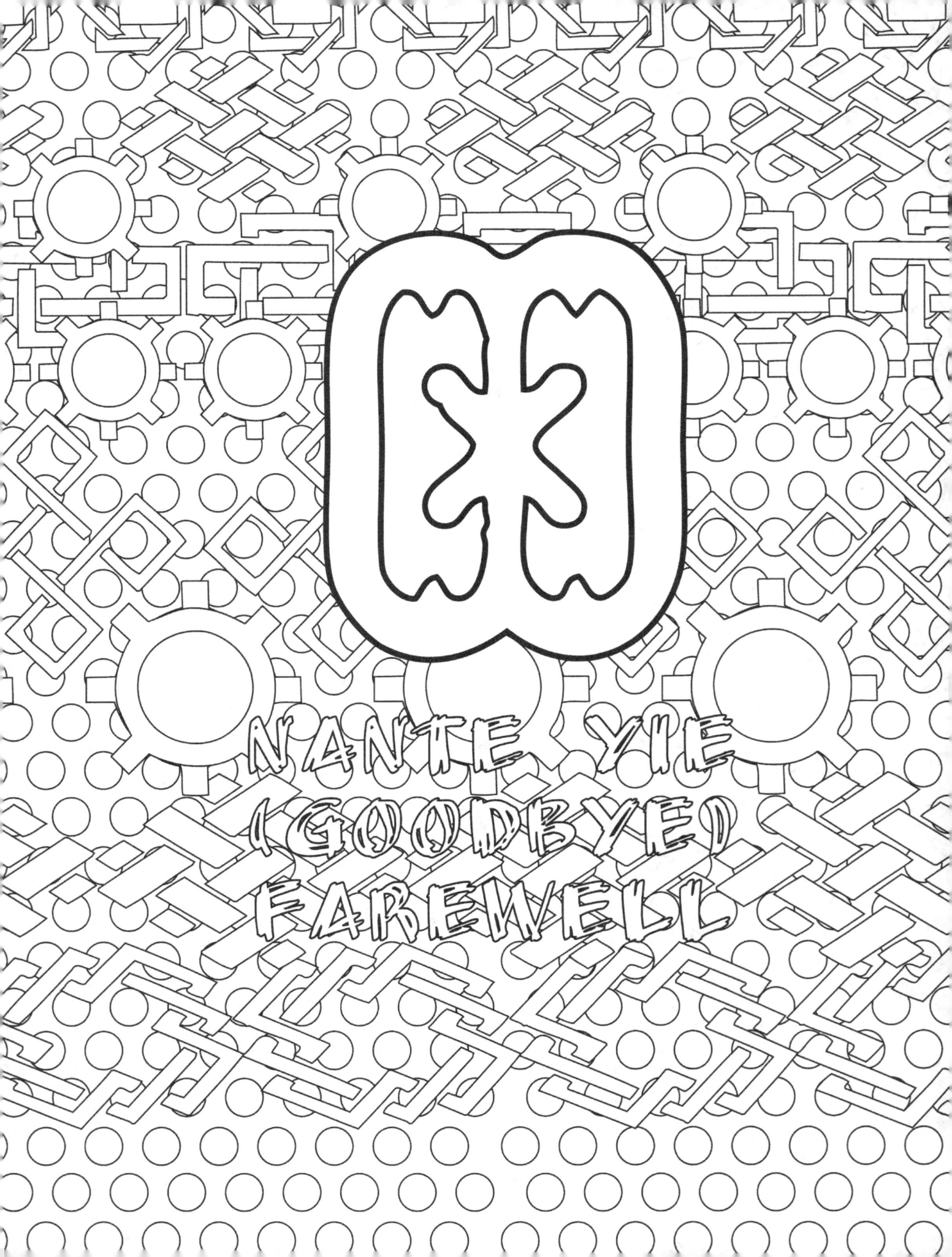

NANTE YIE
(GOODBYE)
FAREWELL

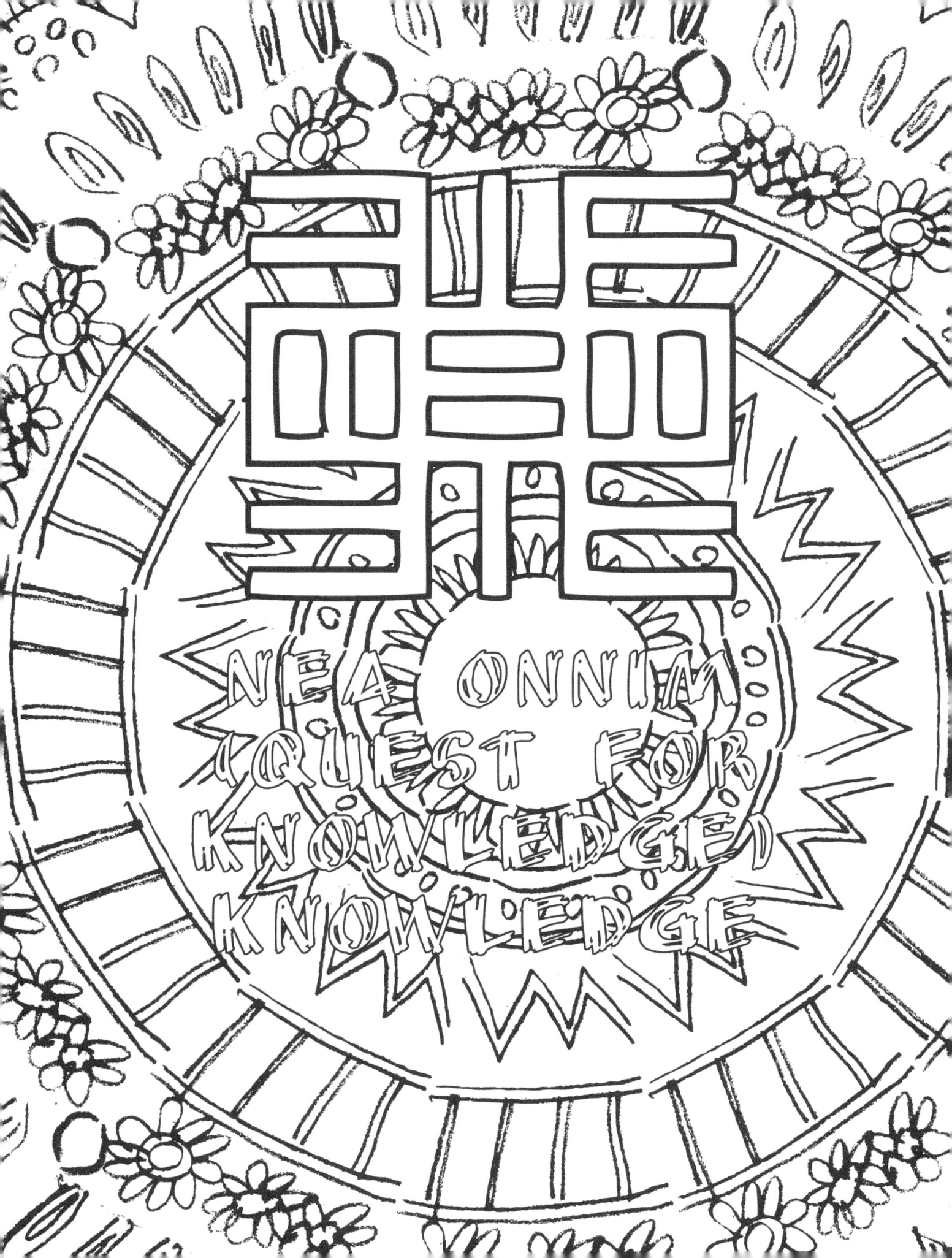

NEA ONNIM (QUEST FOR KNOWLEDGE) KNOWLEDGE

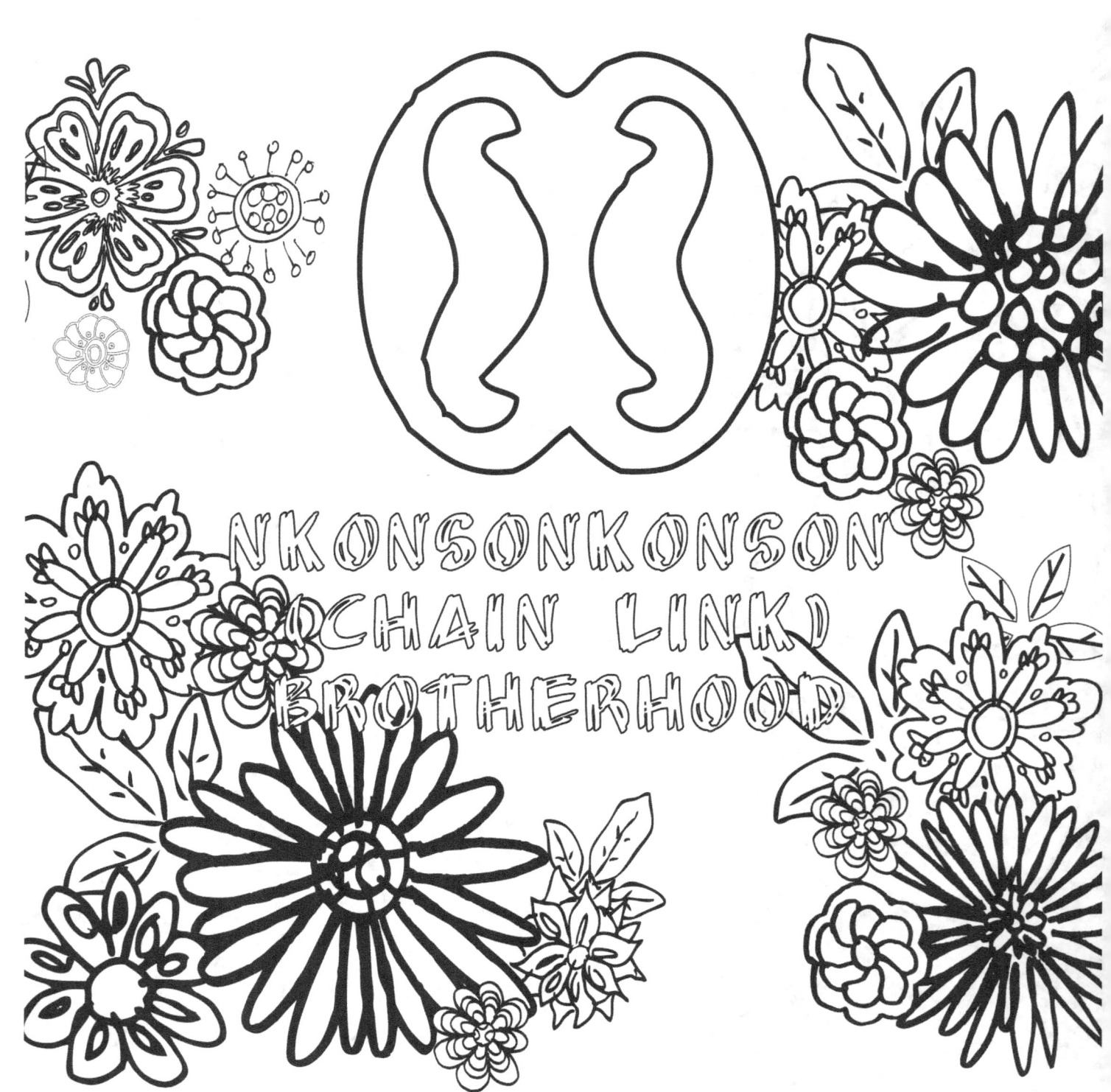

NKONSONKONSON
(CHAIN LINK)
BROTHERHOOD

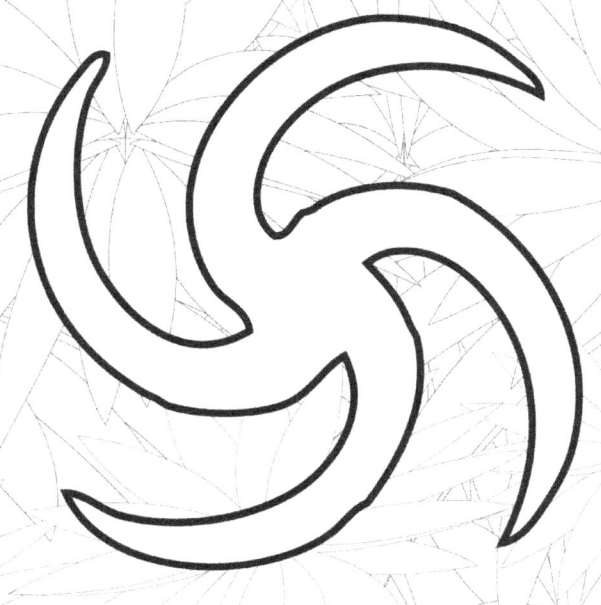

NKOTIMSEFO MPUA
(COURT ATTENDANTS
HAIR STYLE)
LOYALTY

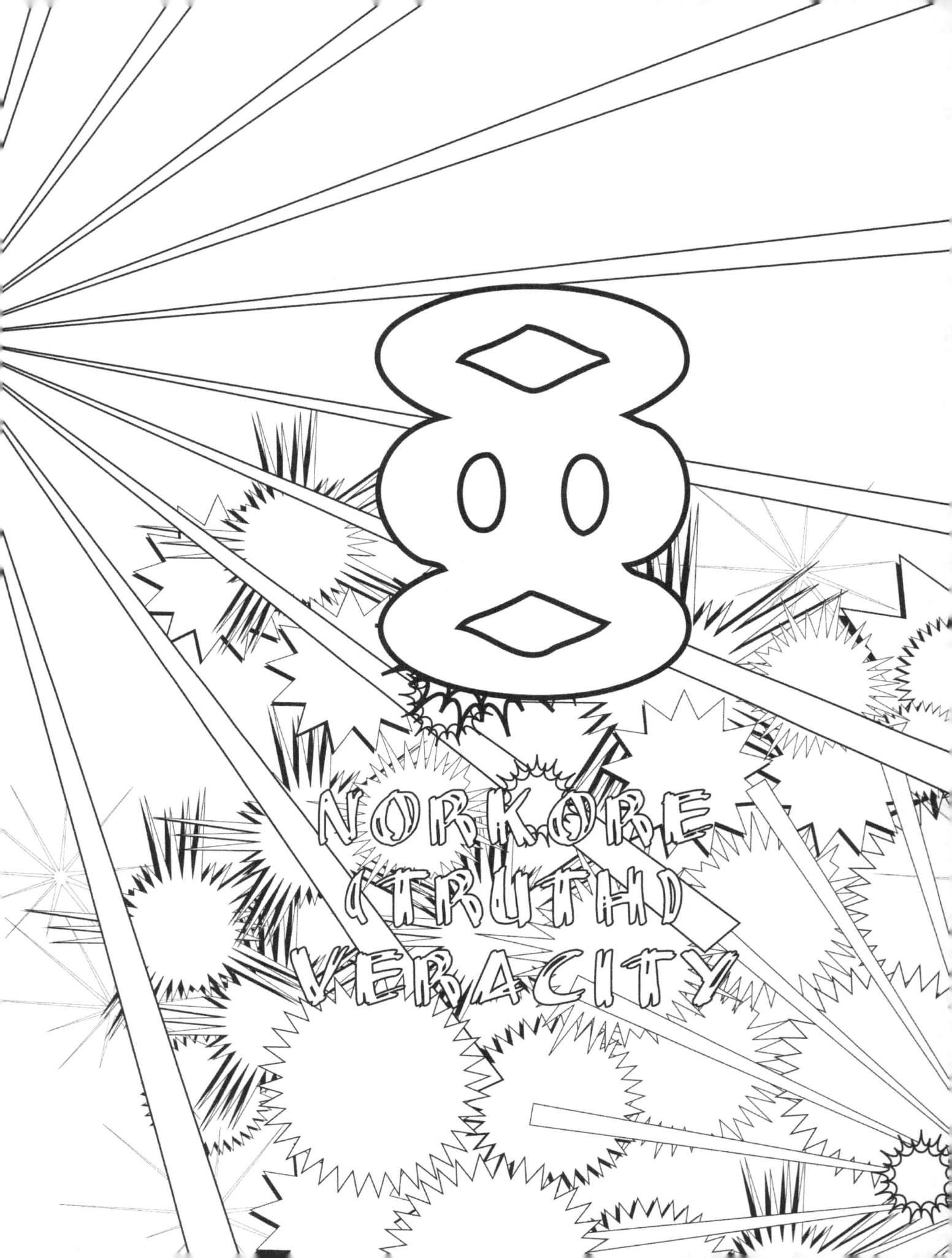

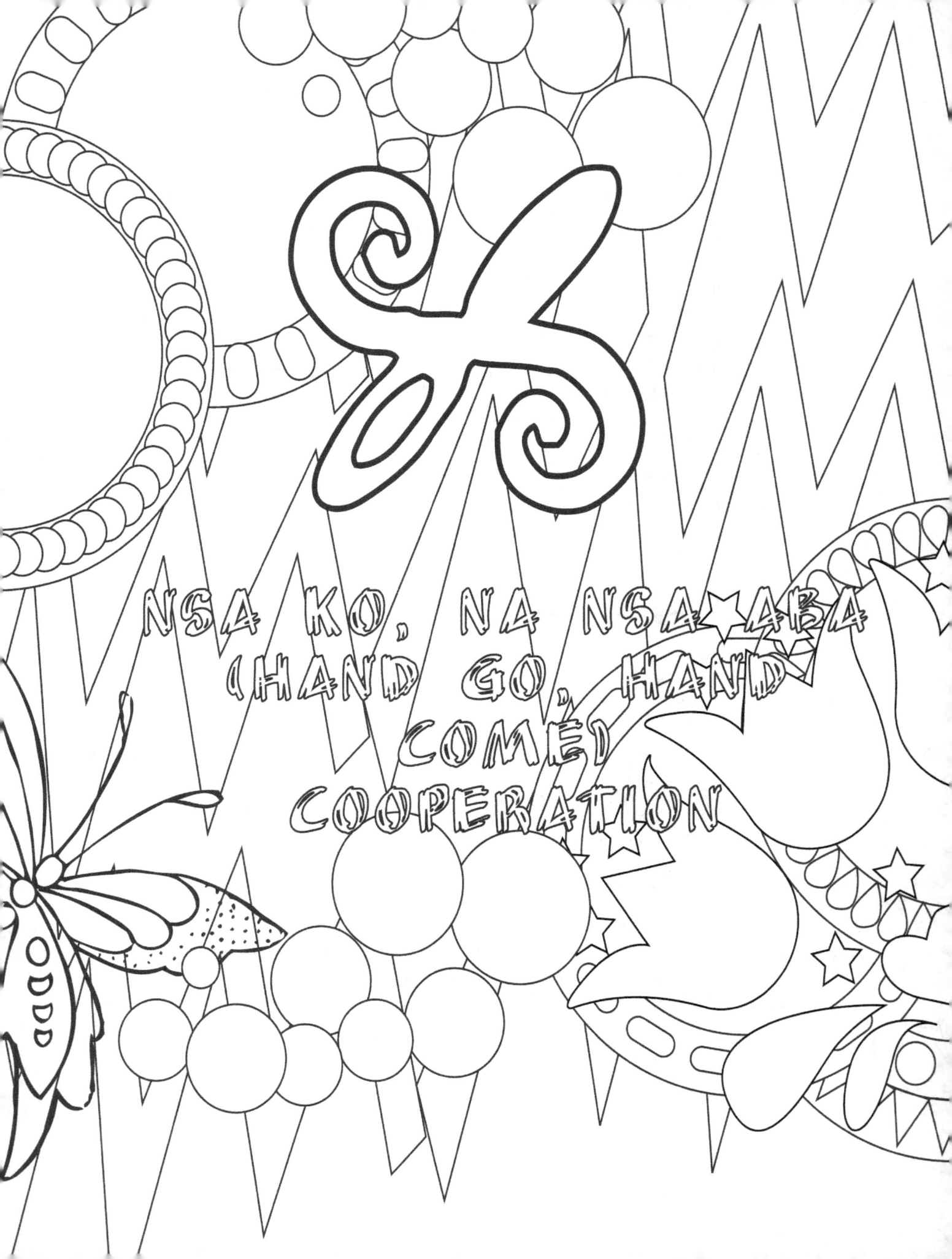

NSA KO, NA NSA ABA
(HAND GO, HAND
COME)
COOPERATION

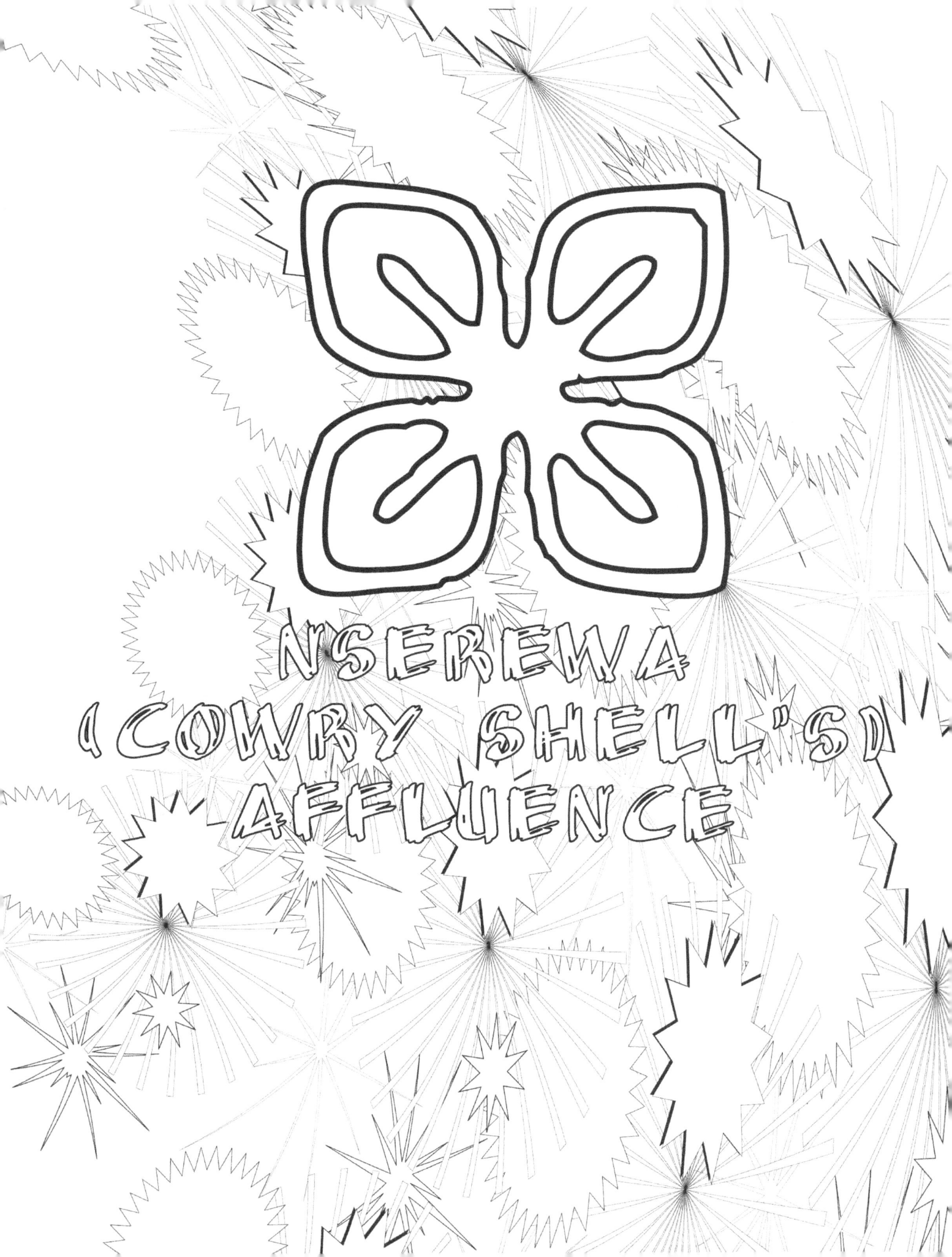

NSEREWA
(COWRY SHELL'S)
AFFLUENCE

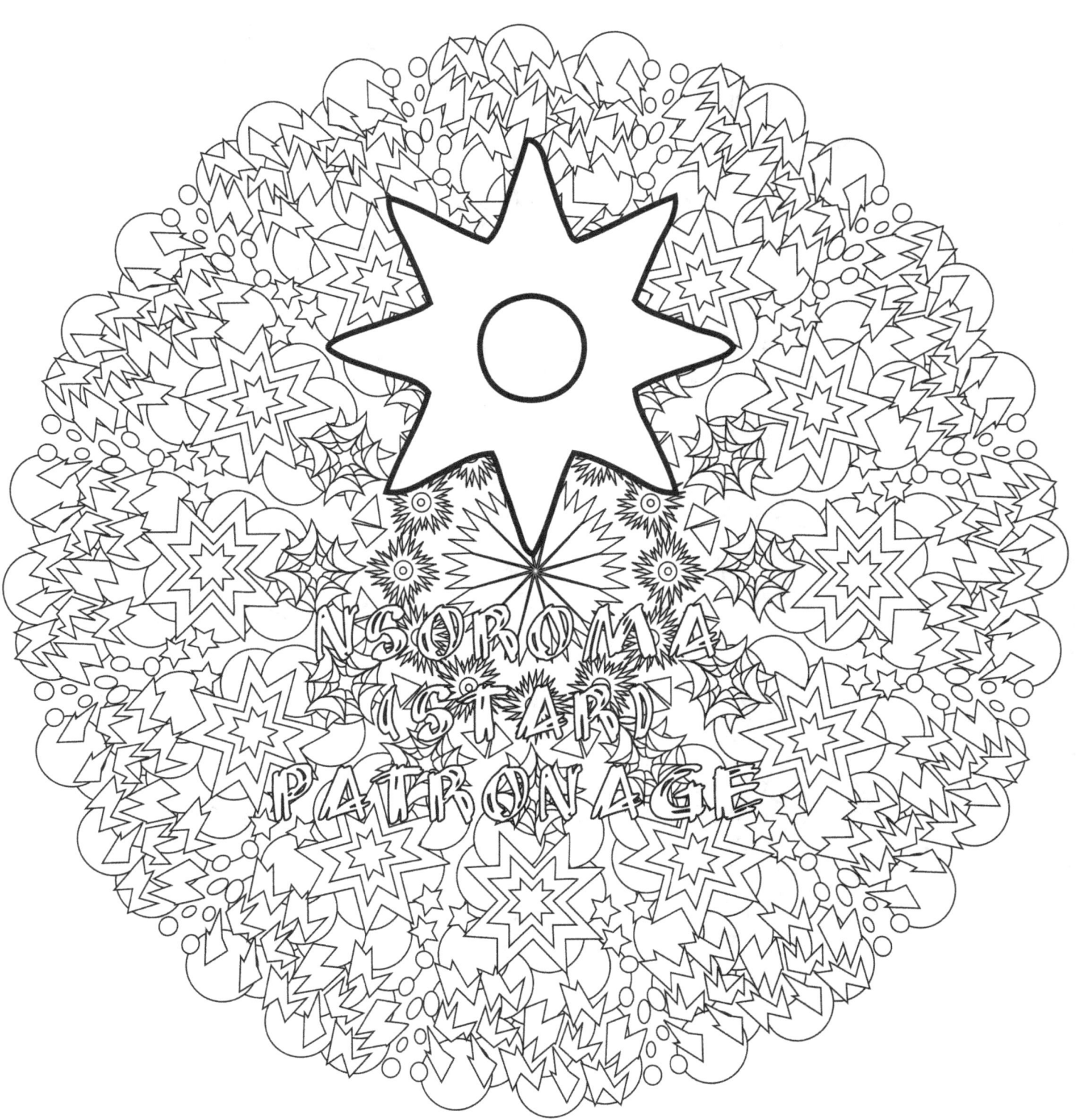

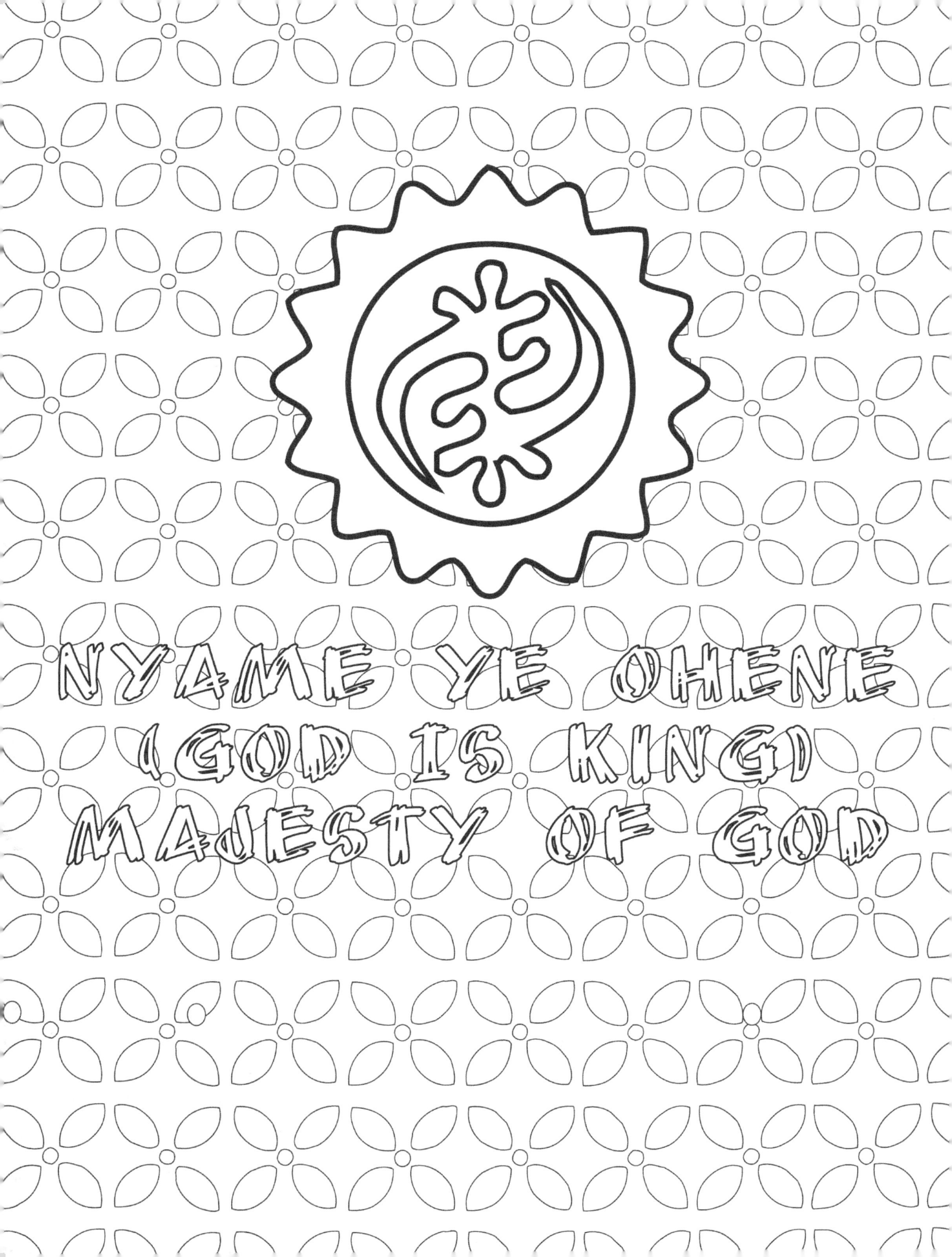

NYAME YE OHENE
(GOD IS KING)
MAJESTY OF GOD

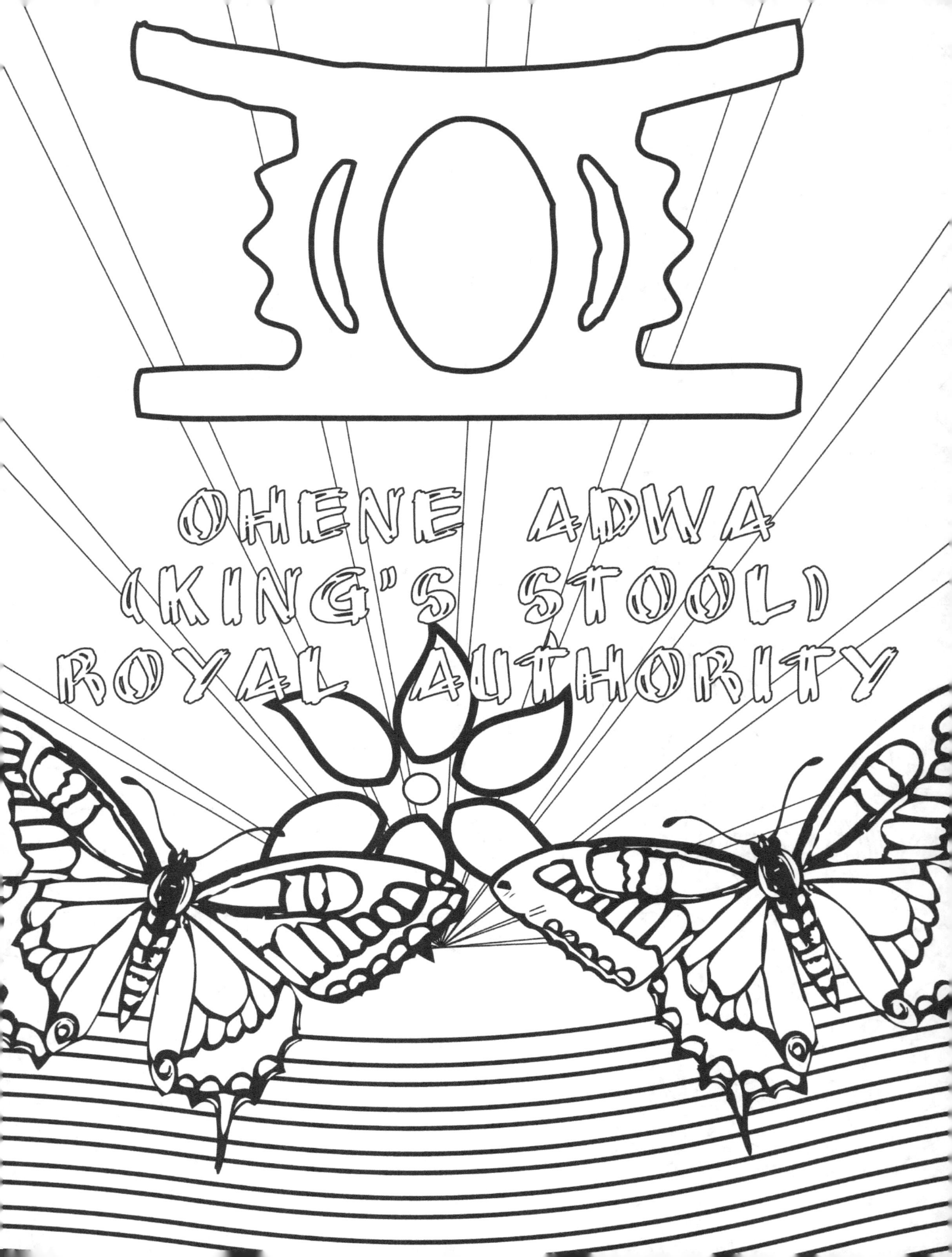

OHENE ADWA
(KING'S STOOL)
ROYAL AUTHORITY

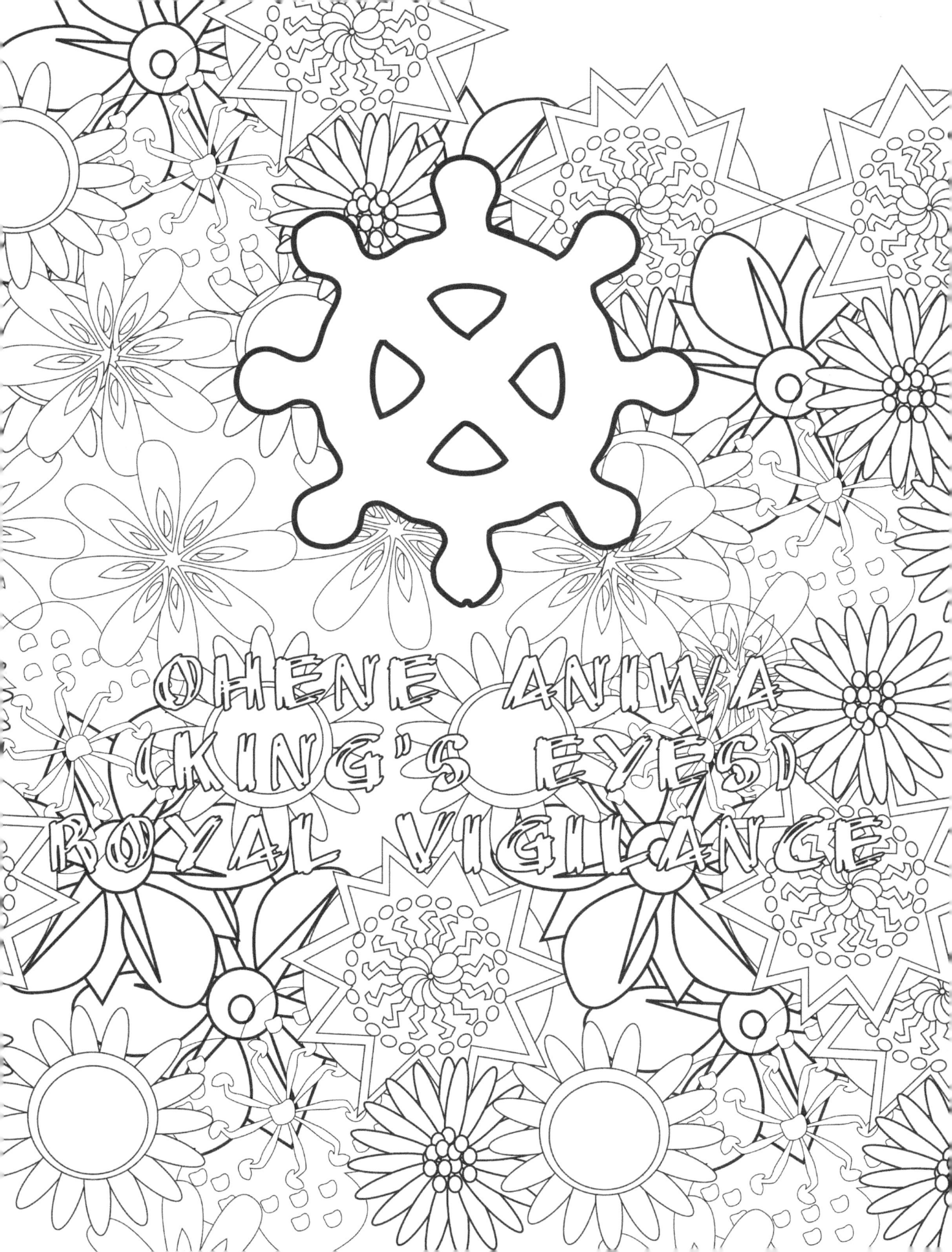

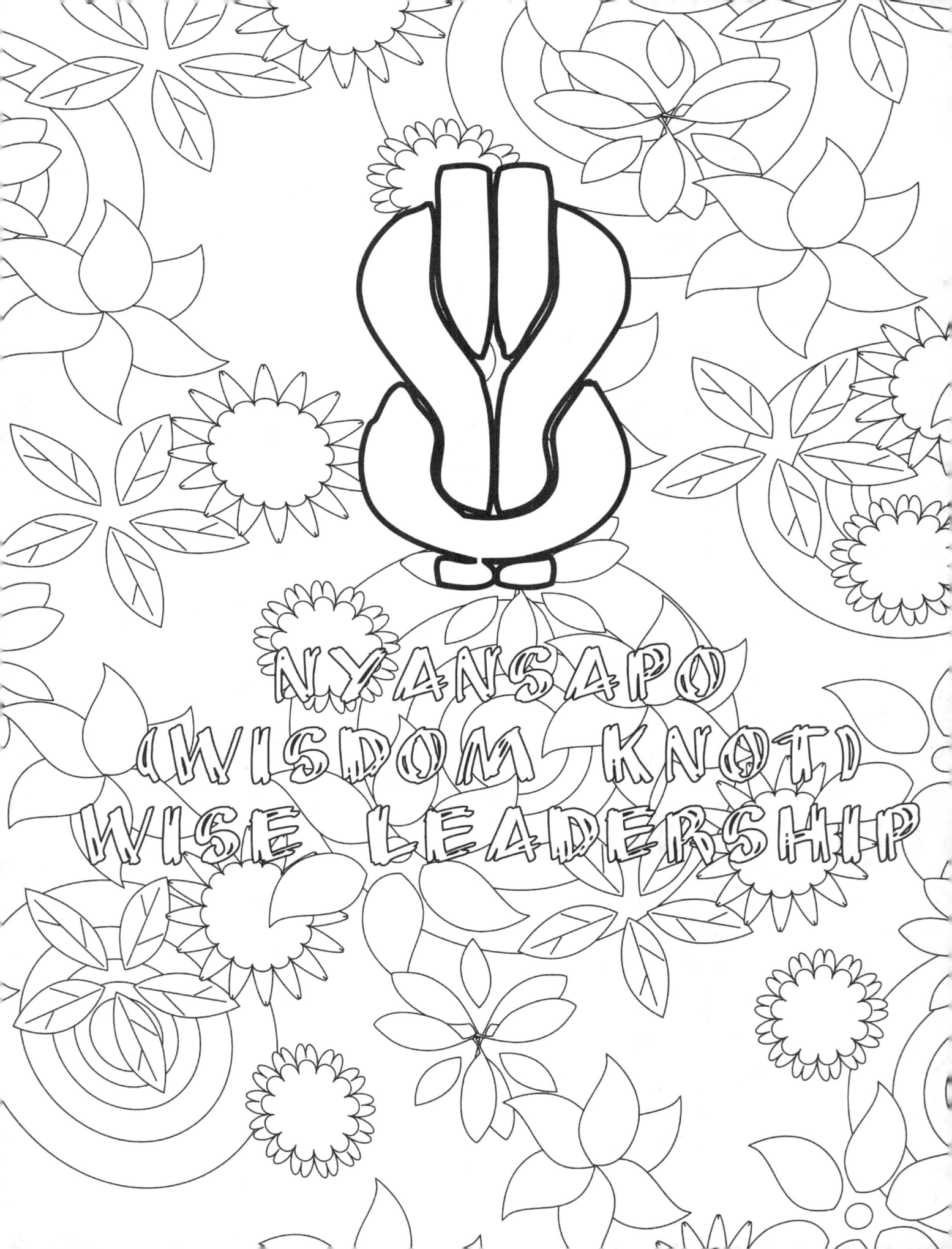

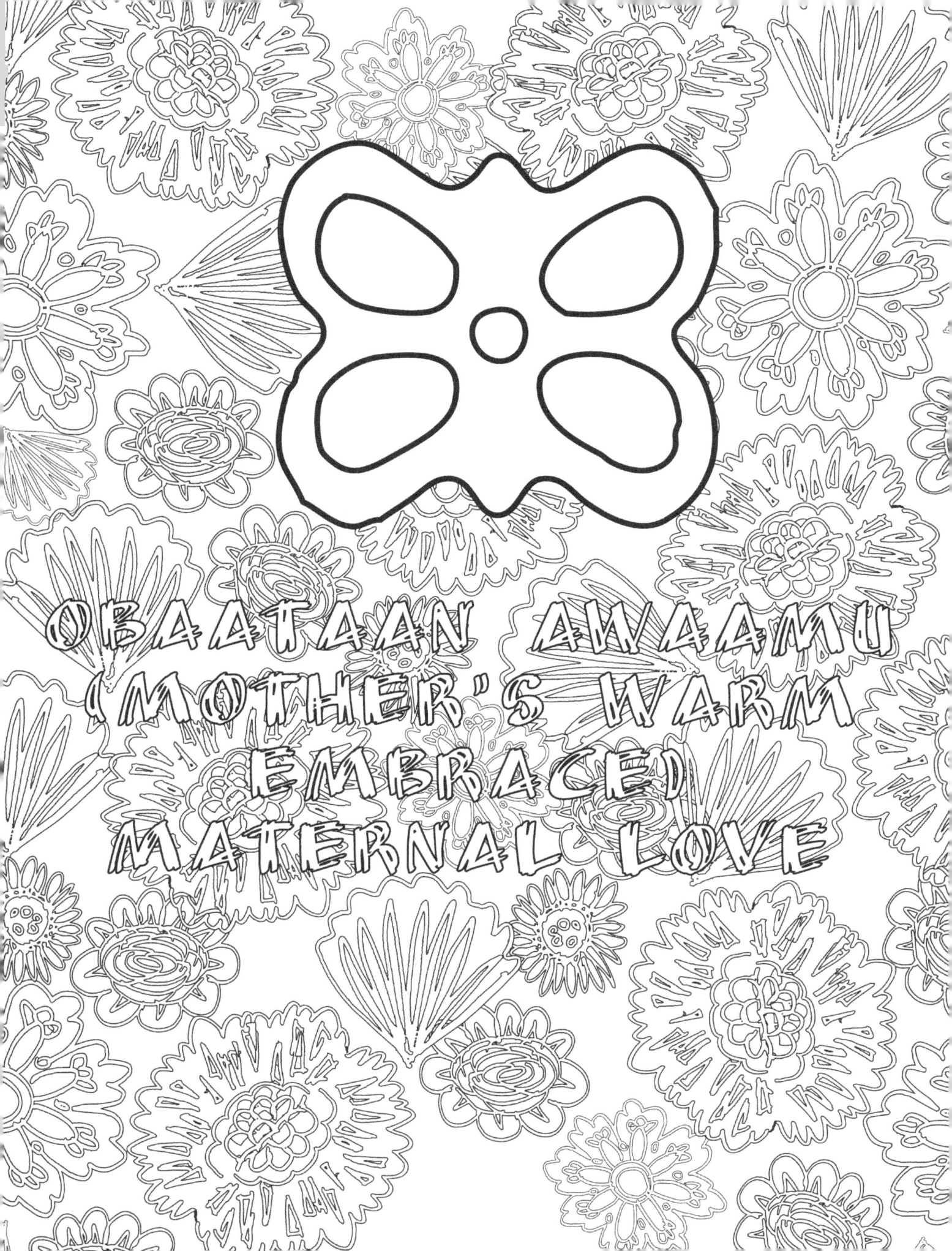

OBAATAAN AWAAMU
(MOTHER'S WARM
EMBRACED
MATERNAL LOVE

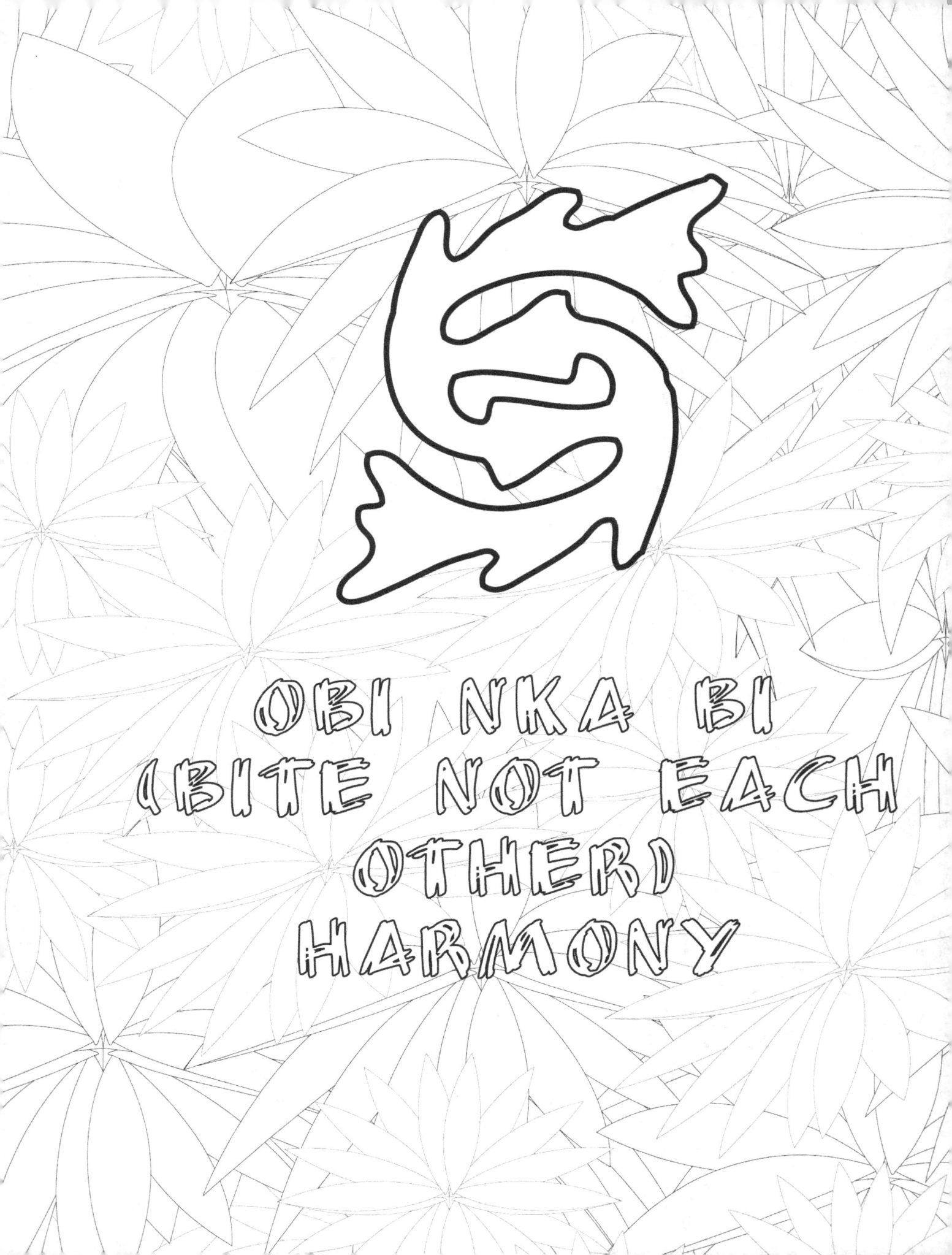

OBI NKA BI
(BITE NOT EACH
OTHER)
HARMONY

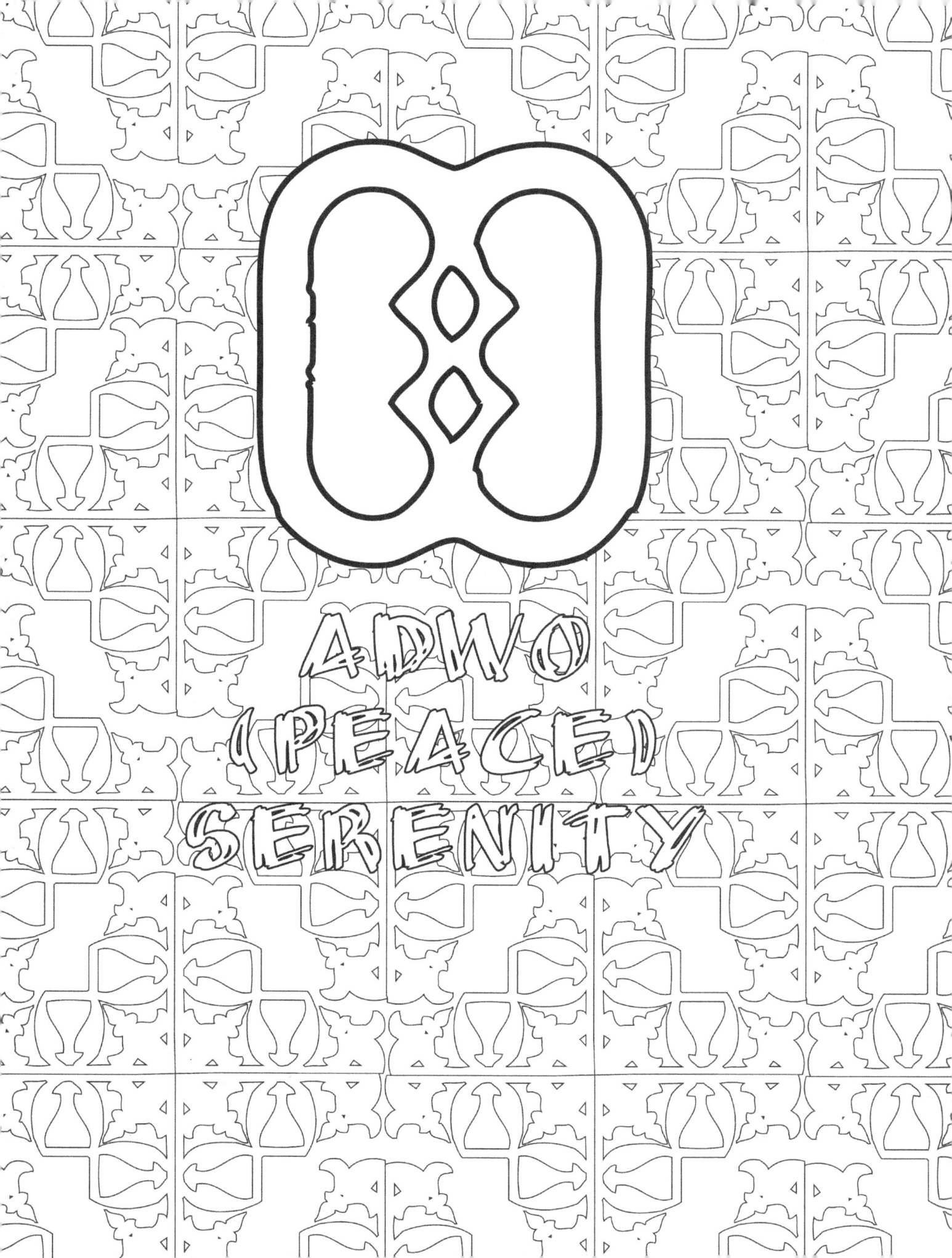

ADWO
(PEACE)
SERENITY

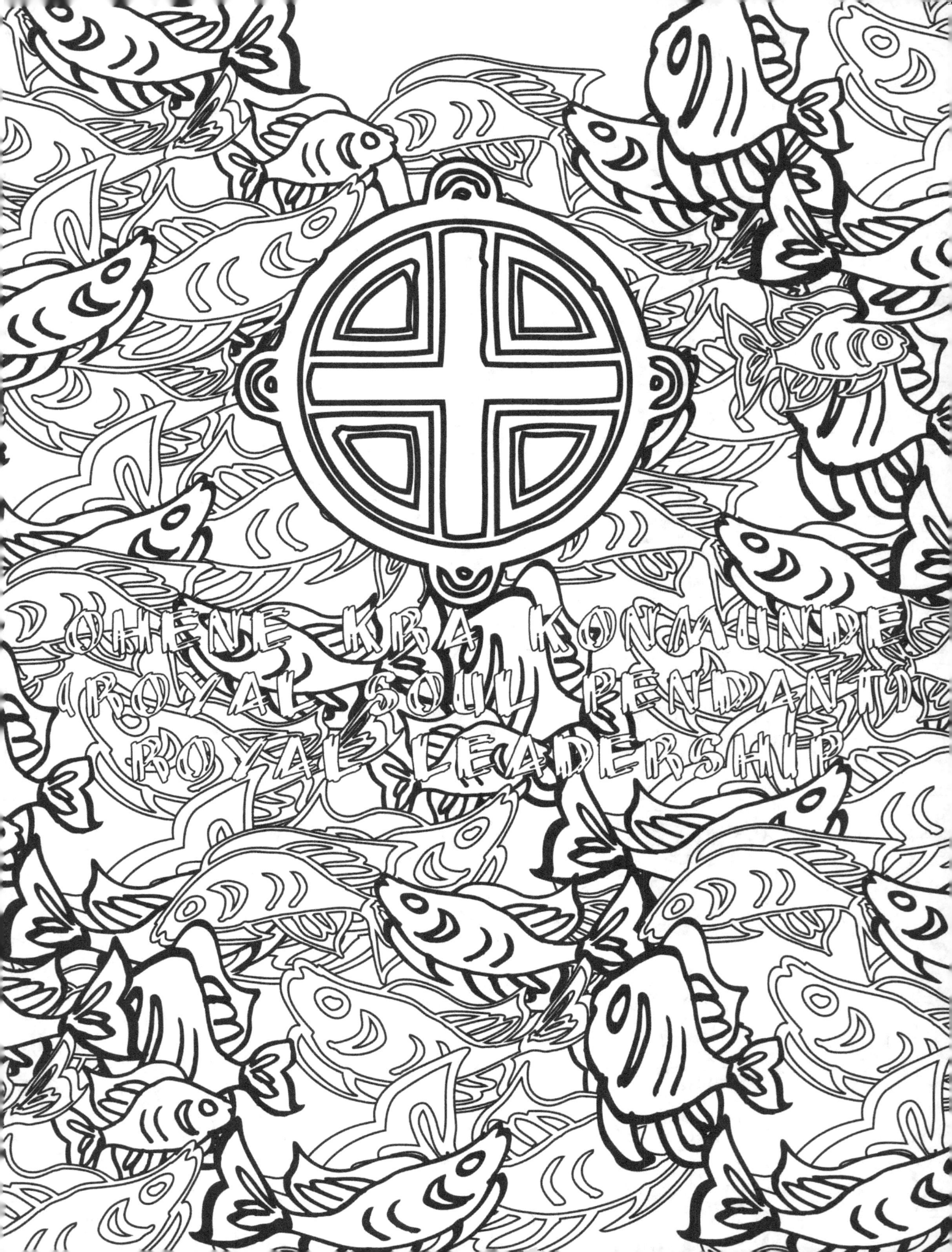

OHENE KRA KONMUNDE
(ROYAL SOUL PENDANT)
ROYAL LEADERSHIP

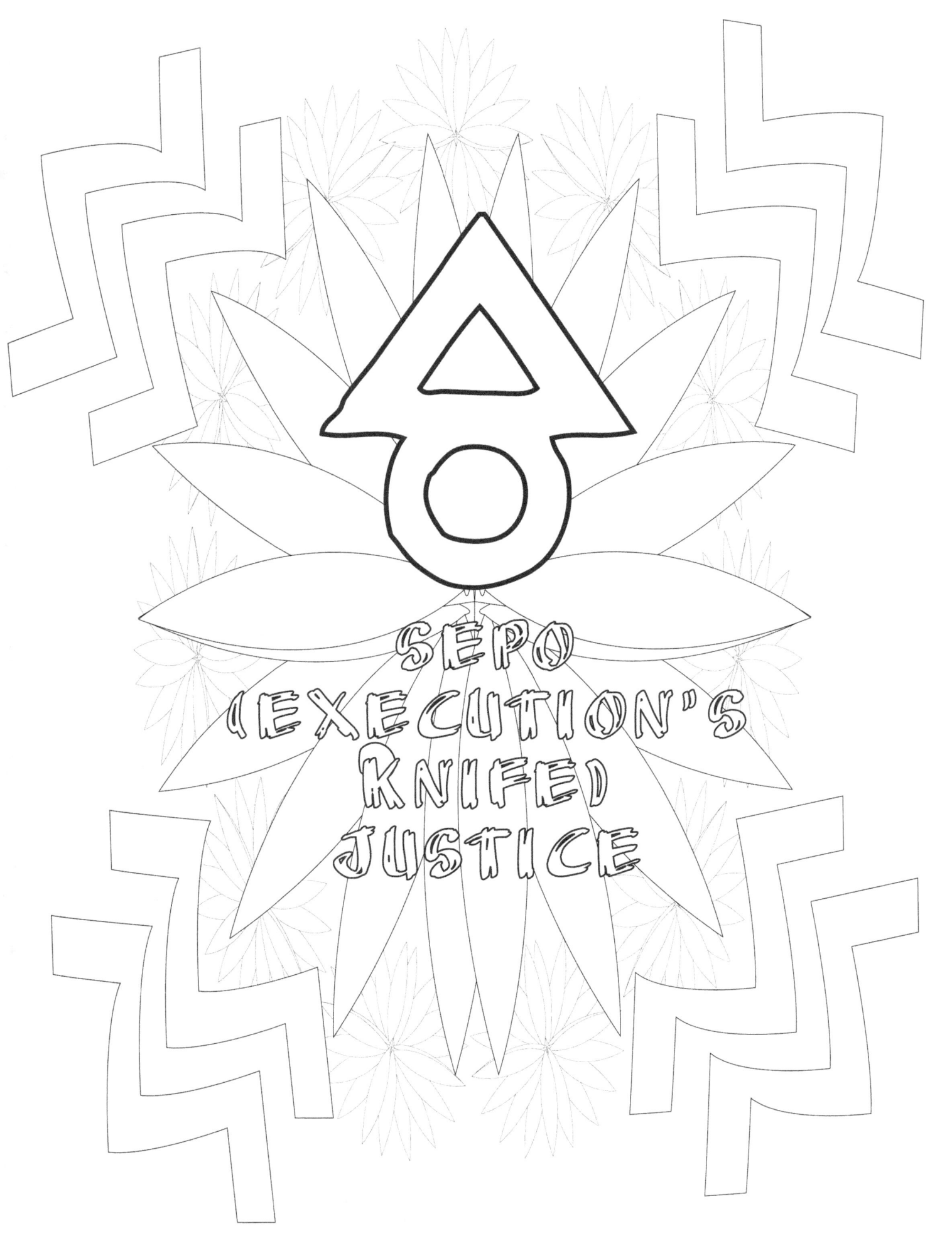

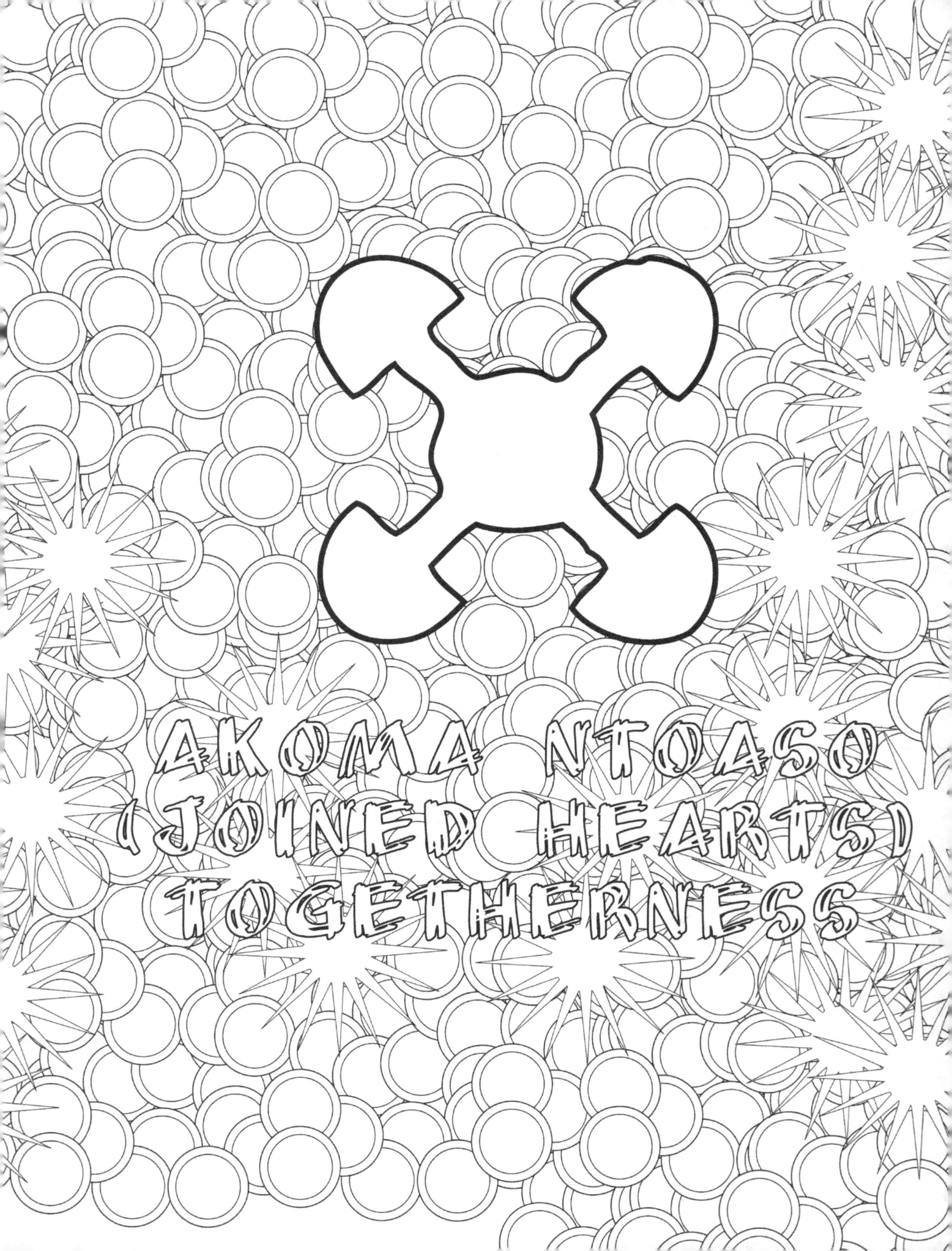

AKOMA NTOASO
(JOINED HEARTS)
TOGETHERNESS

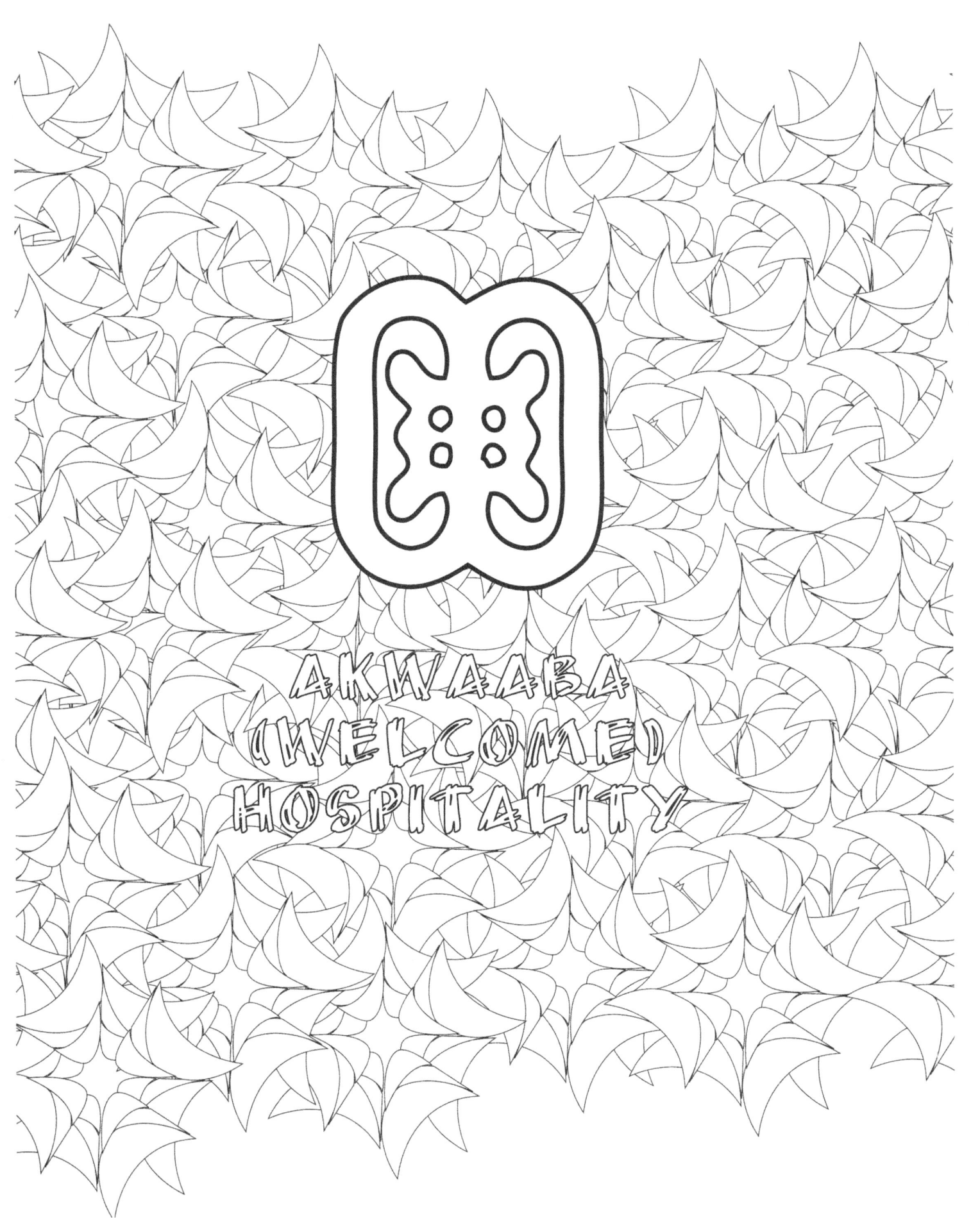

AKWAABA (WELCOME) HOSPITALITY

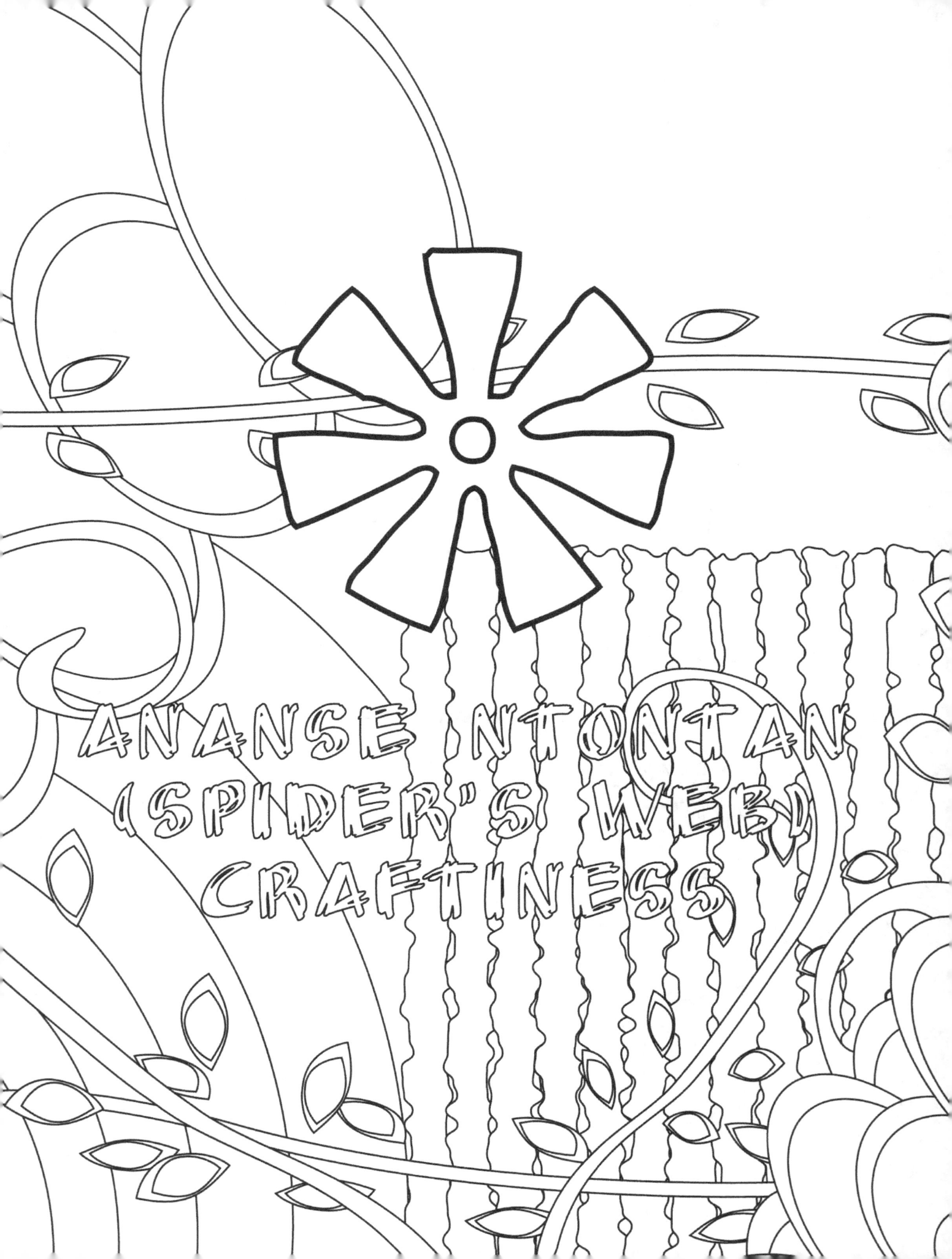

ANANSE NTONTAN
(SPIDER'S WEB)
CRAFTINESS

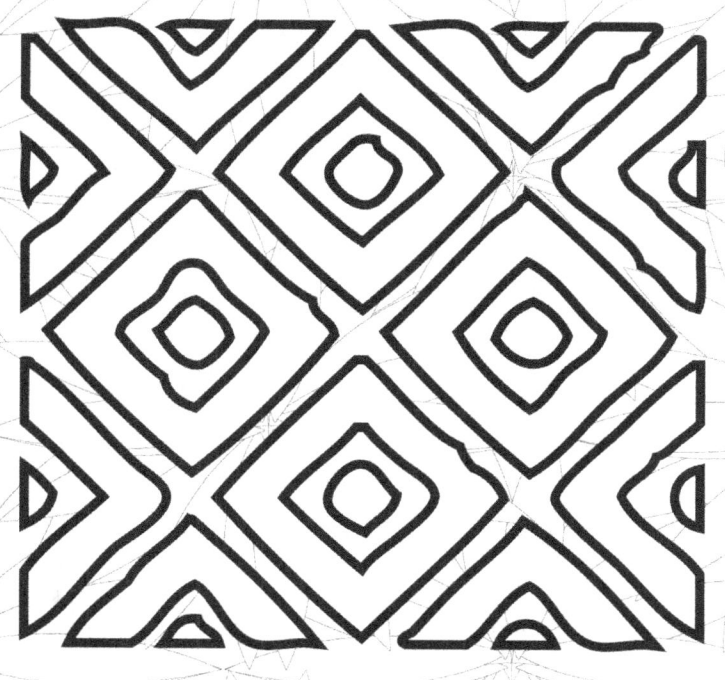

ANI BERE A ENSO GYA
(RED EYES CAN'T SPARK
FLAMES)
DISCIPLINE

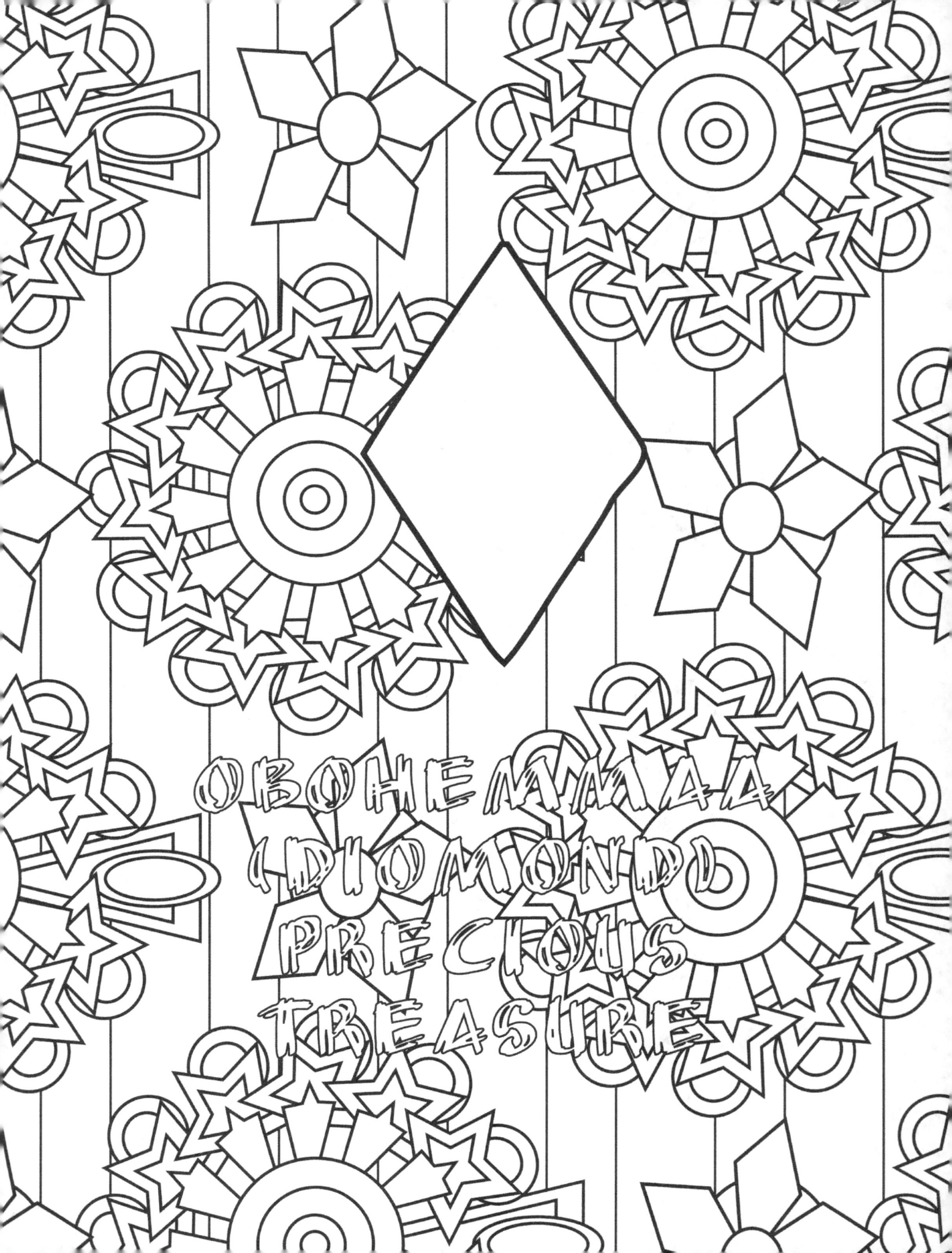

OBOHEMMAA DIOMOND PRECIOUS TREASURE

OHENE KYE
(KING'S CROWN)
ROYAL POWER

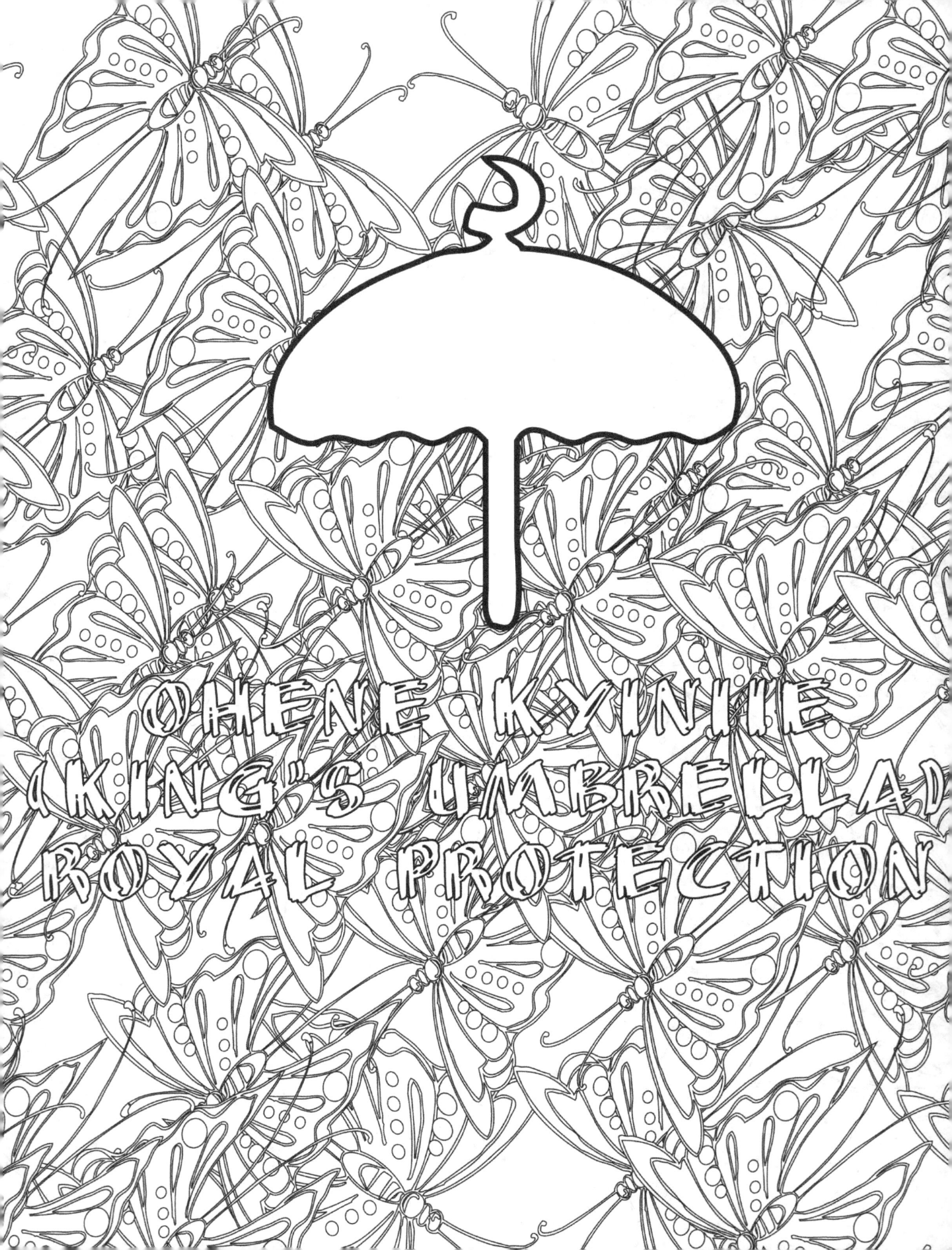

OHENE KYINIIE
(KING'S UMBRELLA)
ROYAL PROTECTION

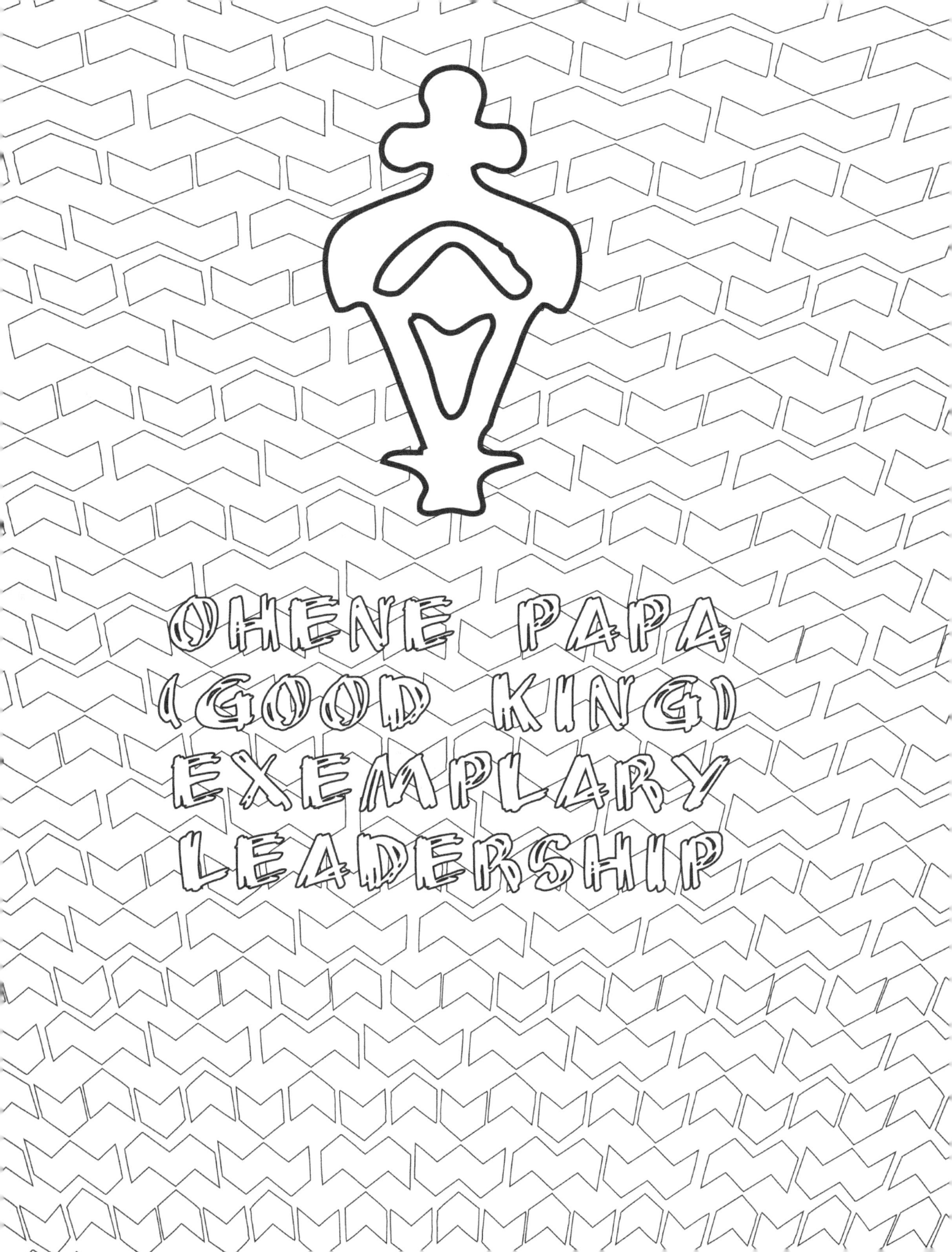

OHENE PAPA
(GOOD KING)
EXEMPLARY
LEADERSHIP

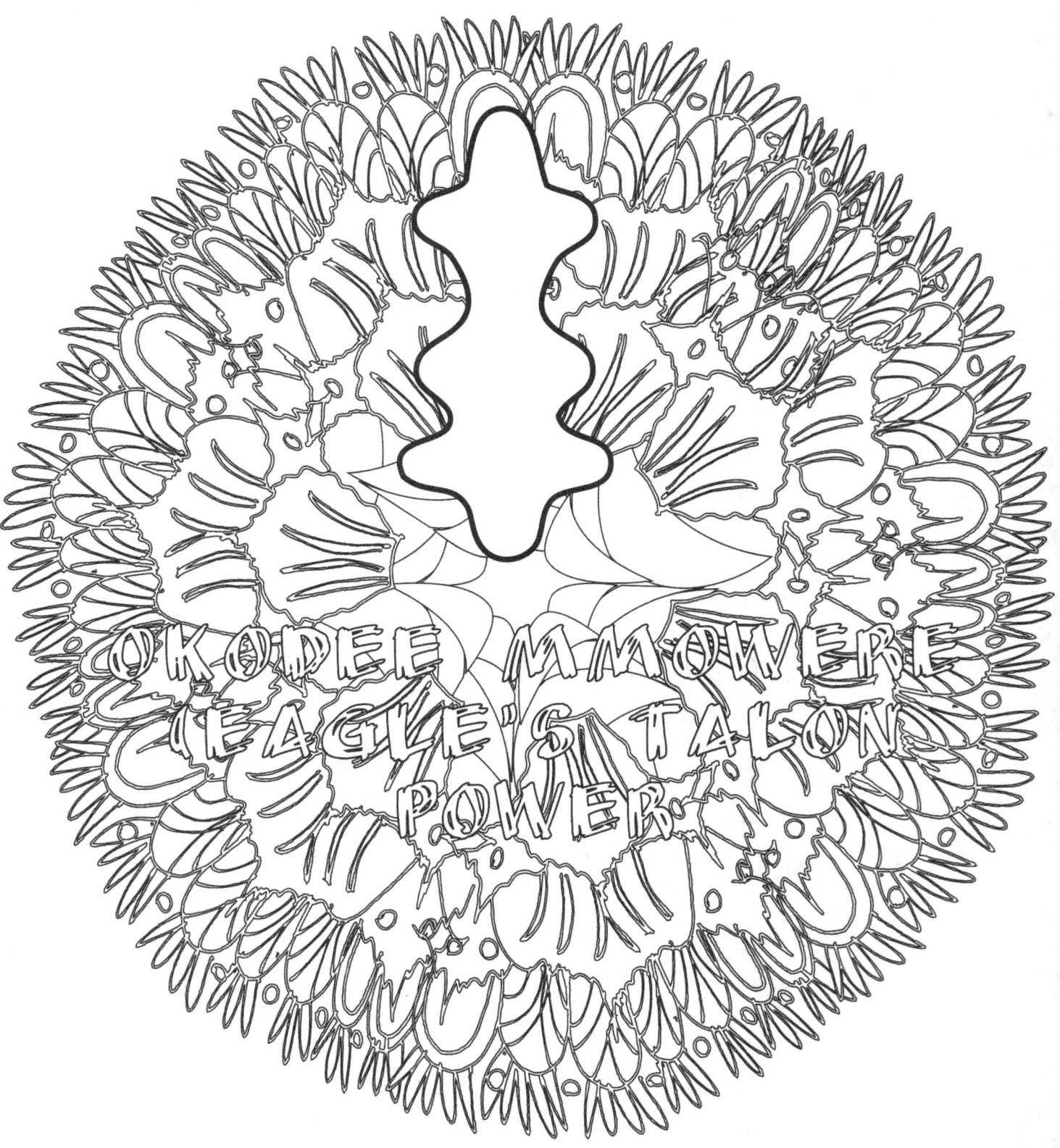

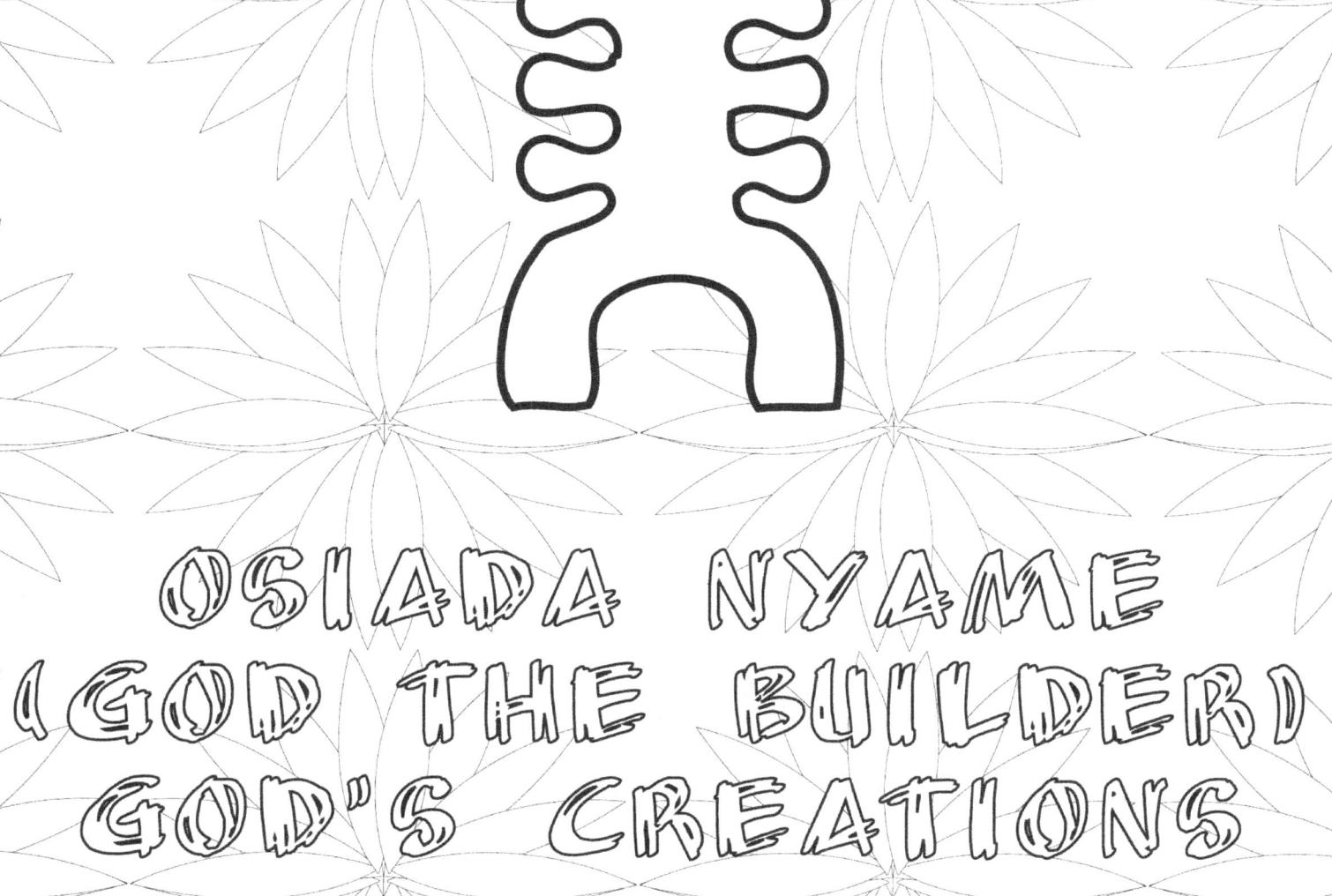

OSIADA NYAME
(GOD THE BUILDER)
GOD'S CREATIONS

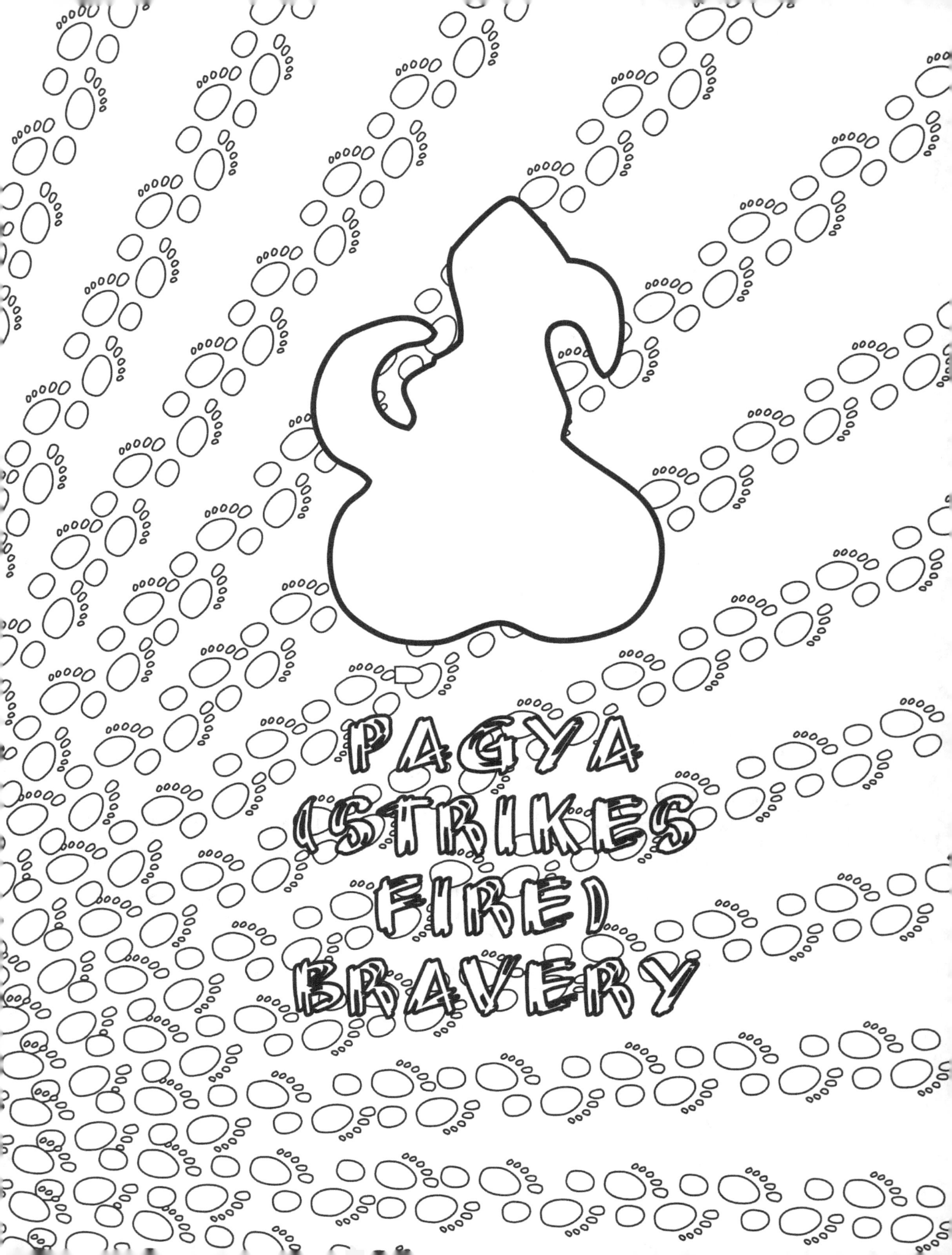

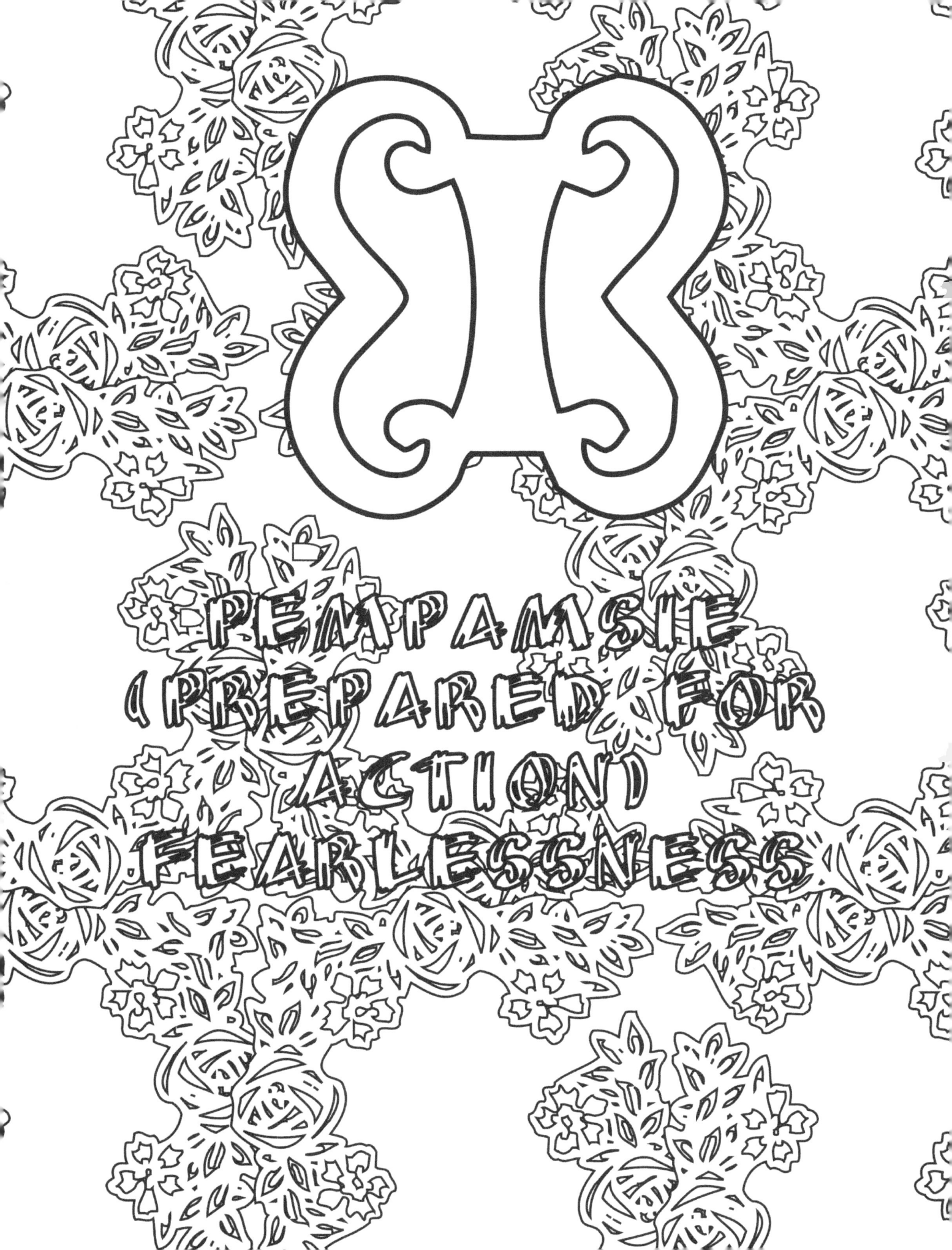

PEMPAMSIE
(PREPARED FOR
ACTION)
FEARLESSNESS

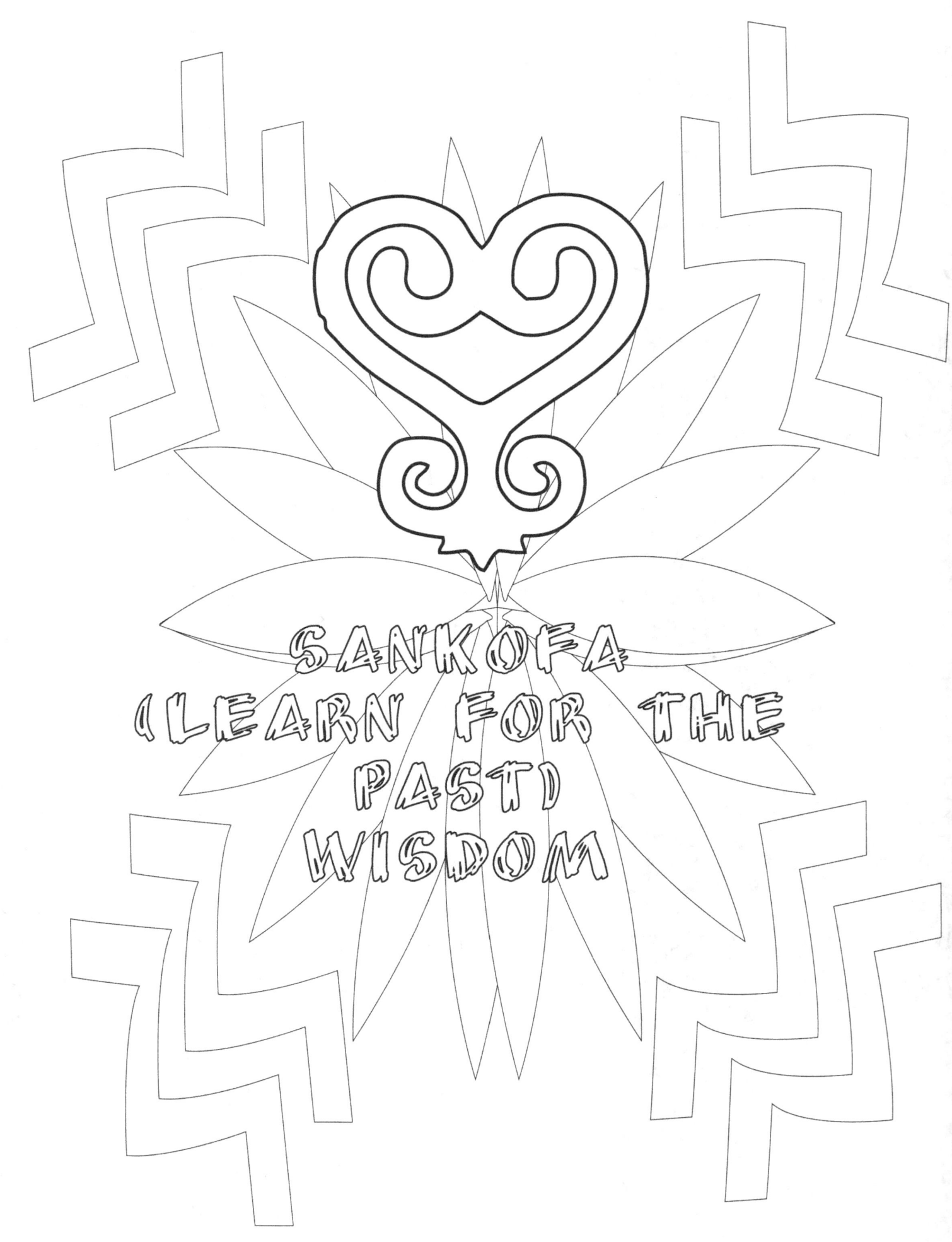

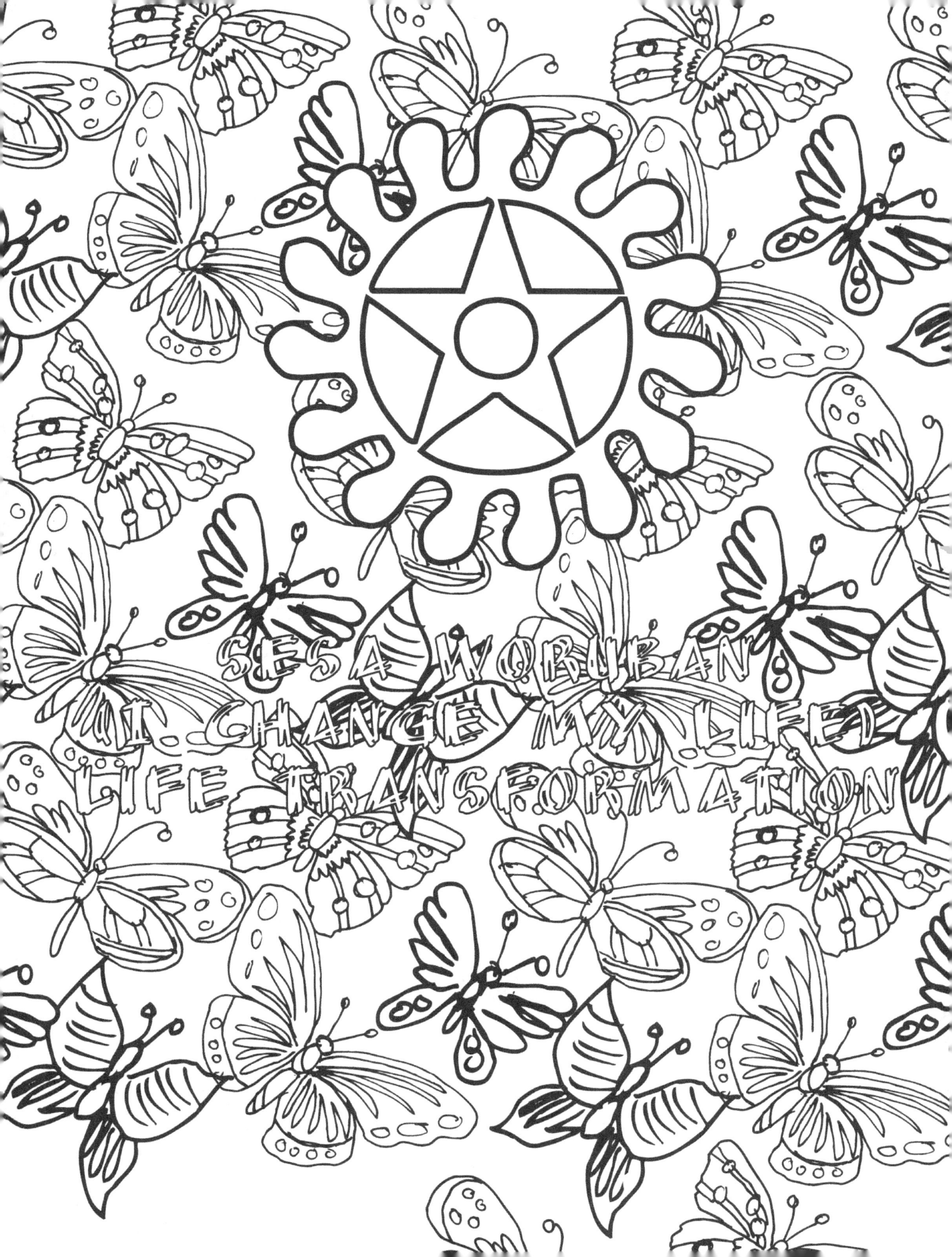

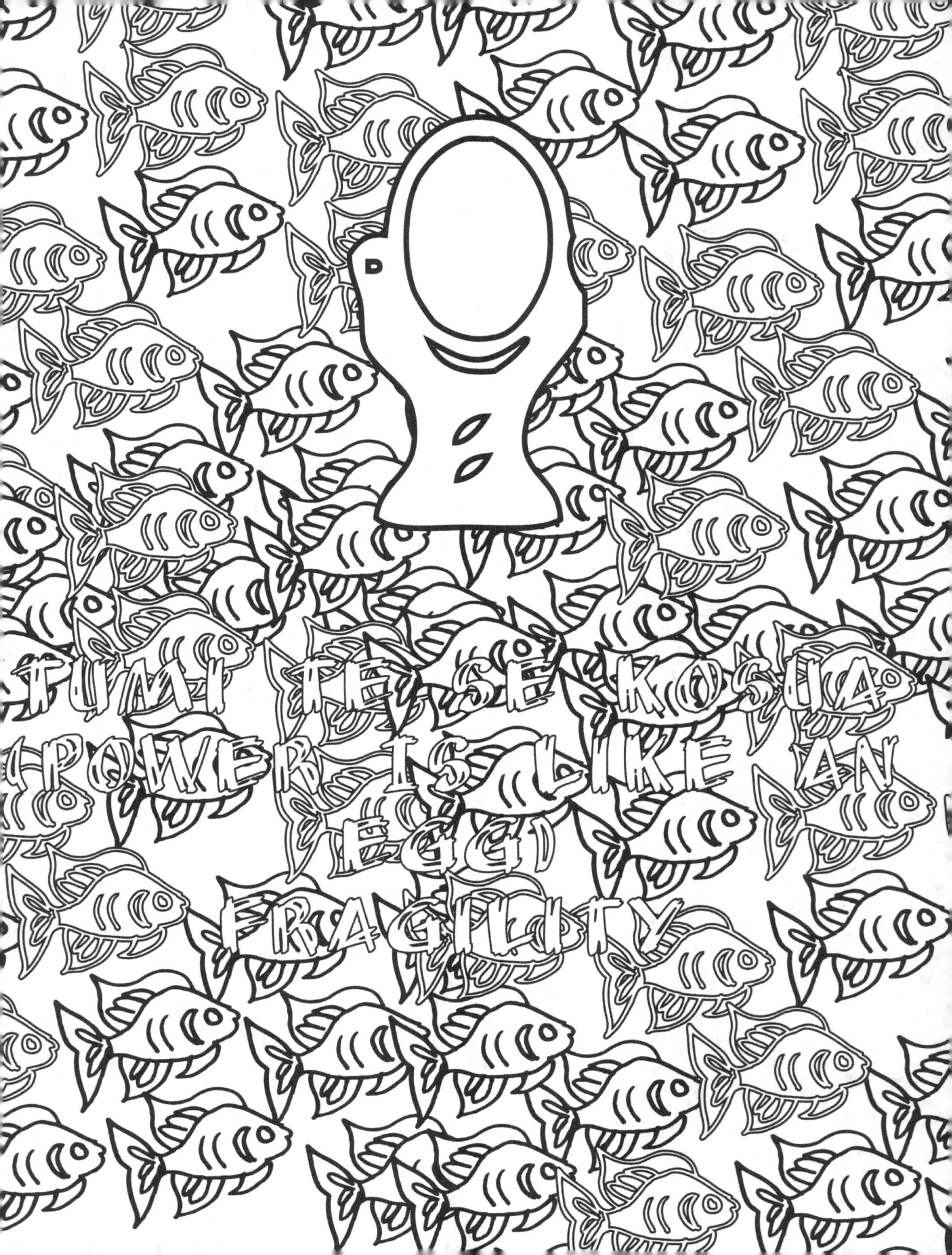

TUMI TESE KOSUA (POWER IS LIKE AN EGG) FRAGILITY

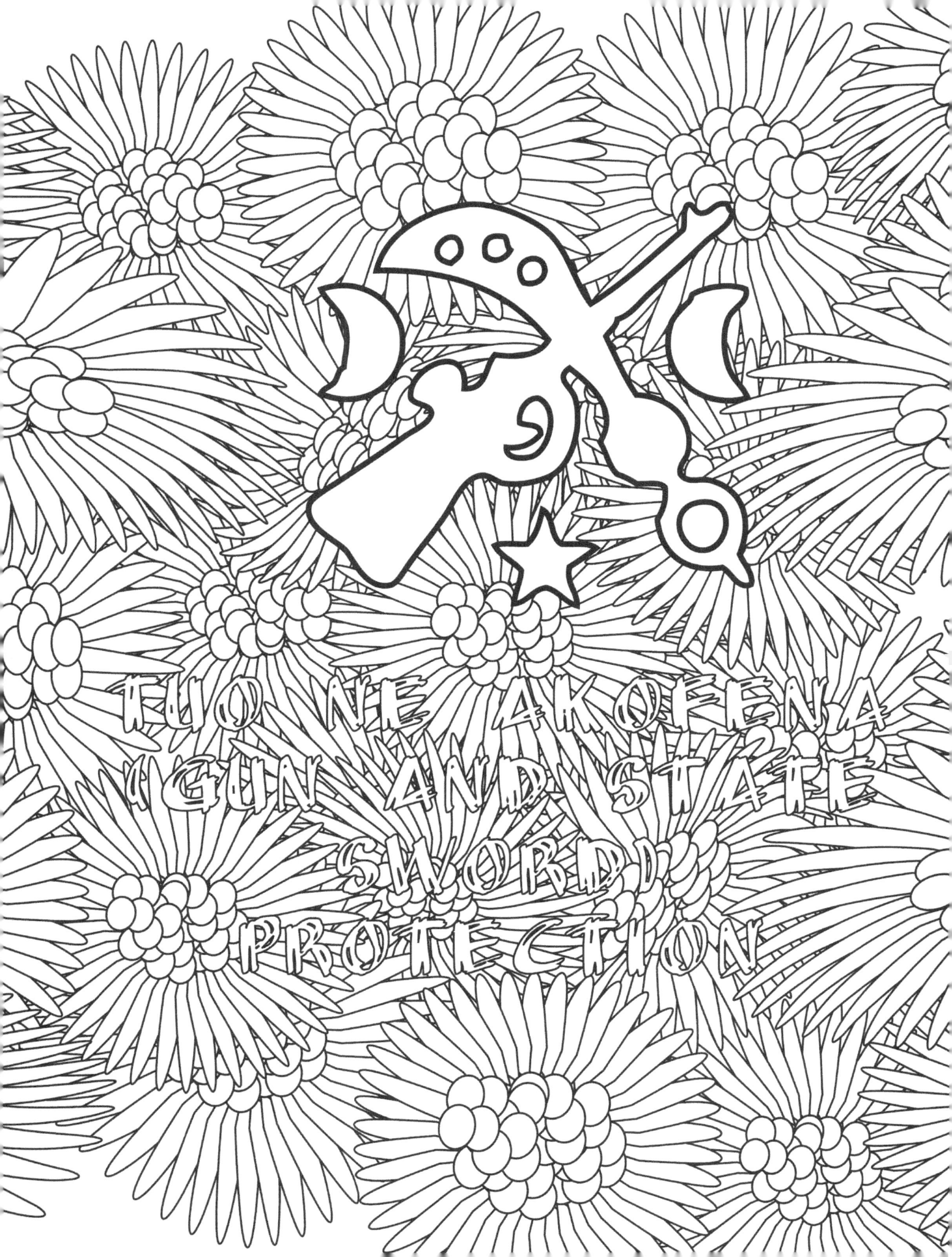

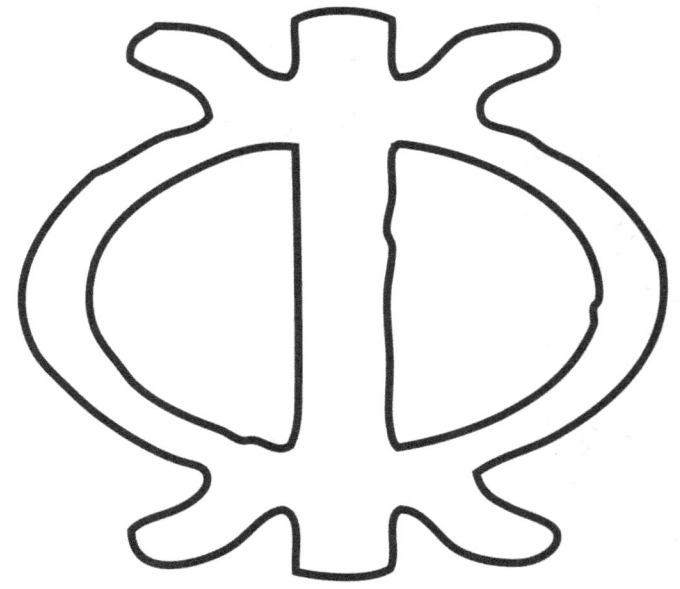

WAWA ABA
(WAWA TREE
SEED)
PERSEVERANCE

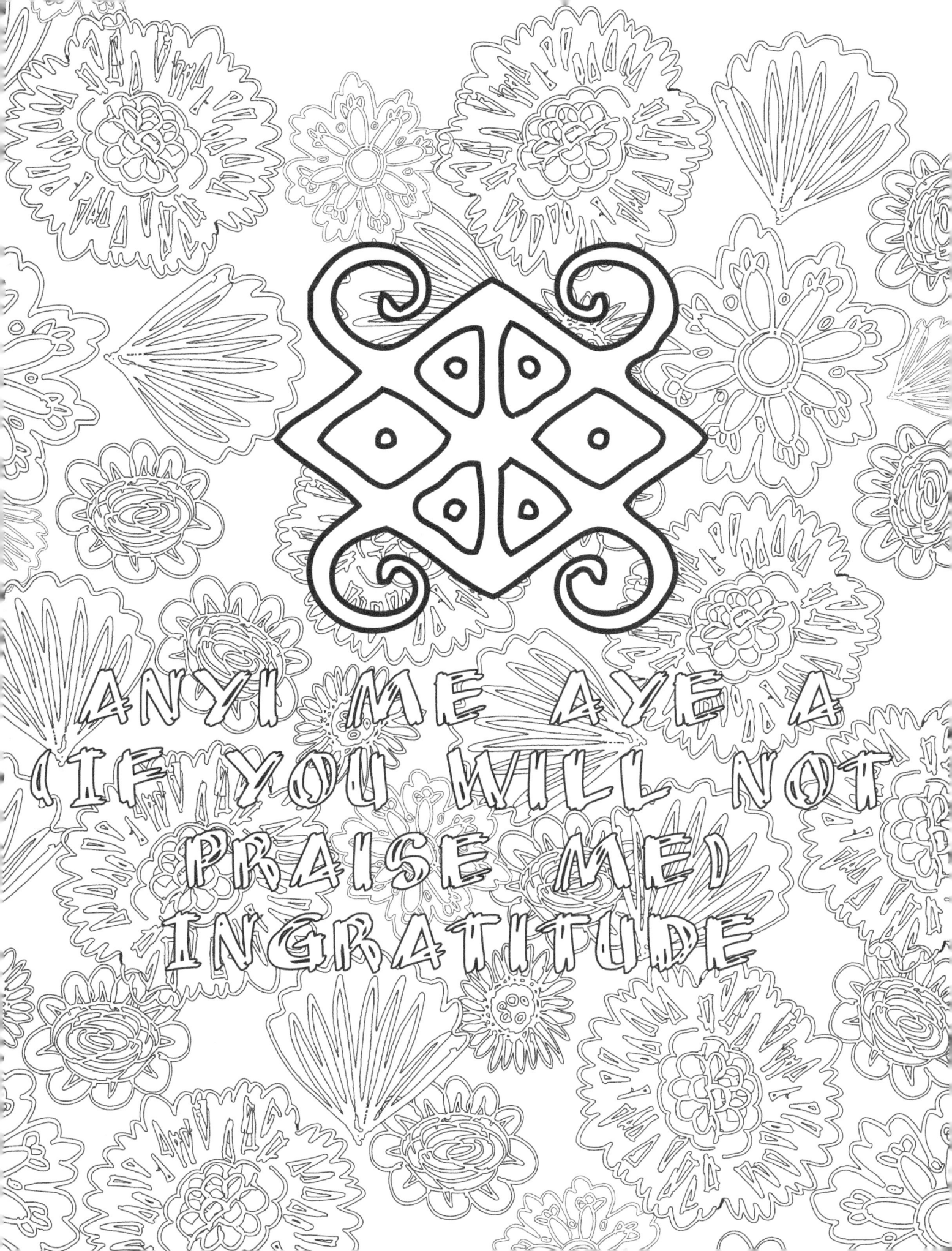

ANYI ME AYE A
(IF YOU WILL NOT
PRAISE ME)
INGRATITUDE

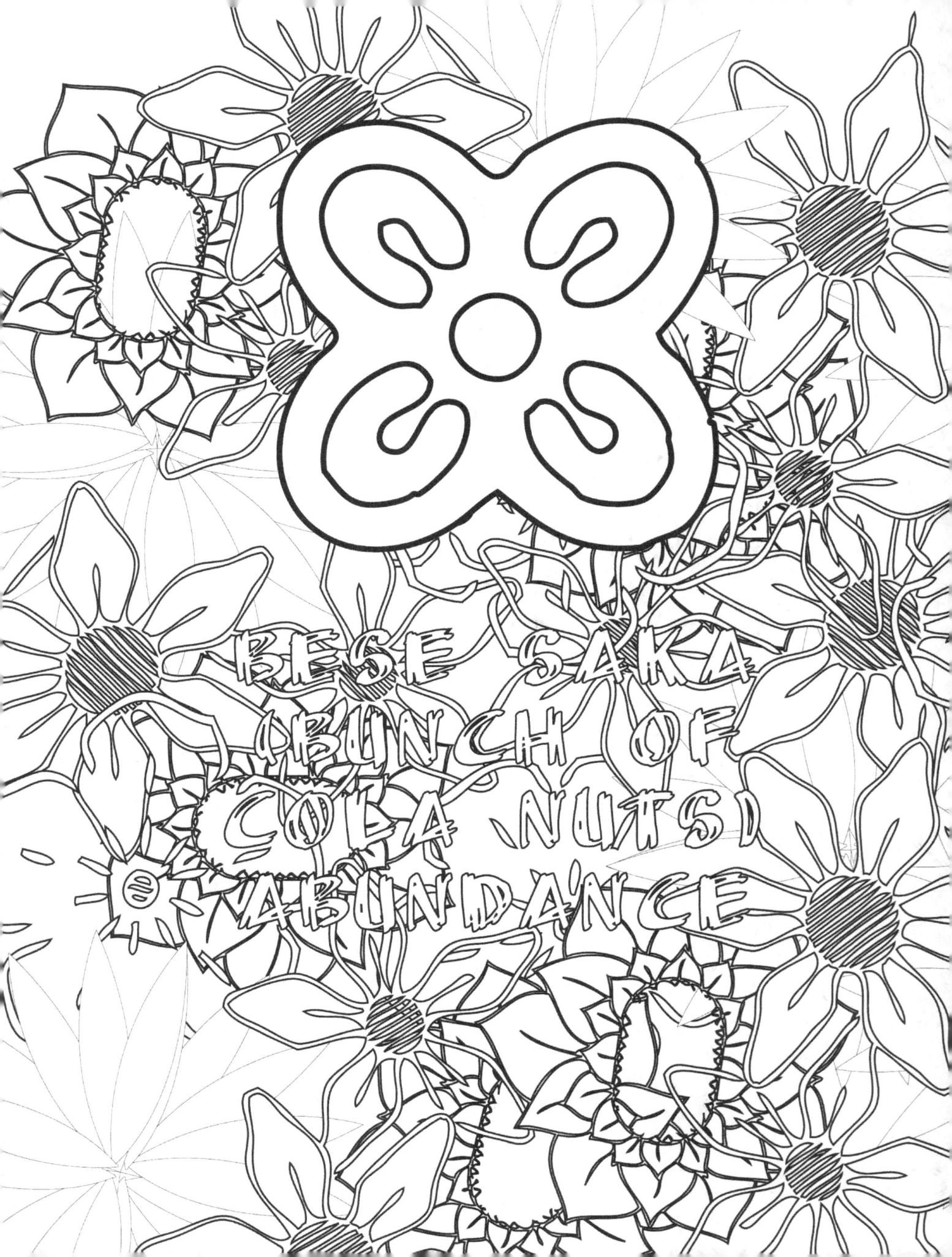

BESE SAKA
(BUNCH OF
COLA NUTS)
ABUNDANCE

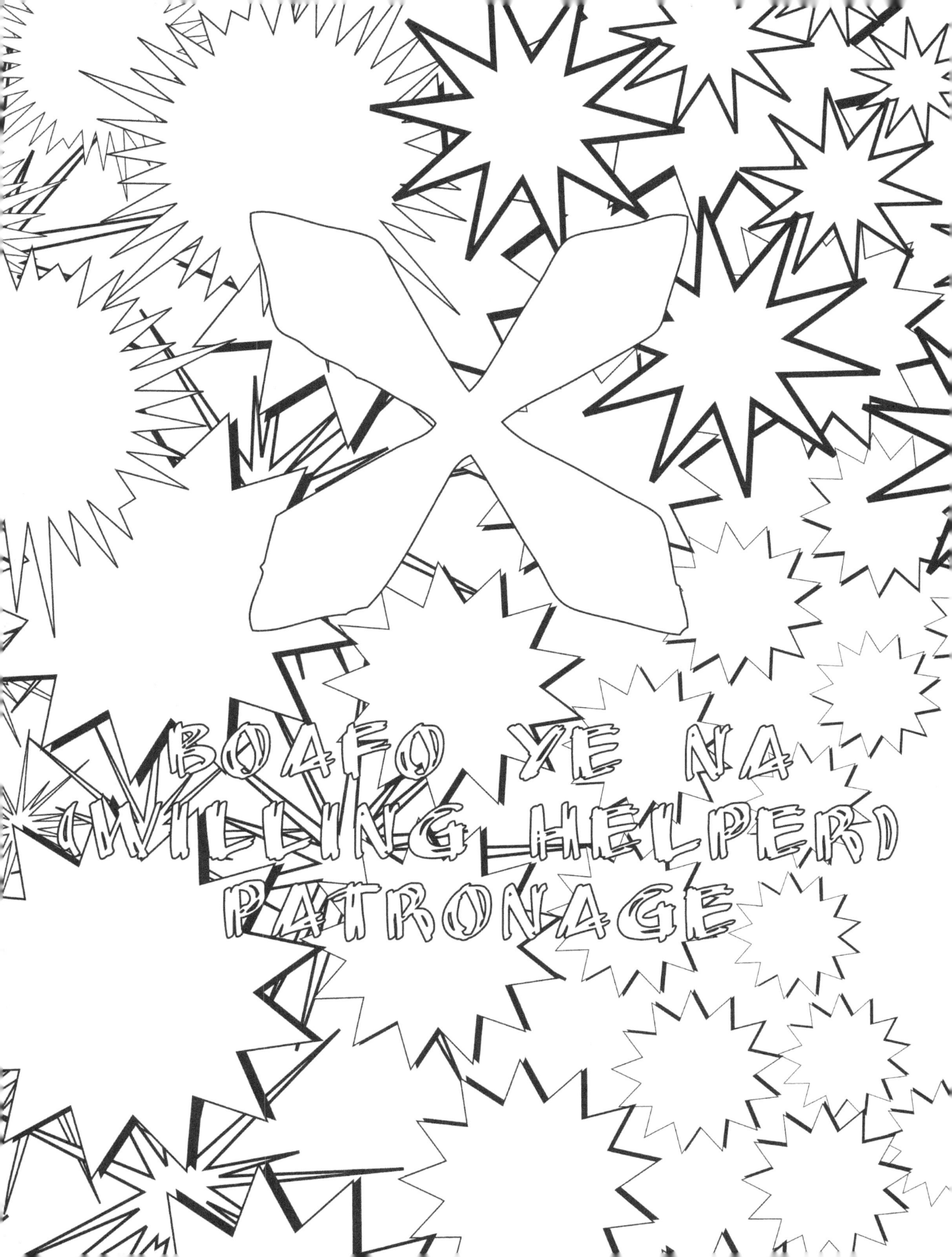

BOAFO YE NA
(WILLING HELPER)
PATRONAGE

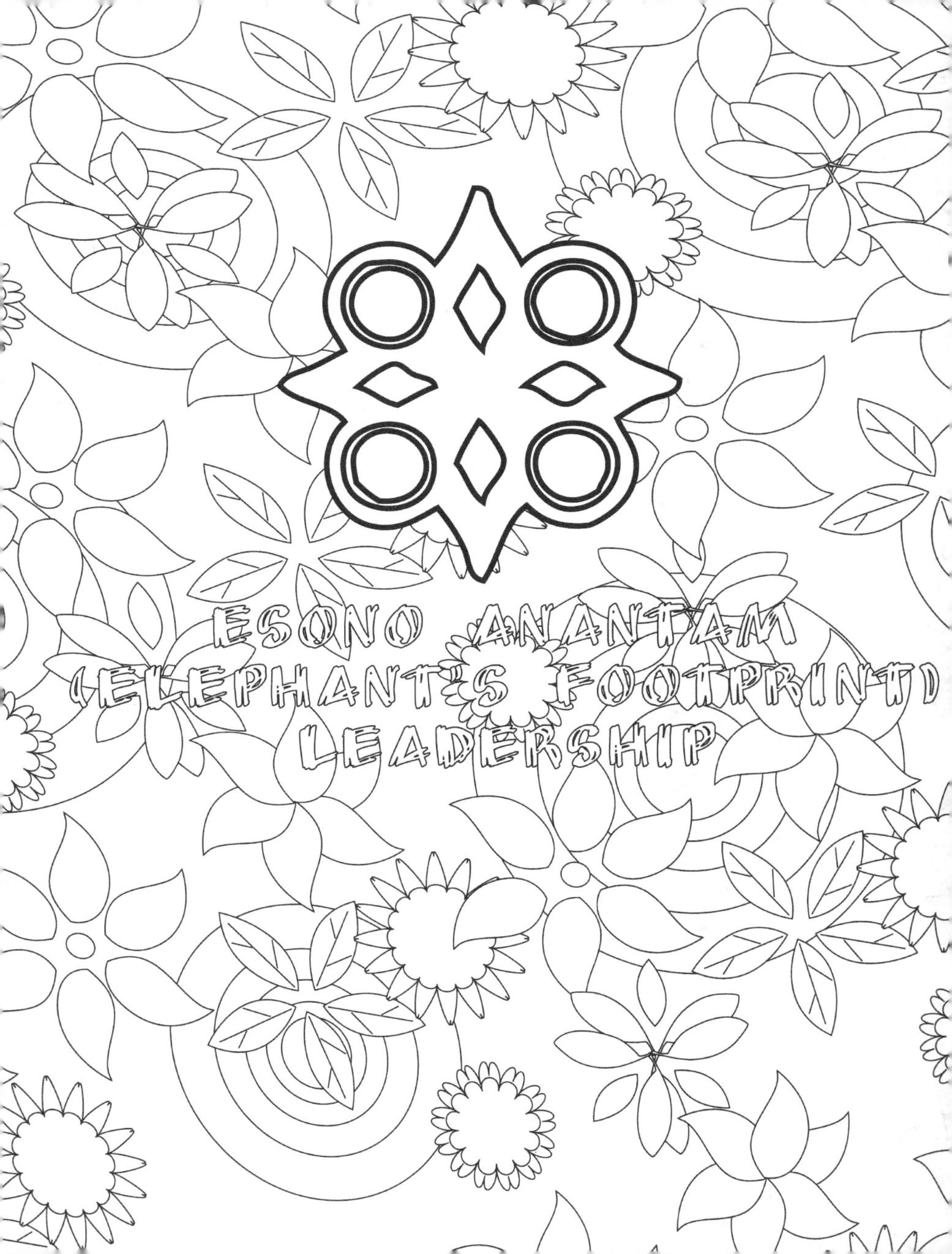

ESONO ANANTAM
(ELEPHANT'S FOOTPRINT)
LEADERSHIP

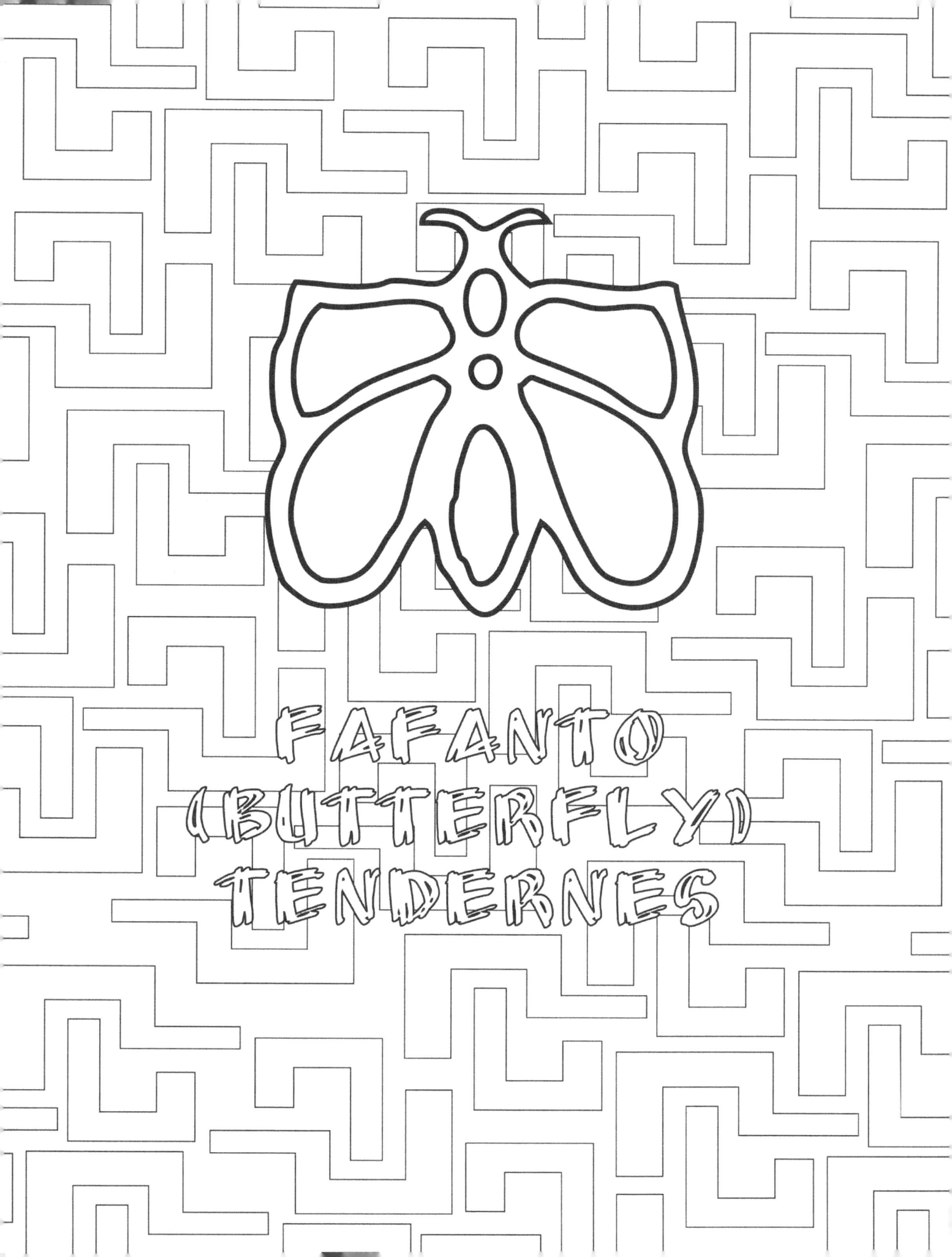

FAFANTO
(BUTTERFLY)
TENDERNES

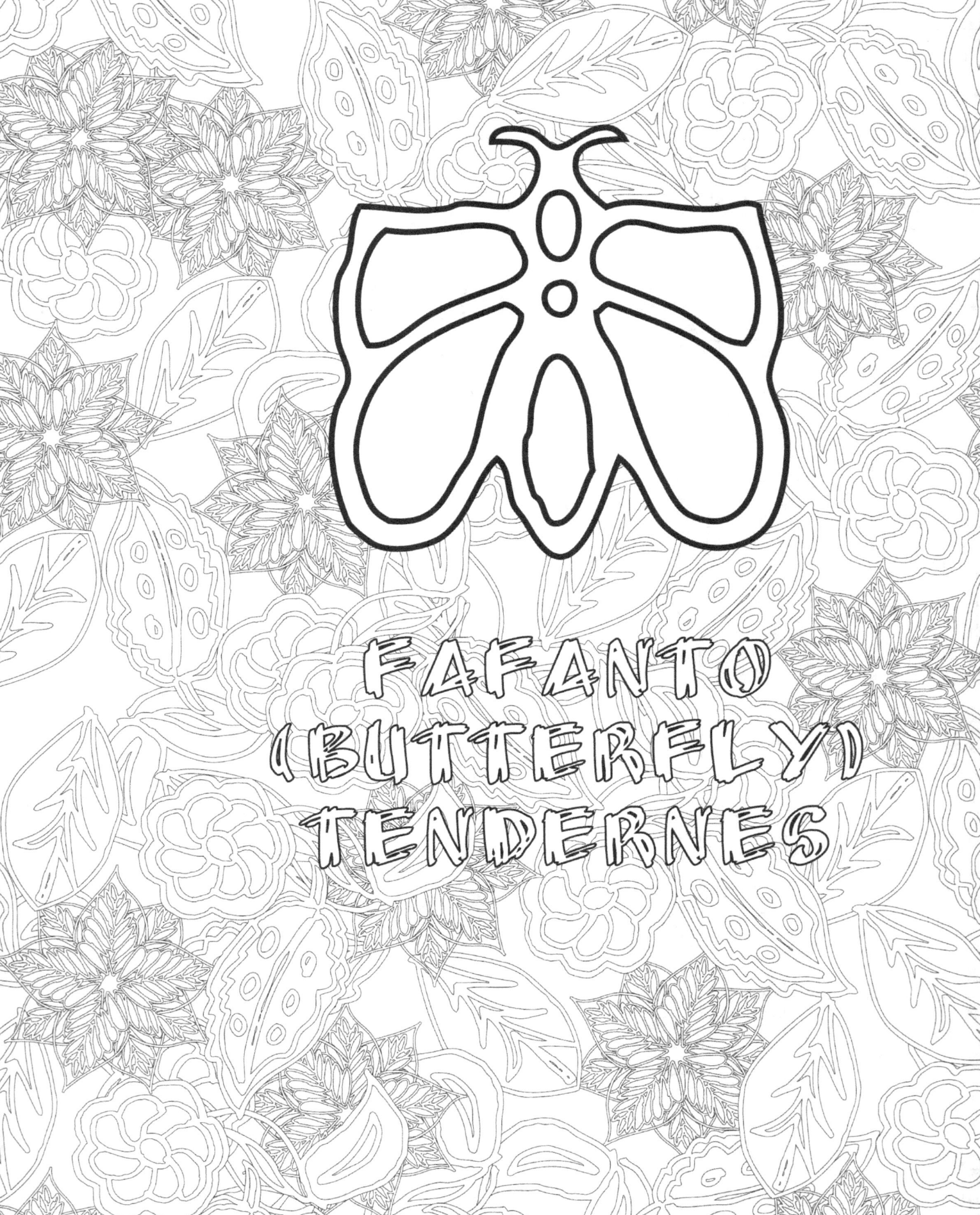

FAFANTO
(BUTTERFLY)
TENDERNES

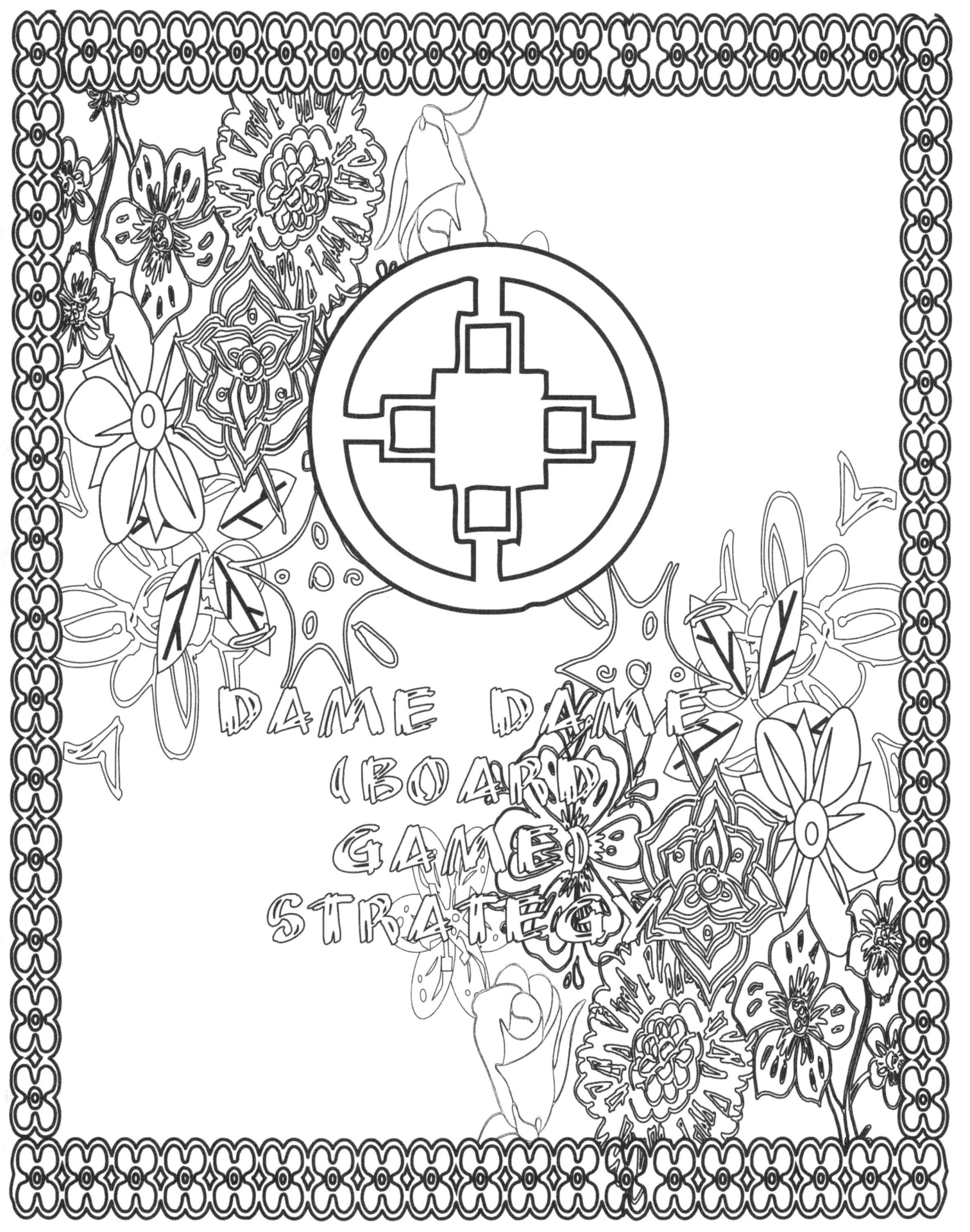

DAME DAME
(BOARD)
GAME
STRATEGY

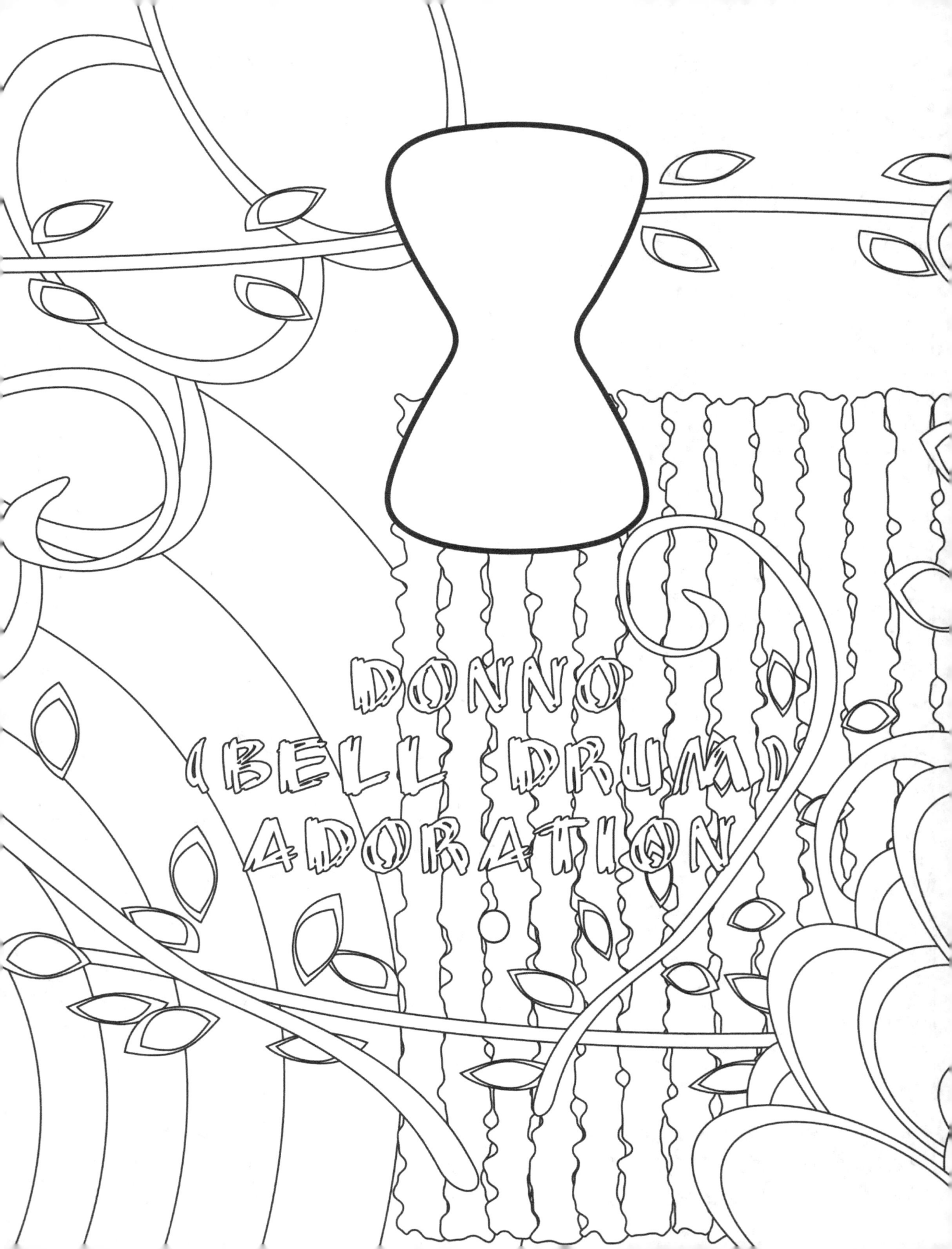

DONNO
(BELL DRUM)
ADORATION

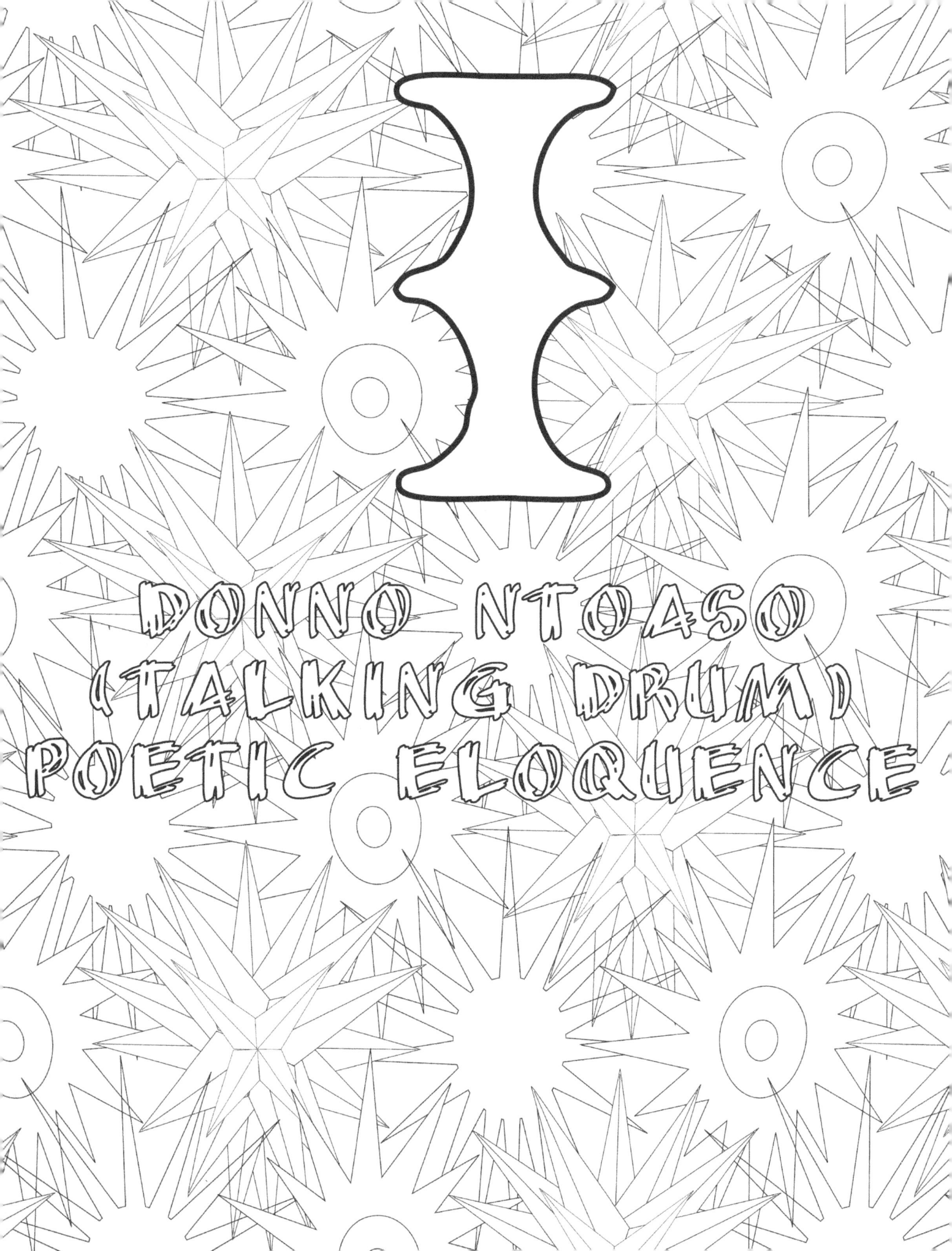

DONNO NTOASO
(TALKING DRUM)
POETIC ELOQUENCE

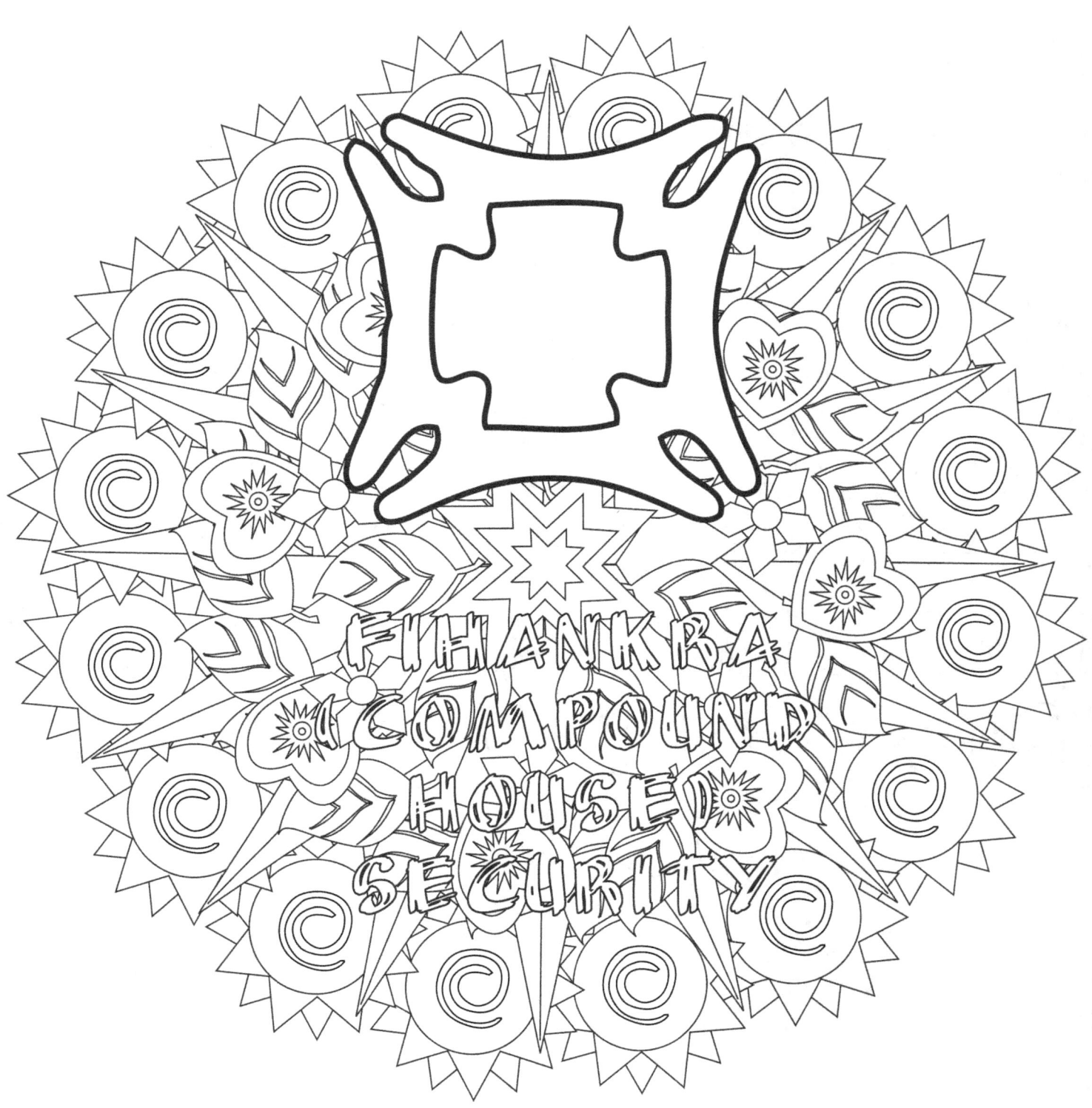

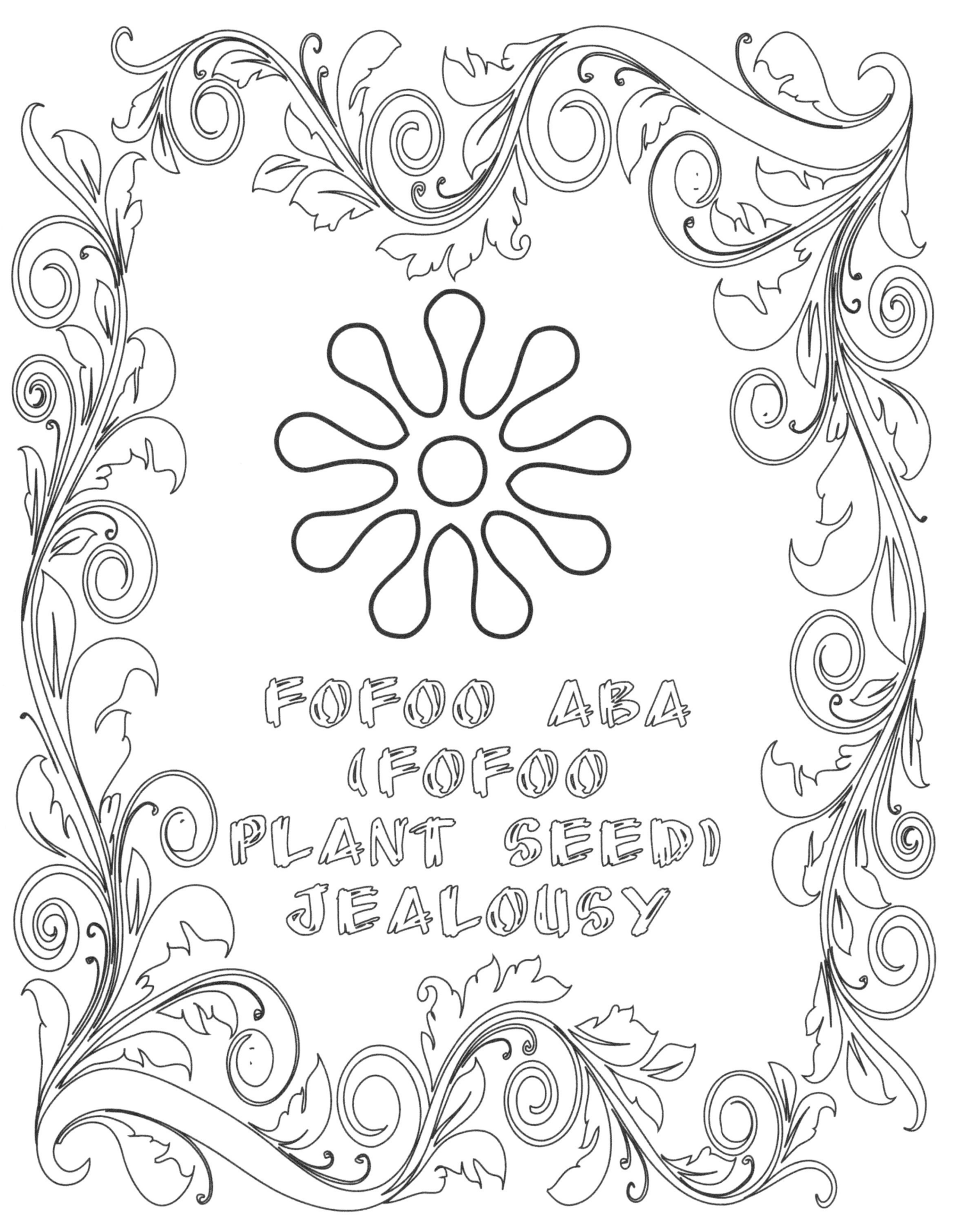

FOFOO ABA
(FOFOO
PLANT SEED)
JEALOUSY

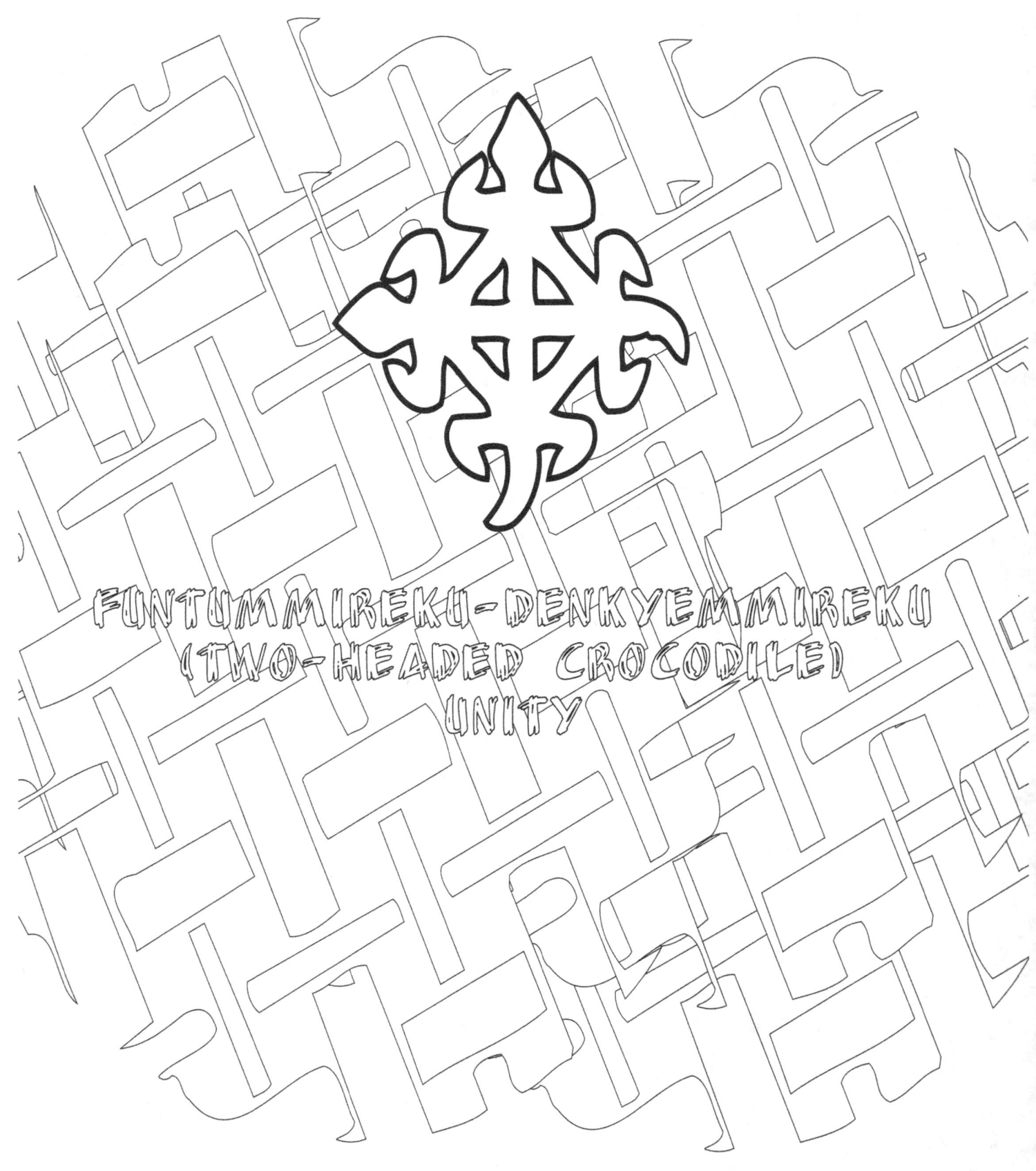

FUNTUMMIREKU-DENKYEMMIREKU
(TWO-HEADED CROCODILE)
UNITY

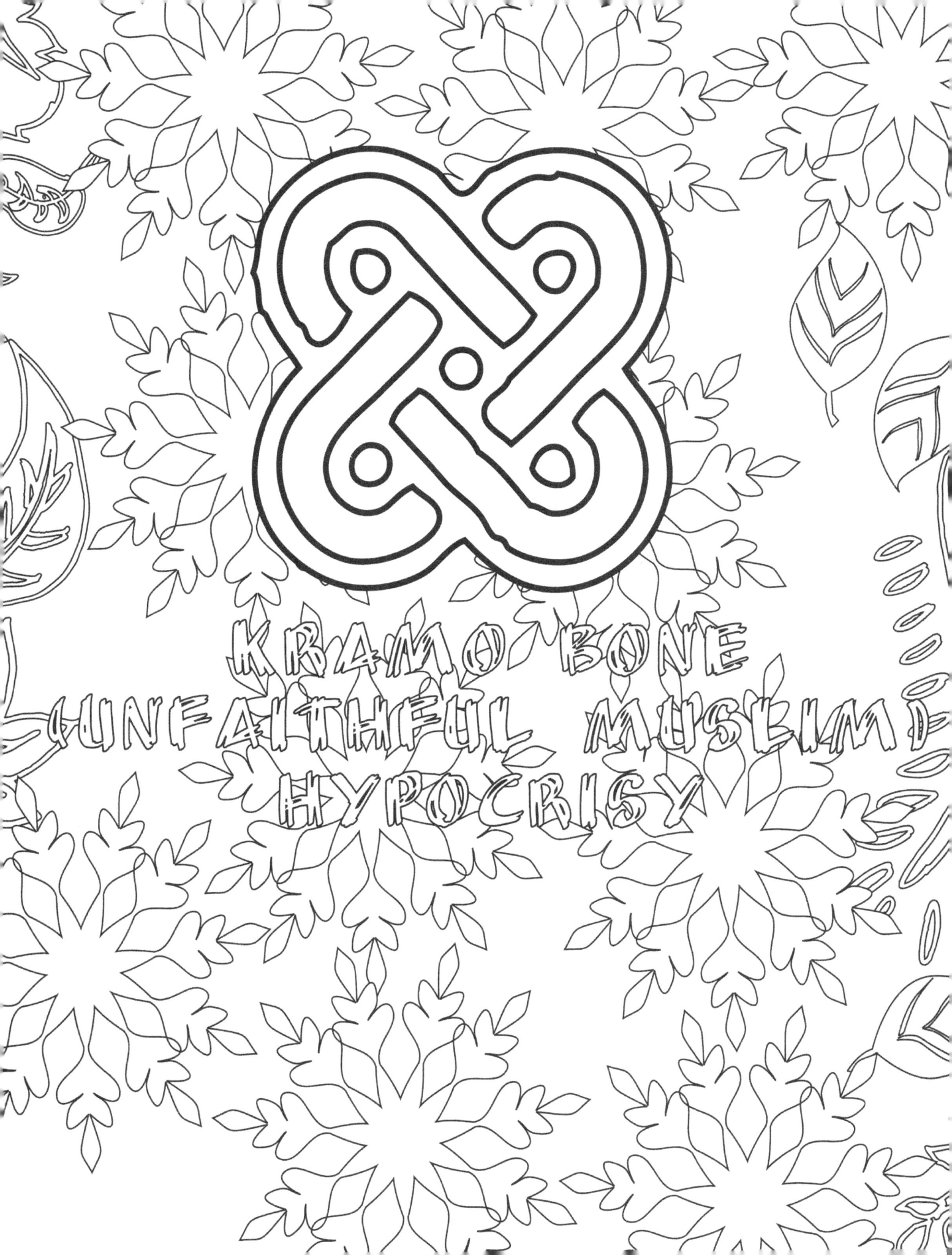

KRAMO BONE
(UNFAITHFUL MUSLIM)
HYPOCRISY

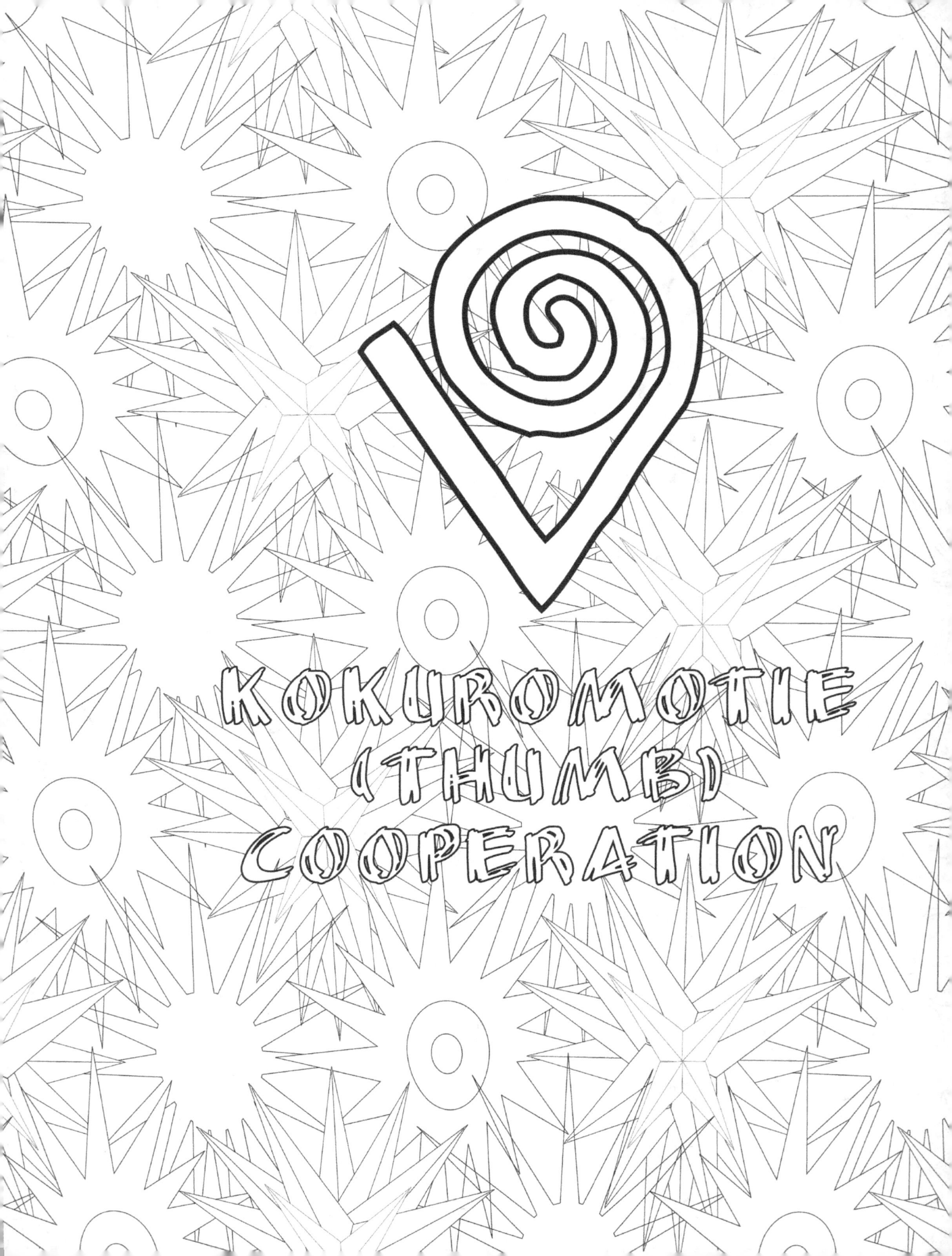

KOKUROMOTIE
(THUMB)
COOPERATION

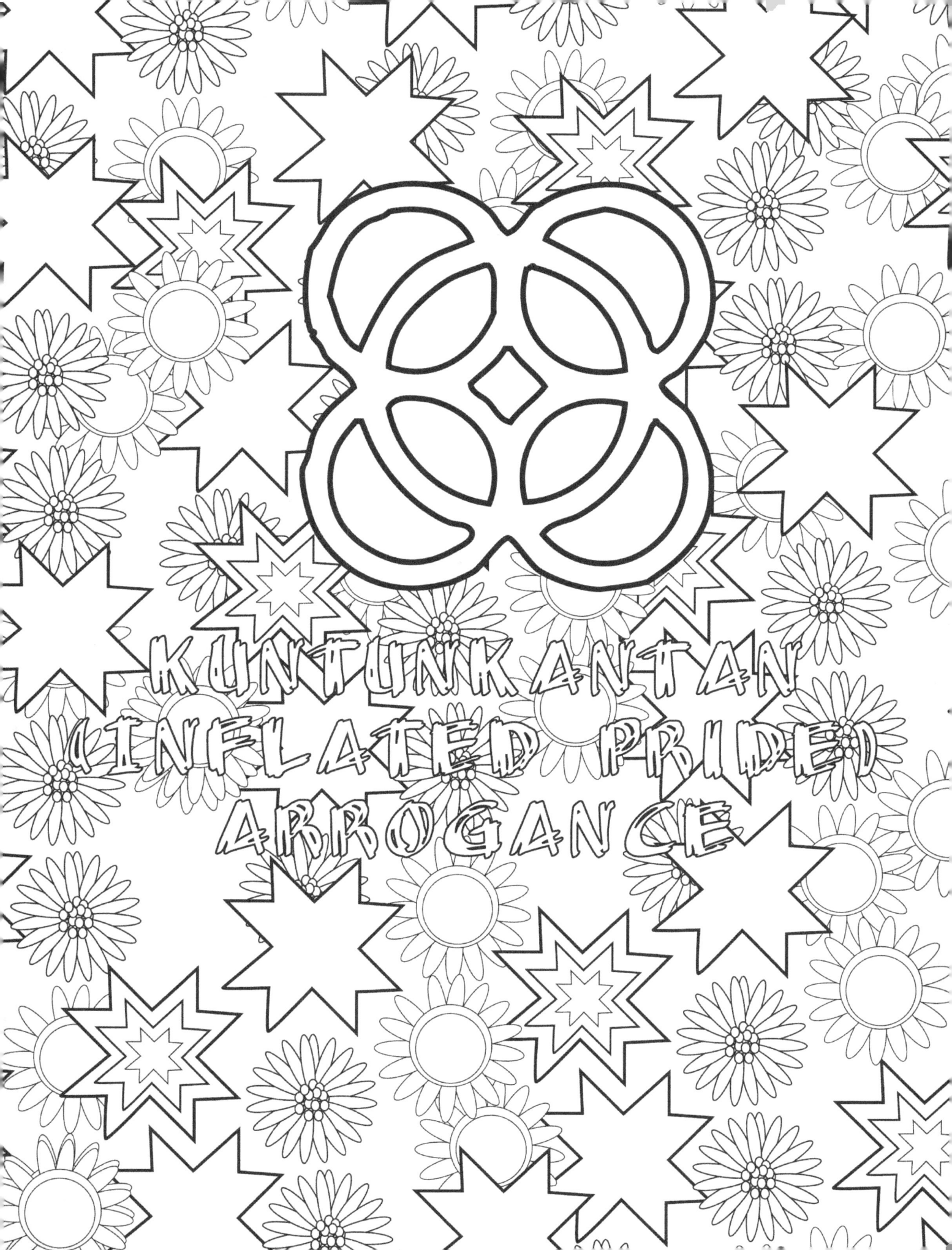

KUNTUNKANTAN

(INFLATED PRIDE)

ARROGANCE

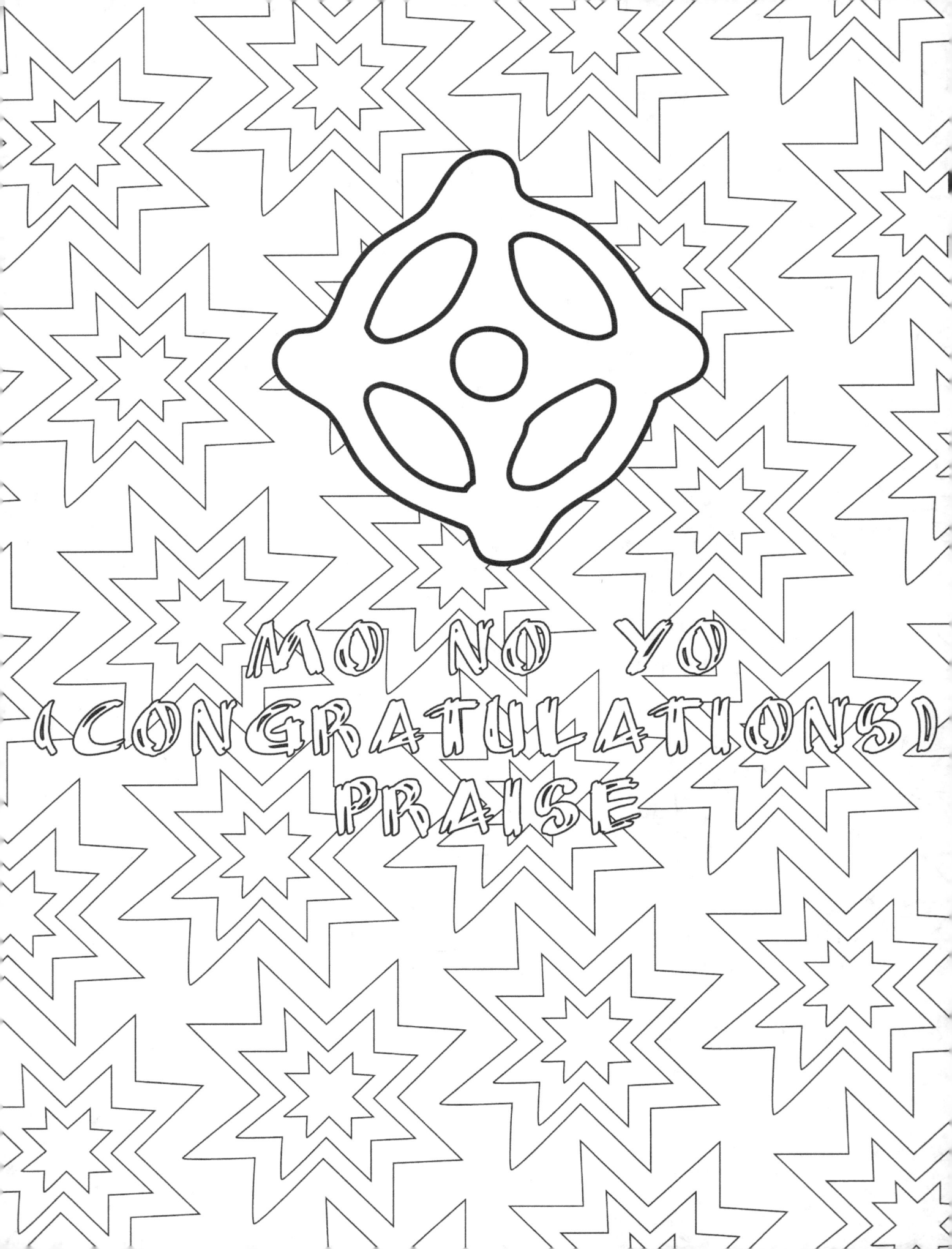

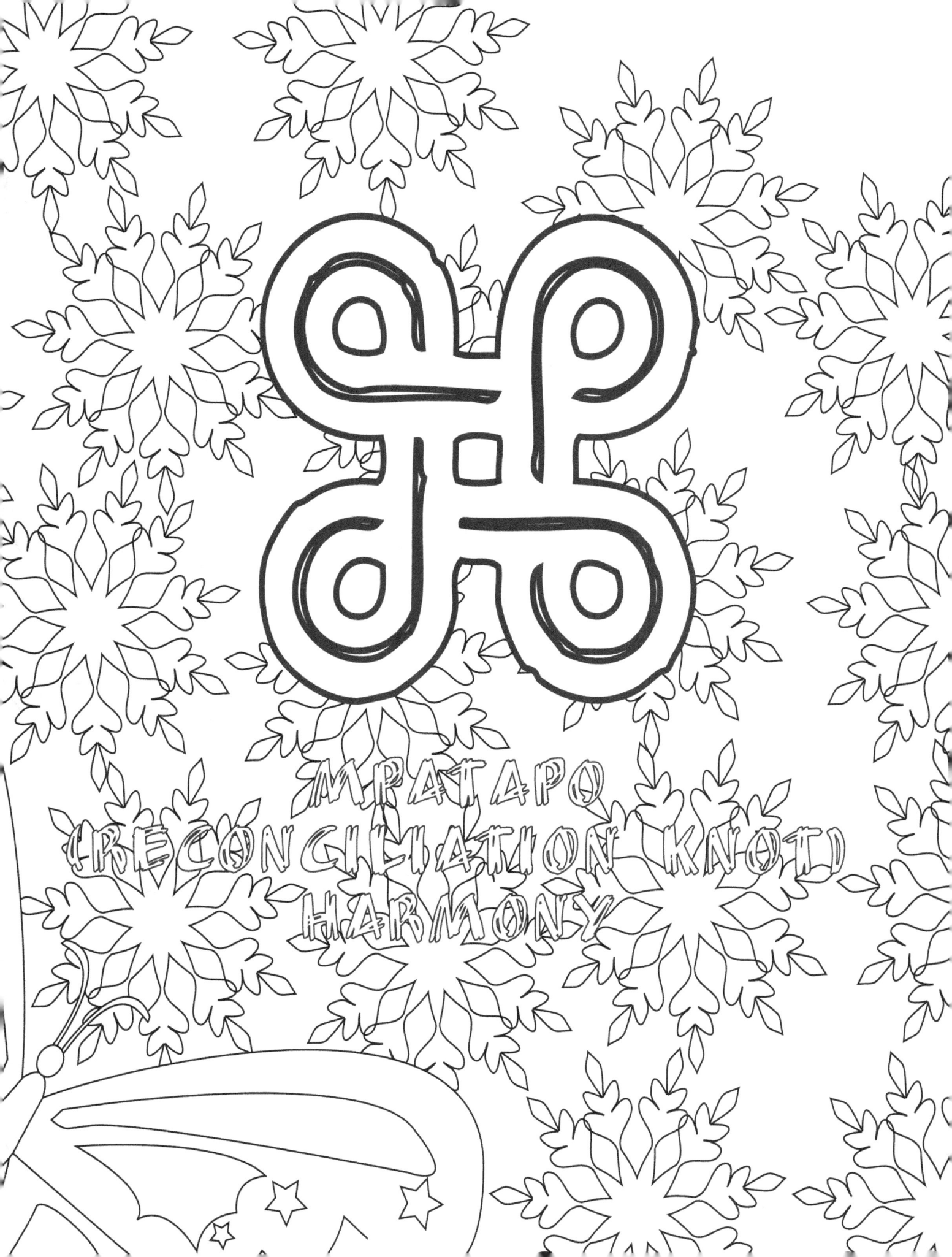

MPATAPO
(RECONCILIATION KNOT)
HARMONY

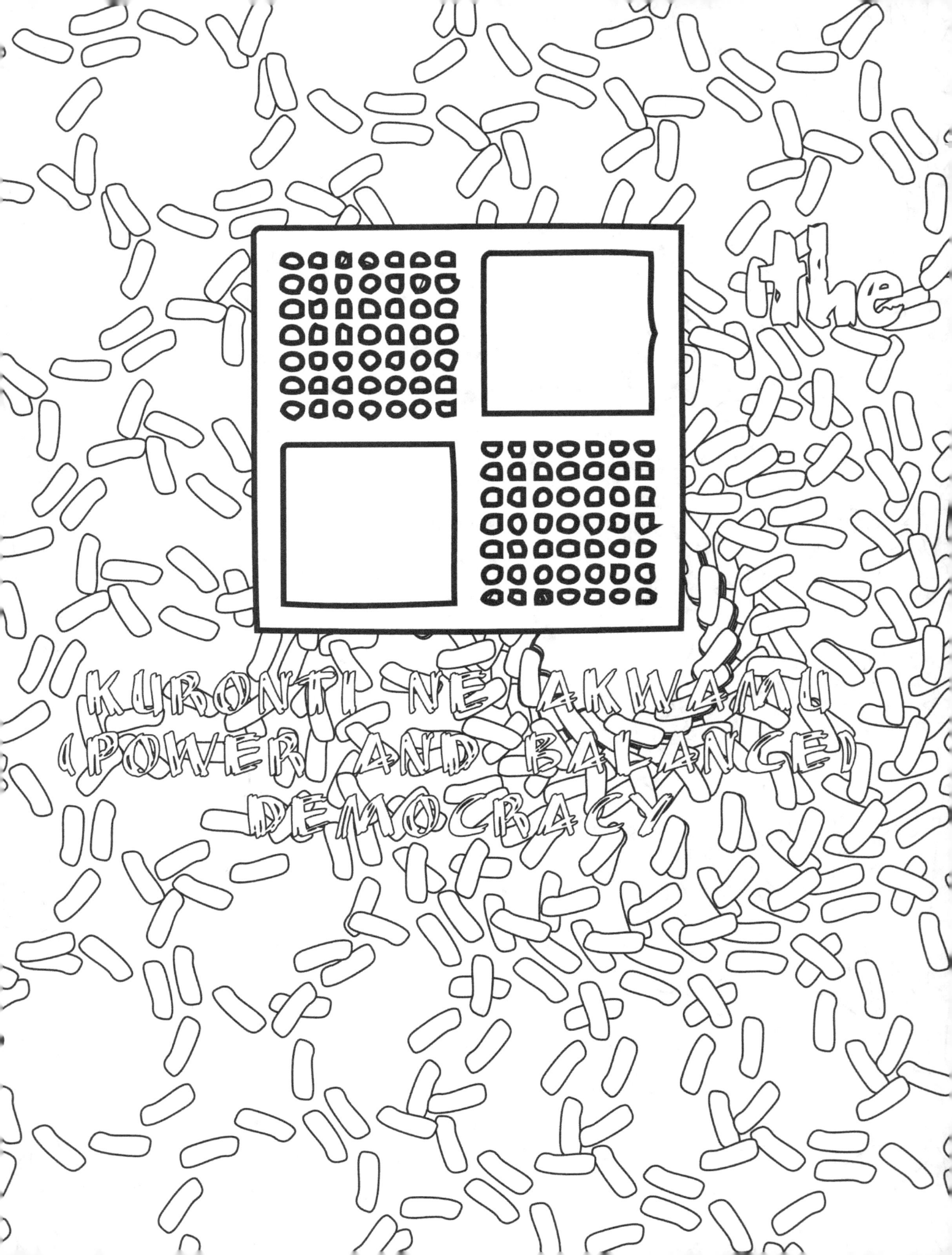

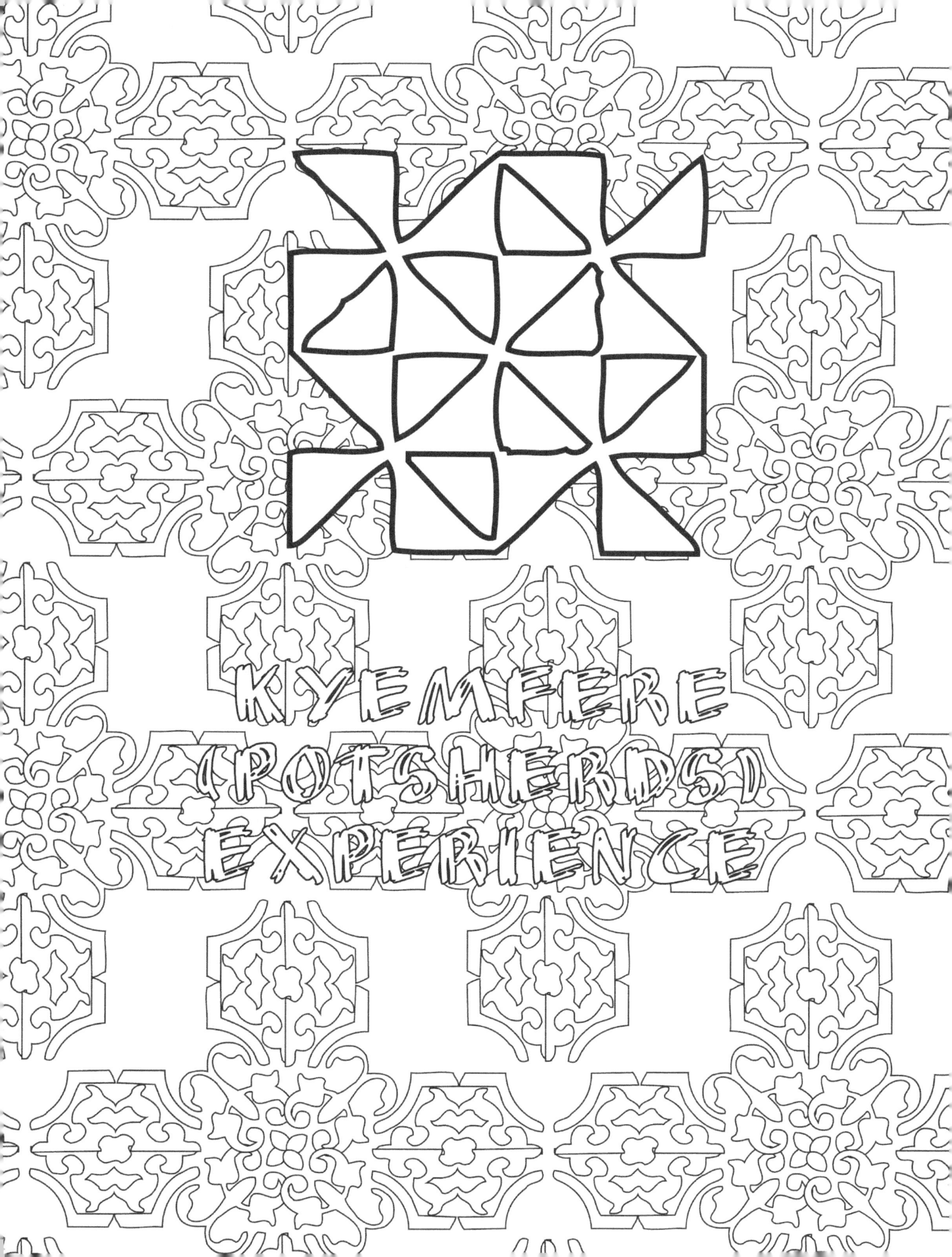

KYEMFERE
(POTSHERDS)
EXPERIENCE

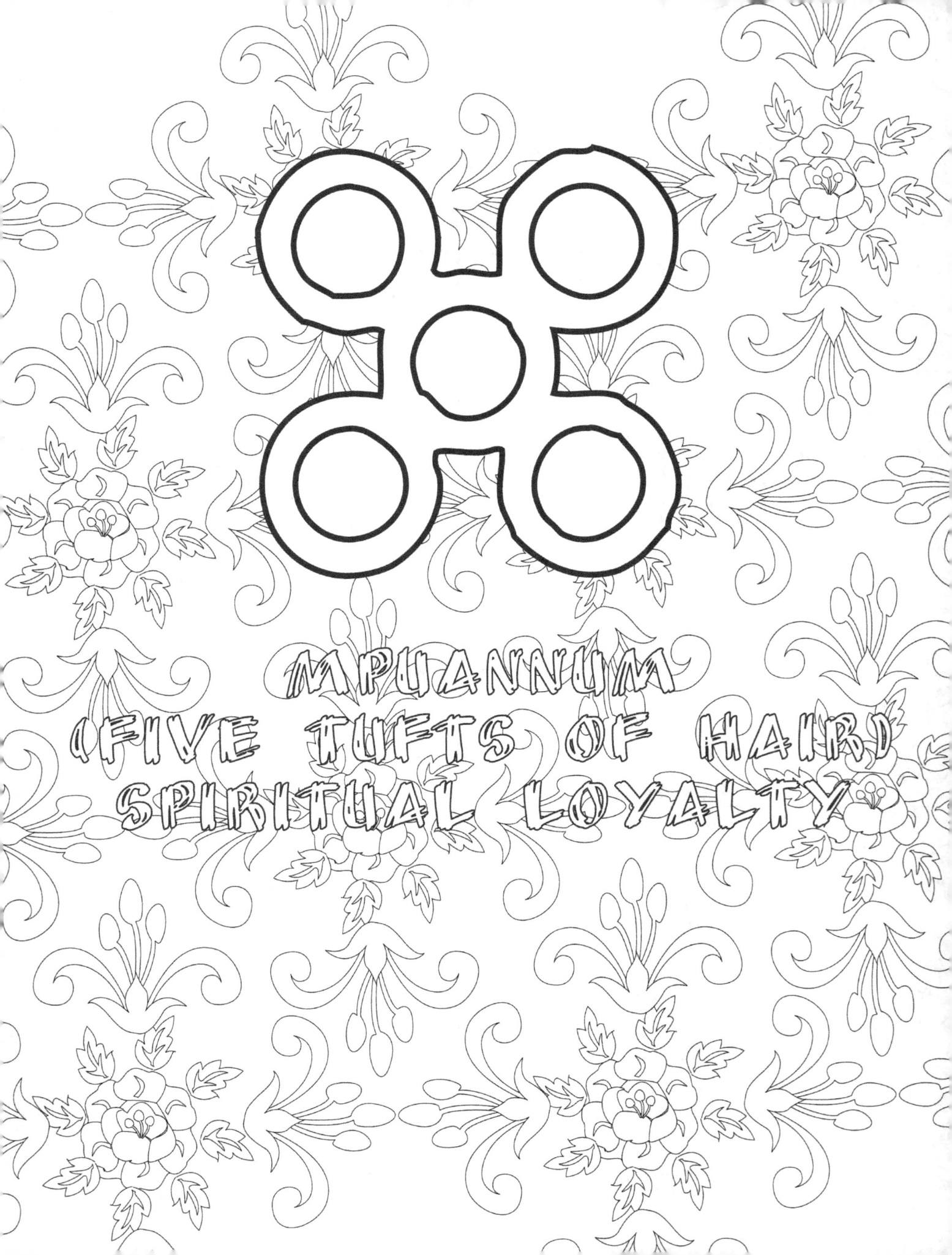

MPUANNUM
(FIVE TUFTS OF HAIR)
SPIRITUAL LOYALTY

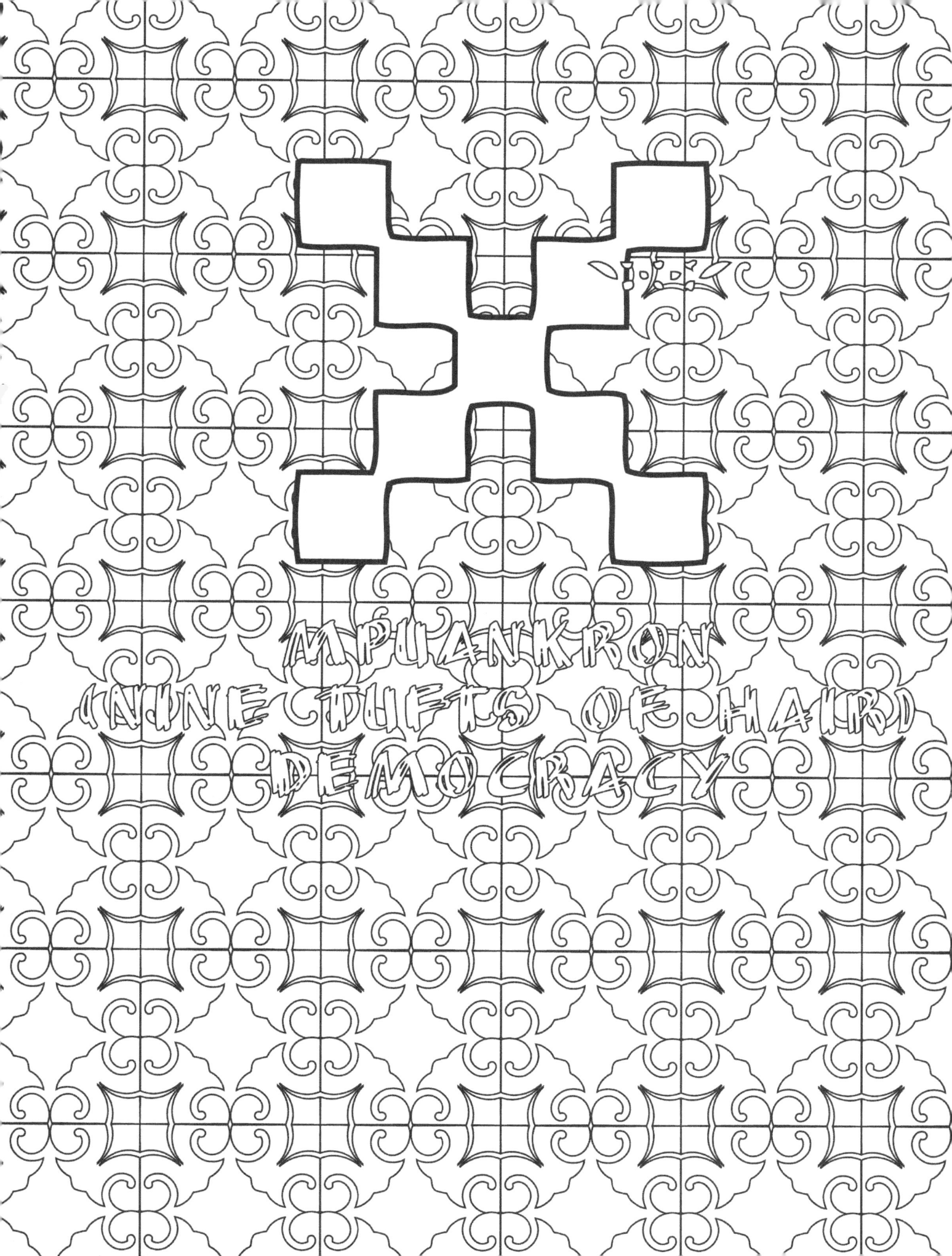

MPUANKRON

(NINE TUFTS OF HAIR)

DEMOCRACY

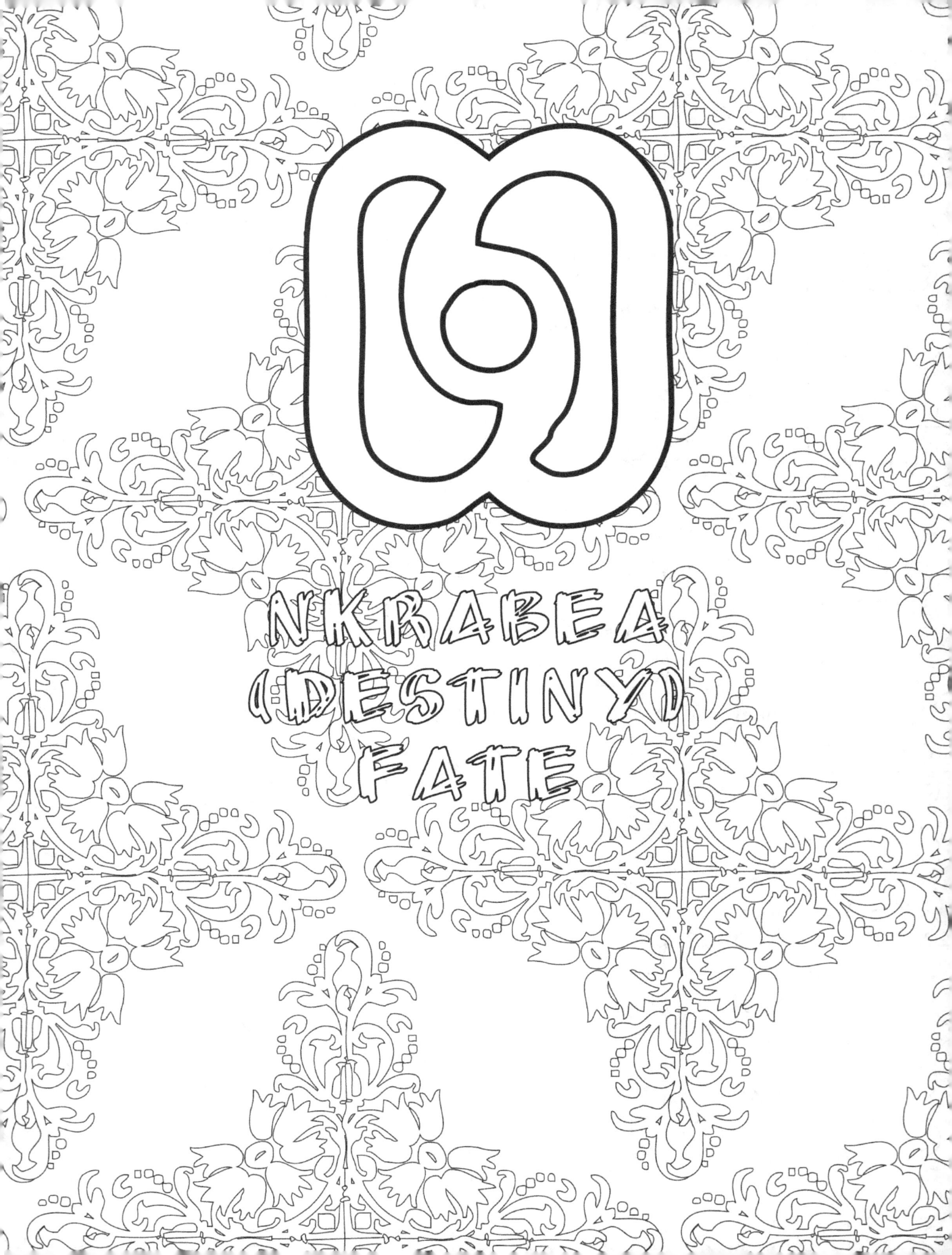

NKRABEA
(DESTINY)
FATE

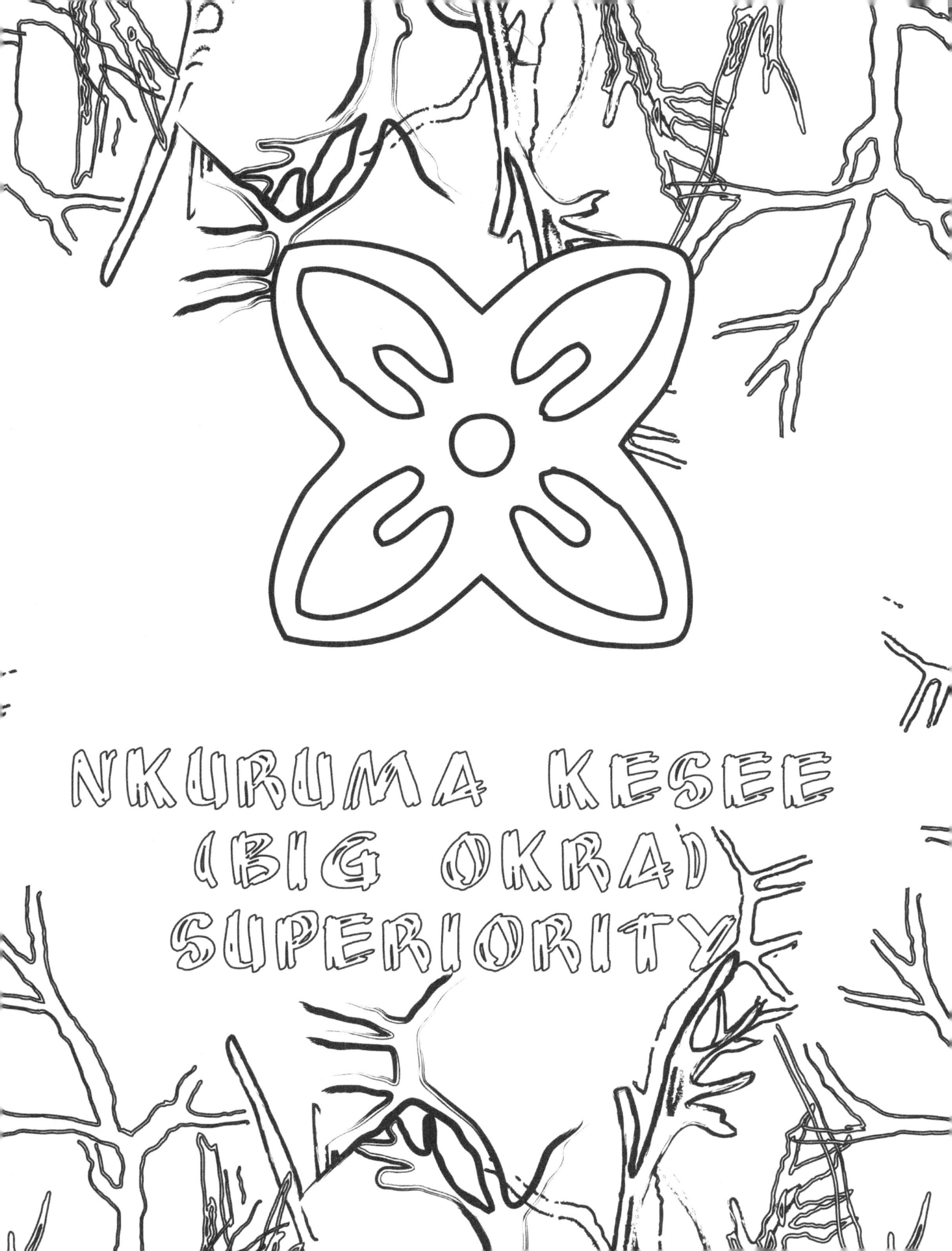

NKURUMA KESEE
(BIG OKRA)
SUPERIORITY

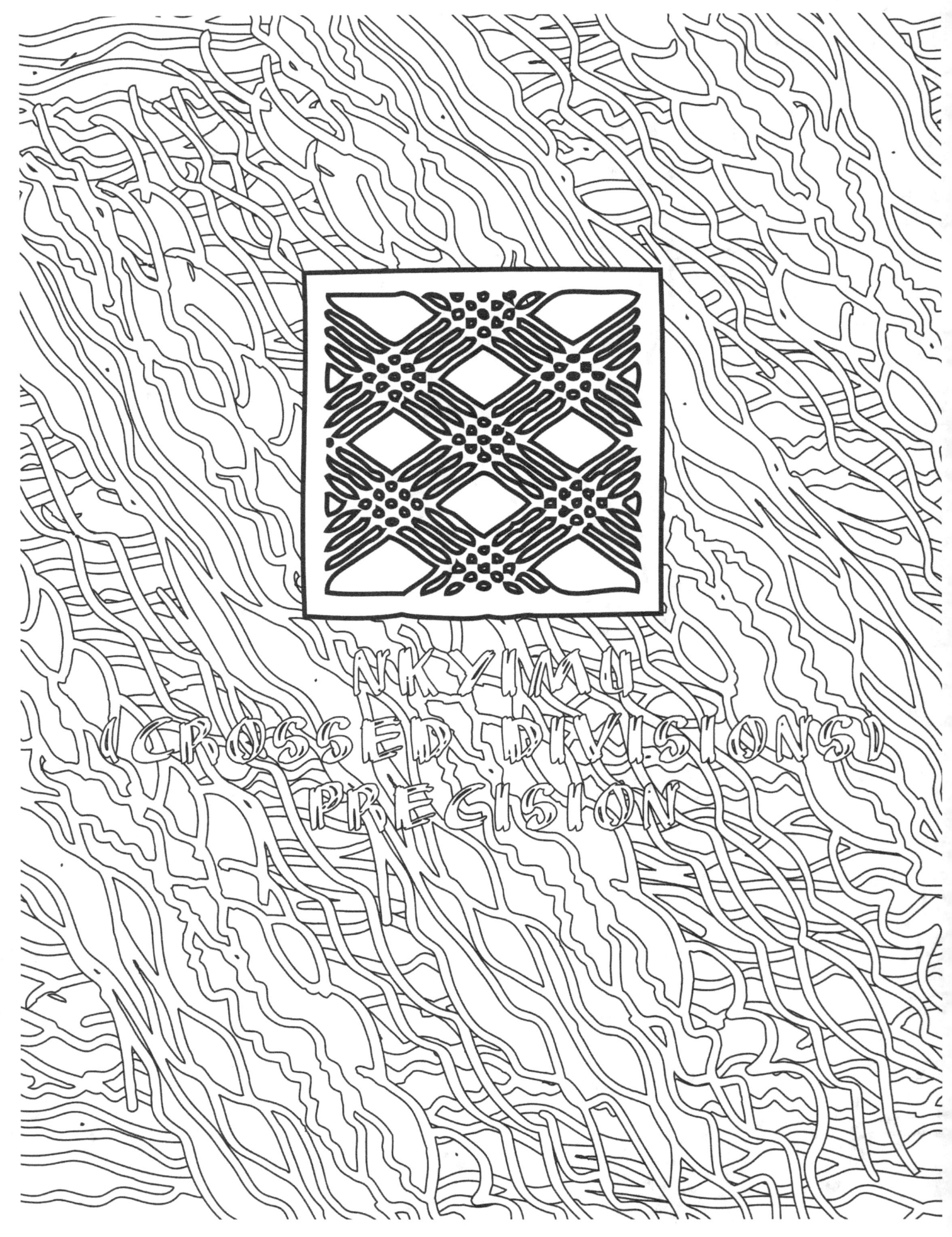

NKYIMU
(CROSSED DIVISIONS)
PRECISION

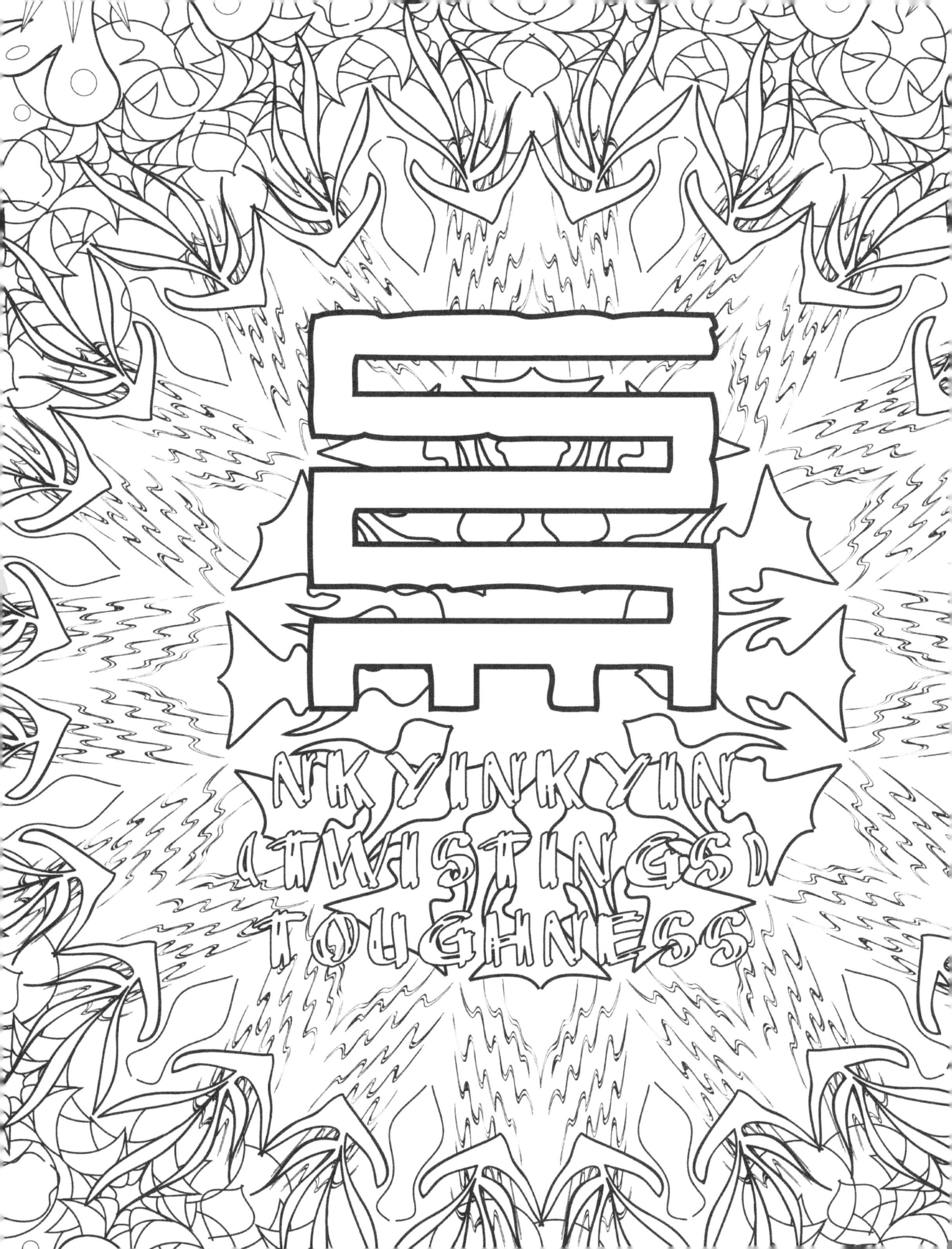

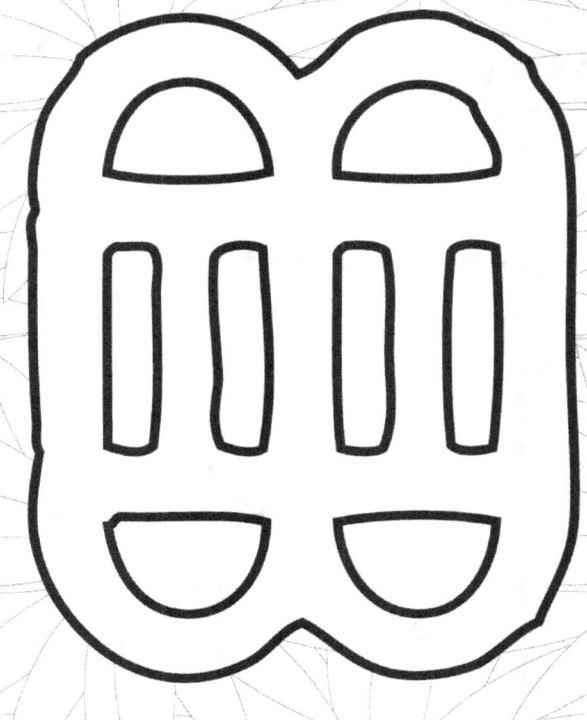

NNAMPO PA BAANU
(TWO GOOD FRIENDS)
FRIENDSHIP

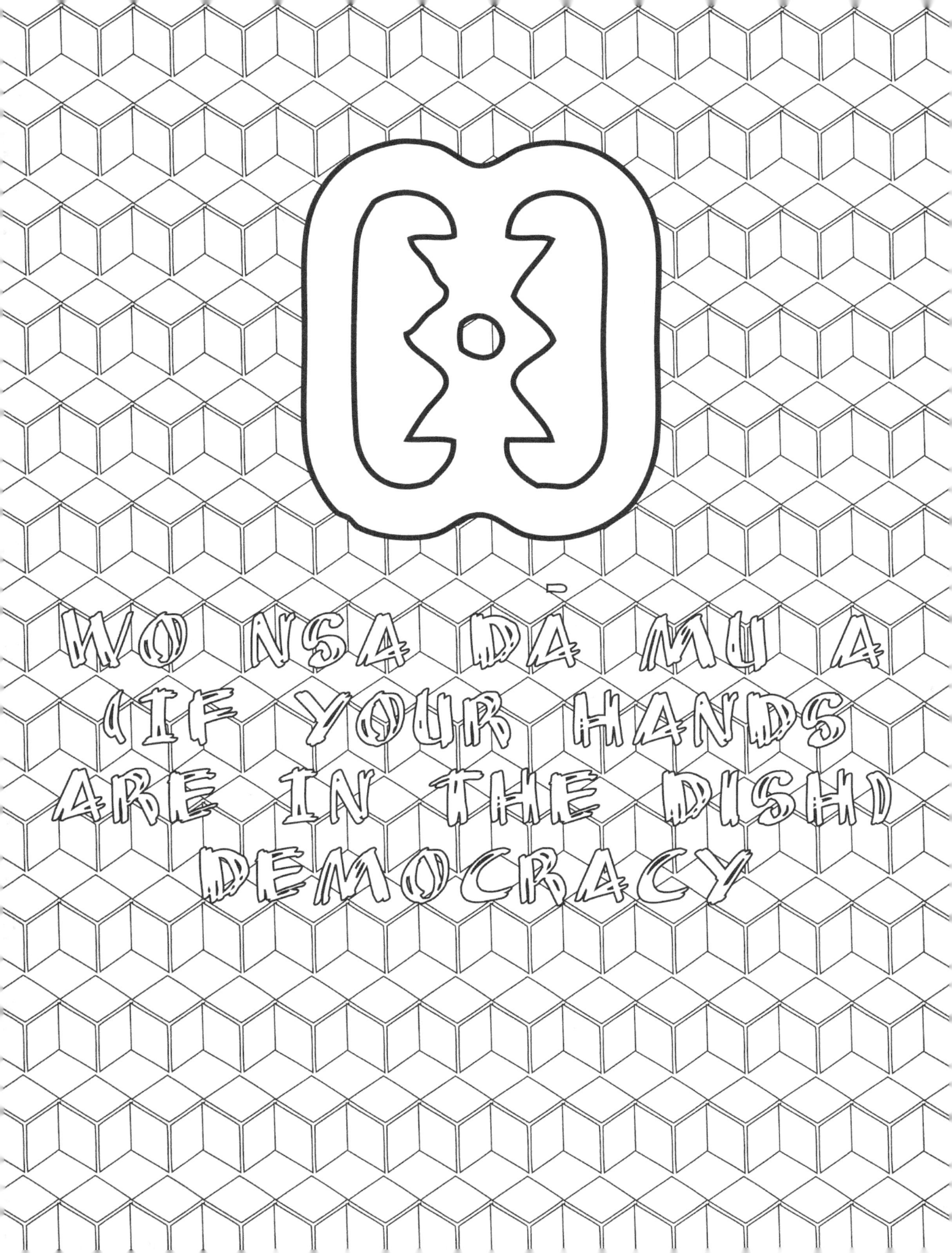

WO NSA DA MUA
(IF YOUR HANDS
ARE IN THE DISH)
DEMOCRACY

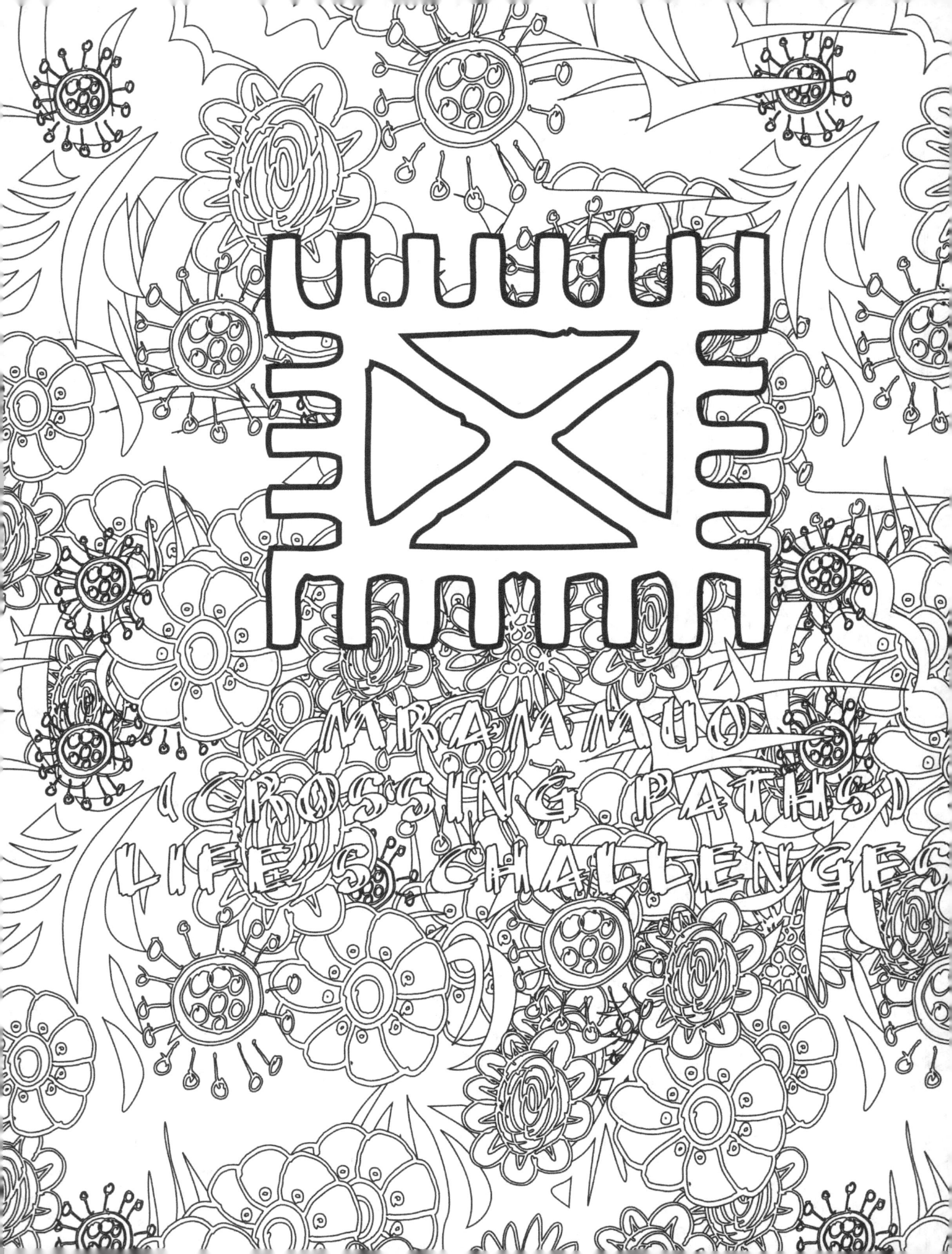

MRAMMUO
(CROSSING PATHS)
LIFE'S CHALLENGES

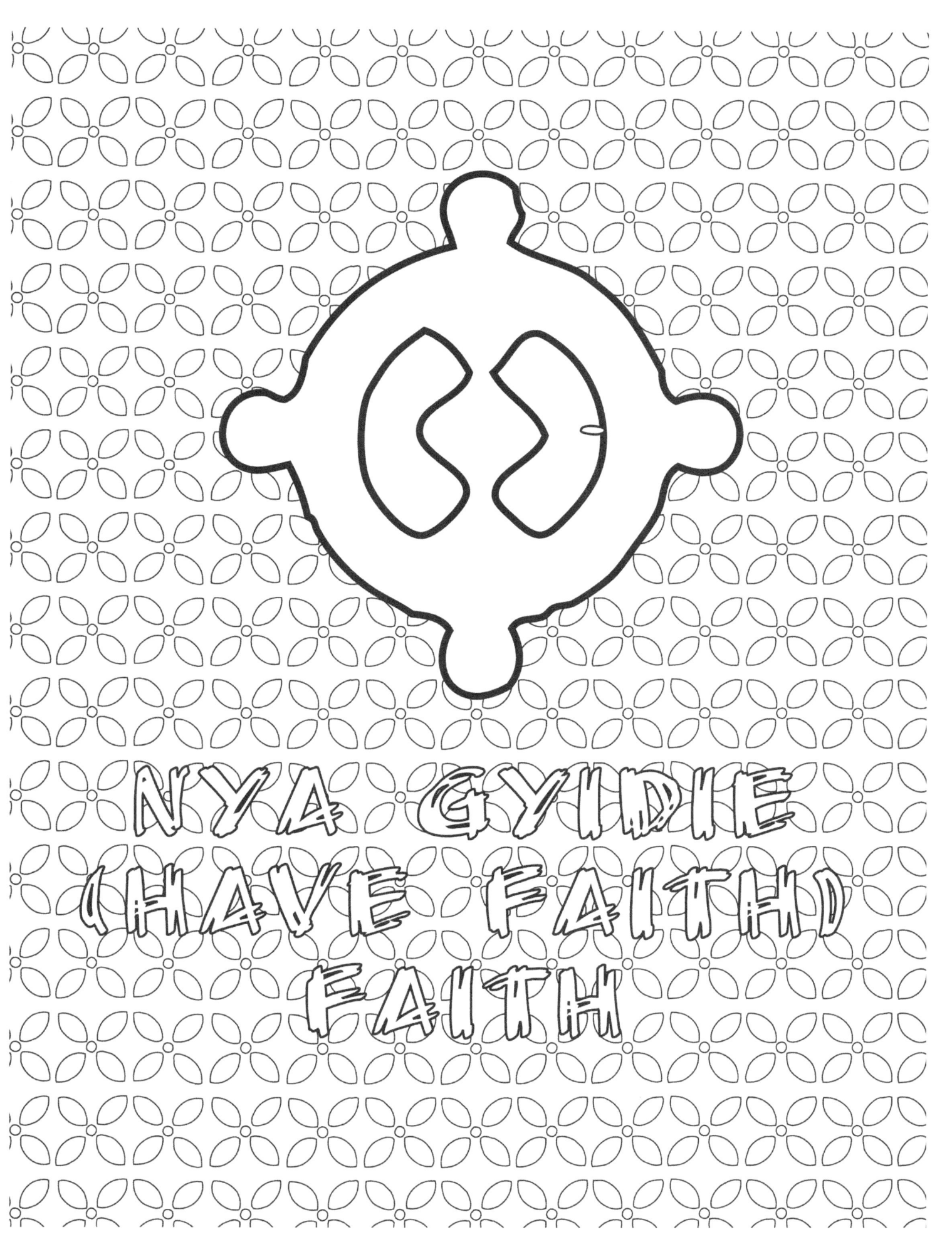

NYA GYIDIE
(HAVE FAITH)
FAITH

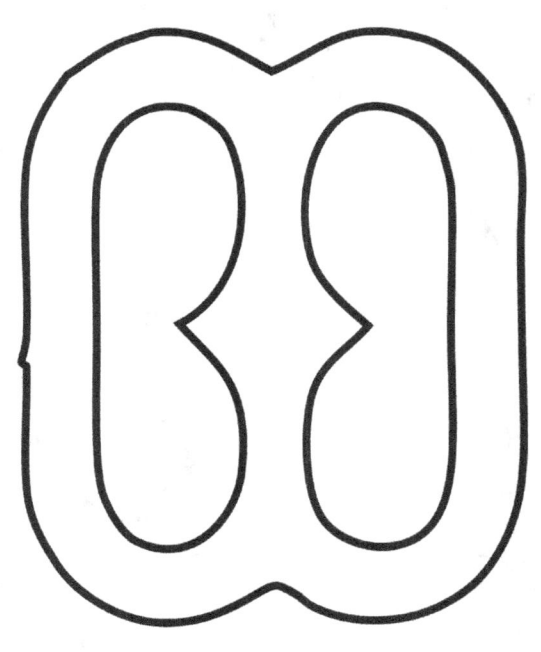

NYAME BIRIDI WO
SORO
(GOD IS WITH ME)
FAITH IN GOD

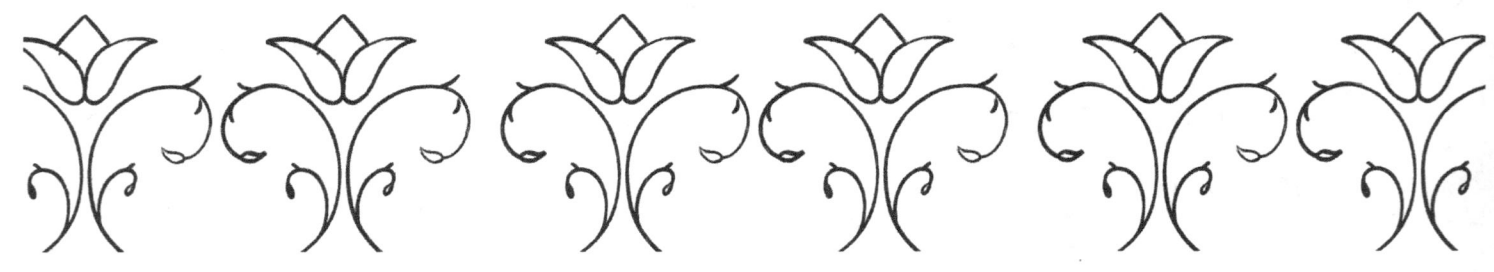

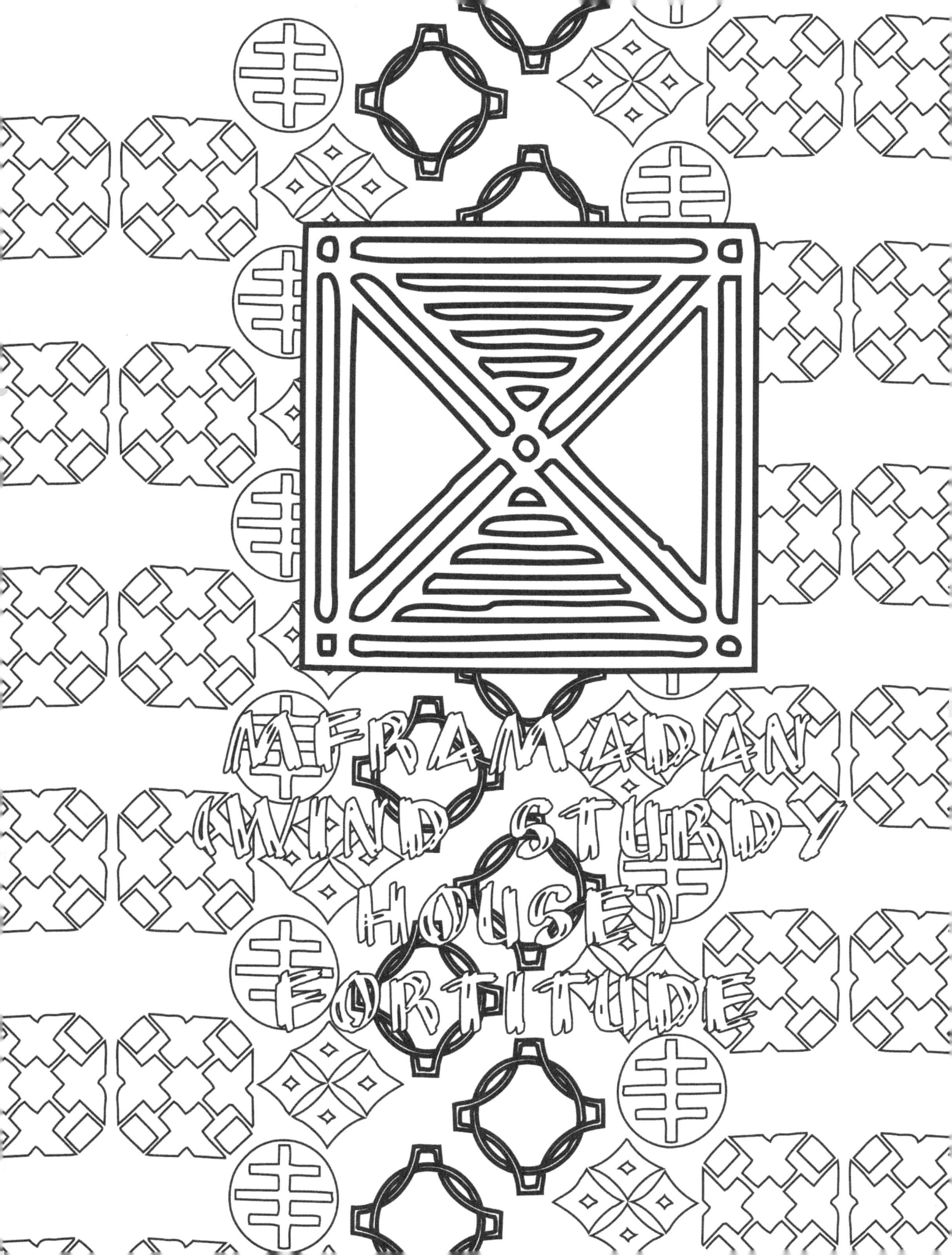

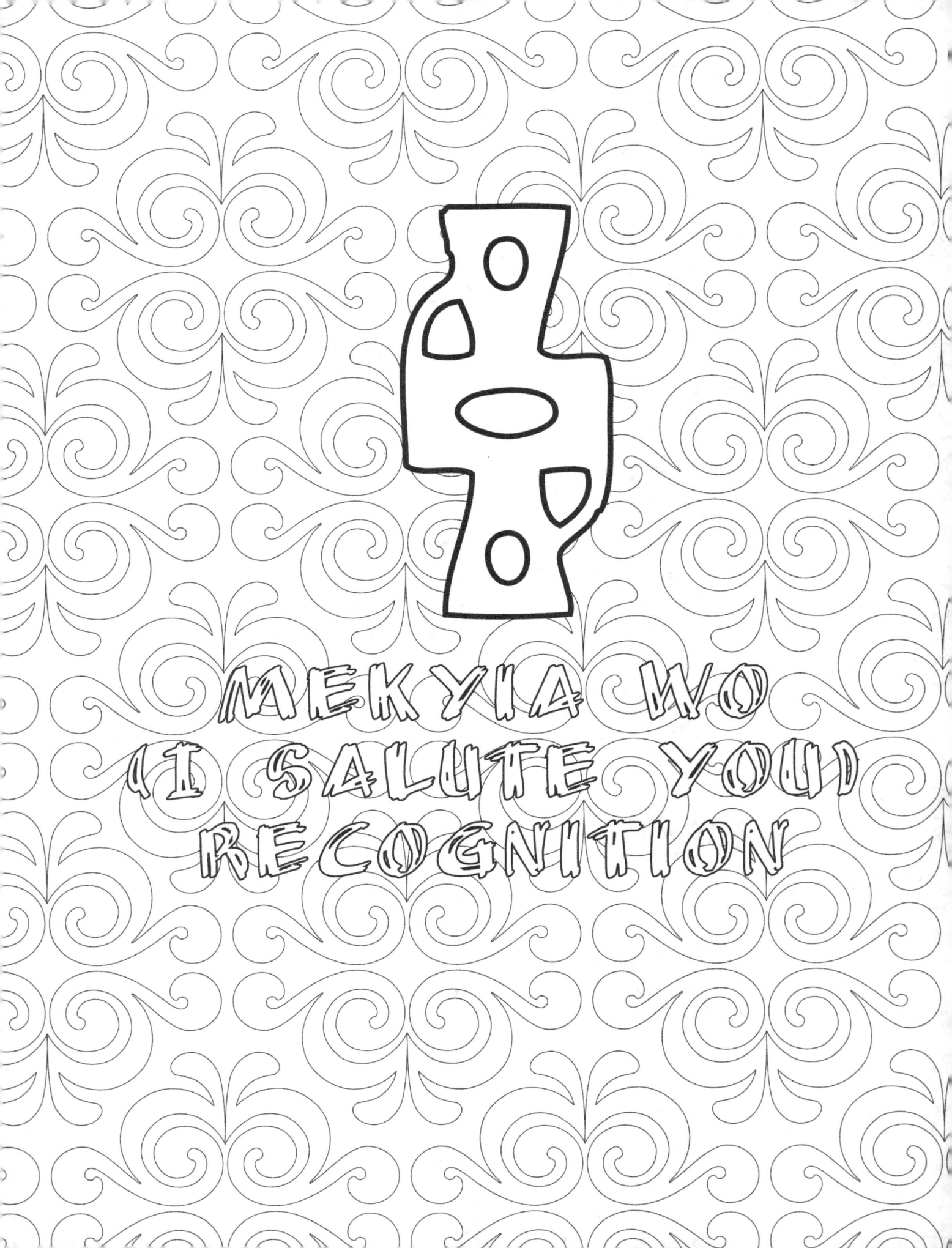

MEKYIA WO
(I SALUTE YOU)
RECOGNITION

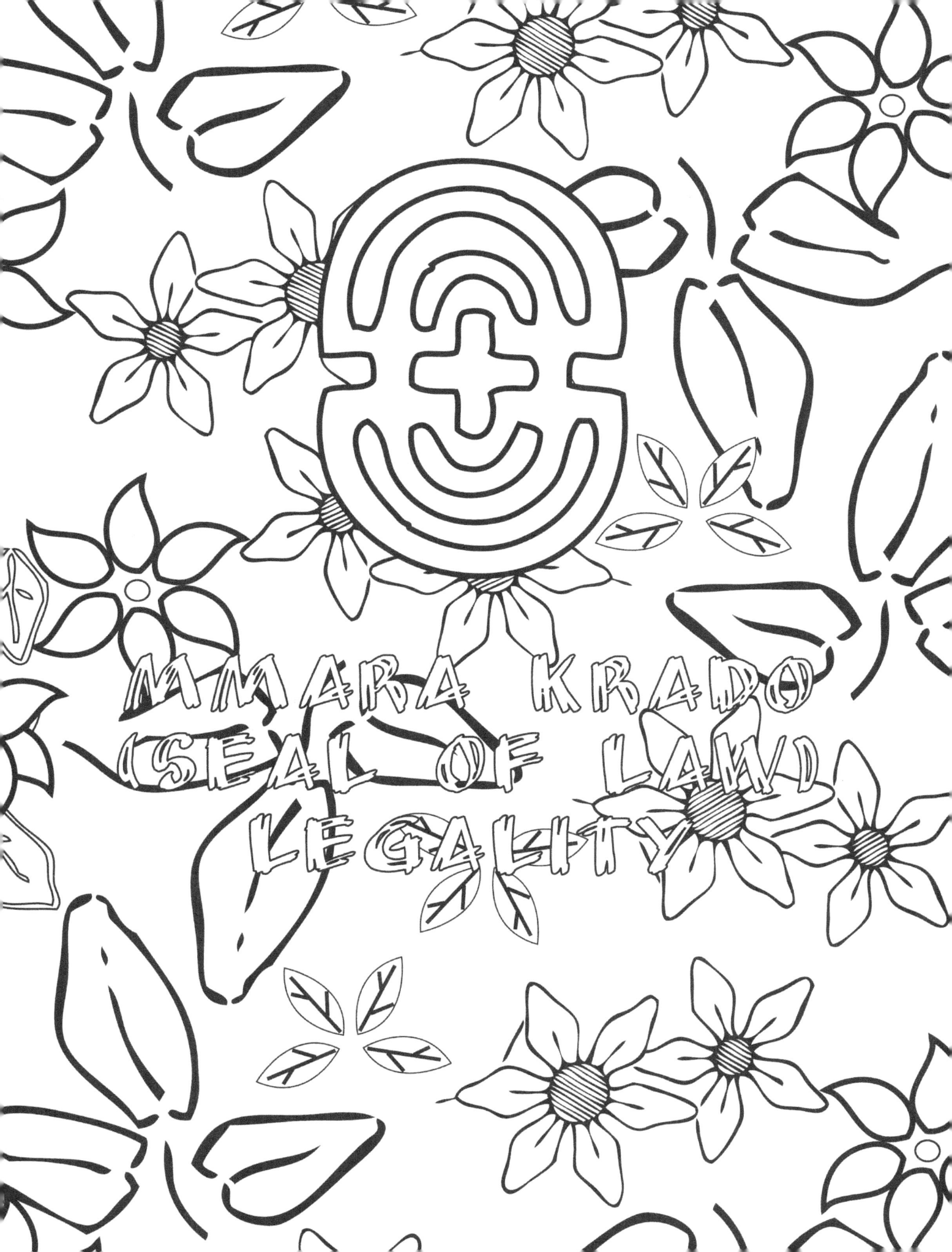

MMARA KRADO
(SEAL OF LAW)
LEGALITY

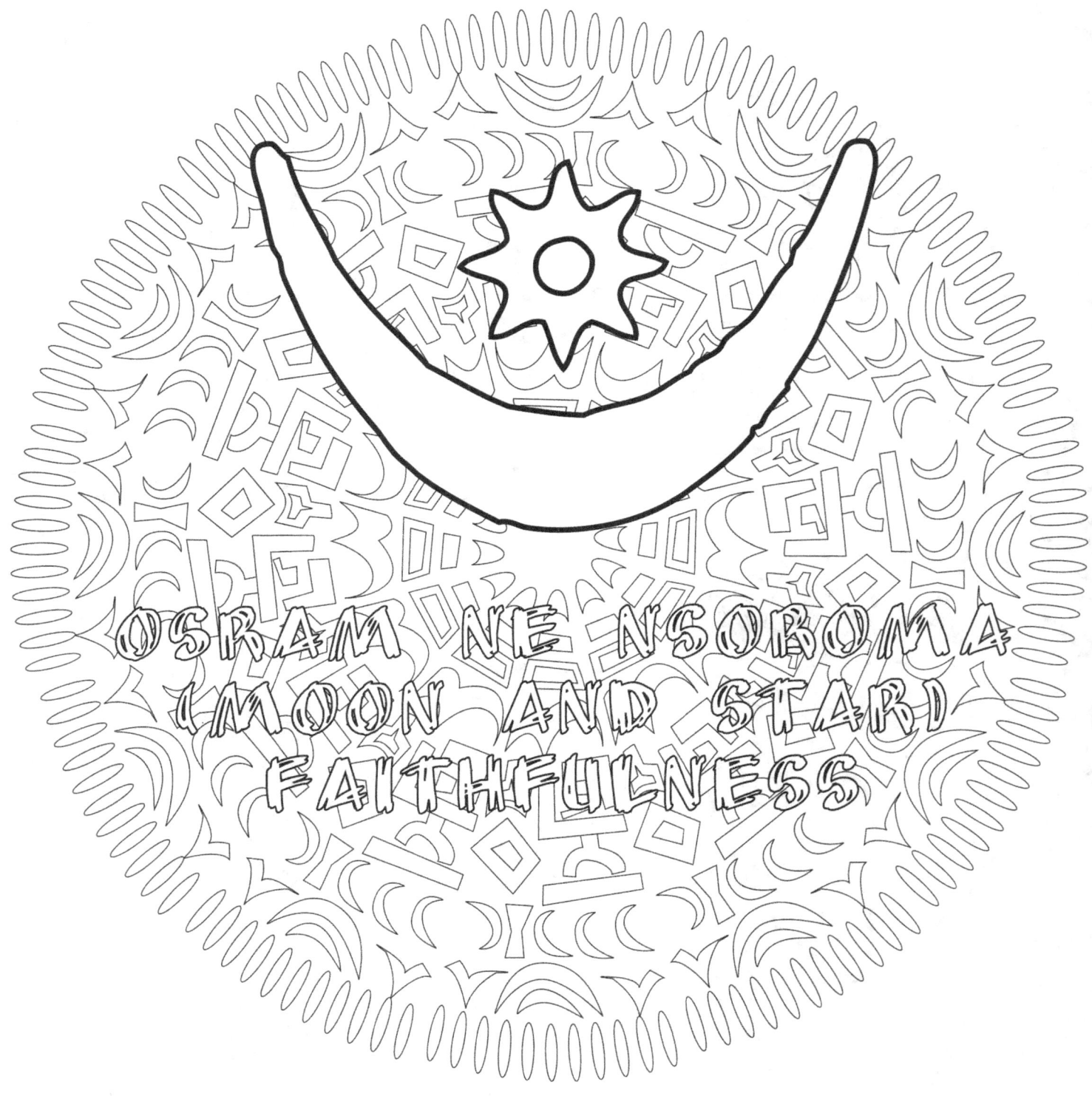

OSRAM NE NSOROMA
(MOON AND STAR)
FAITHFULNESS

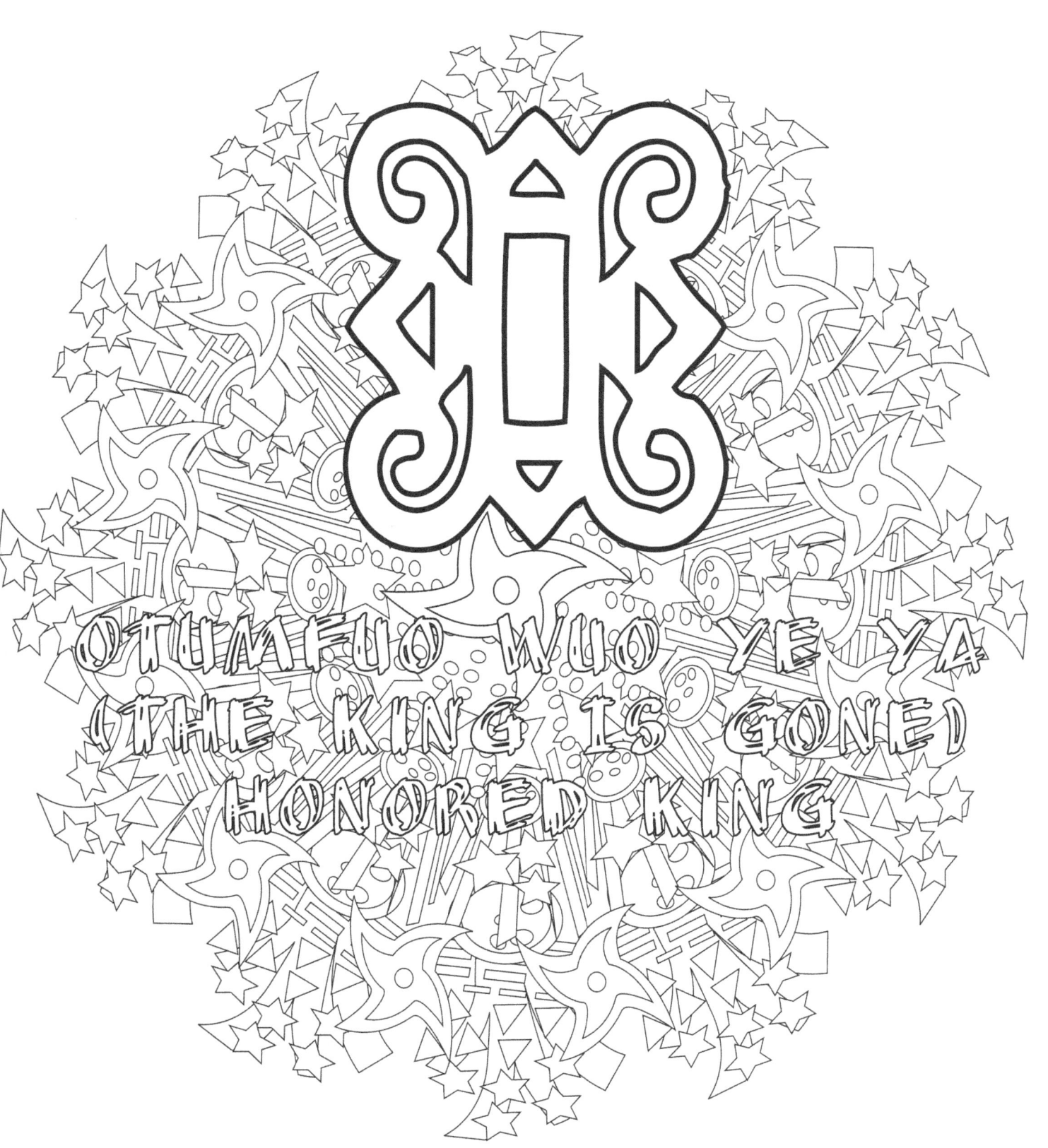

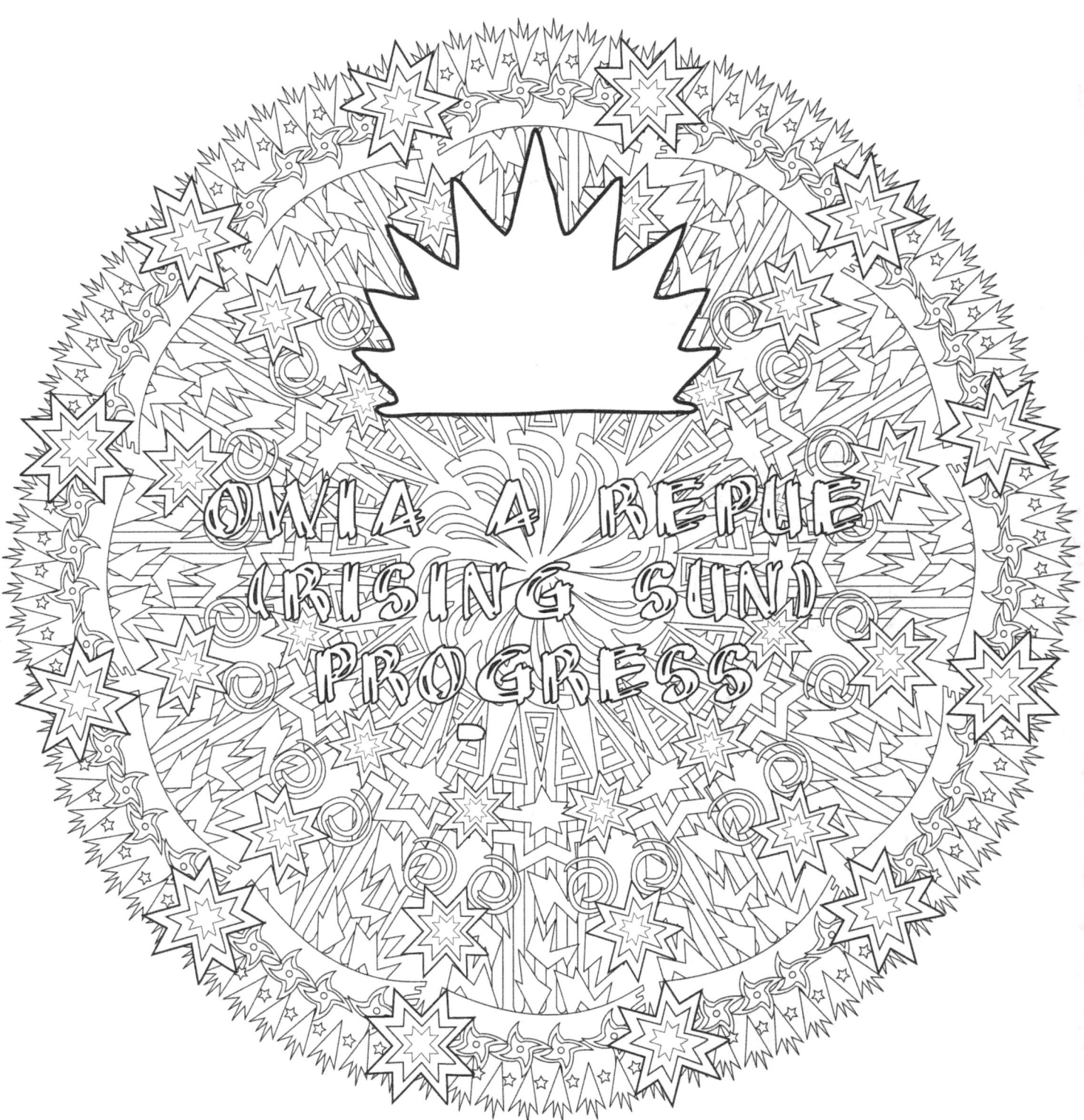

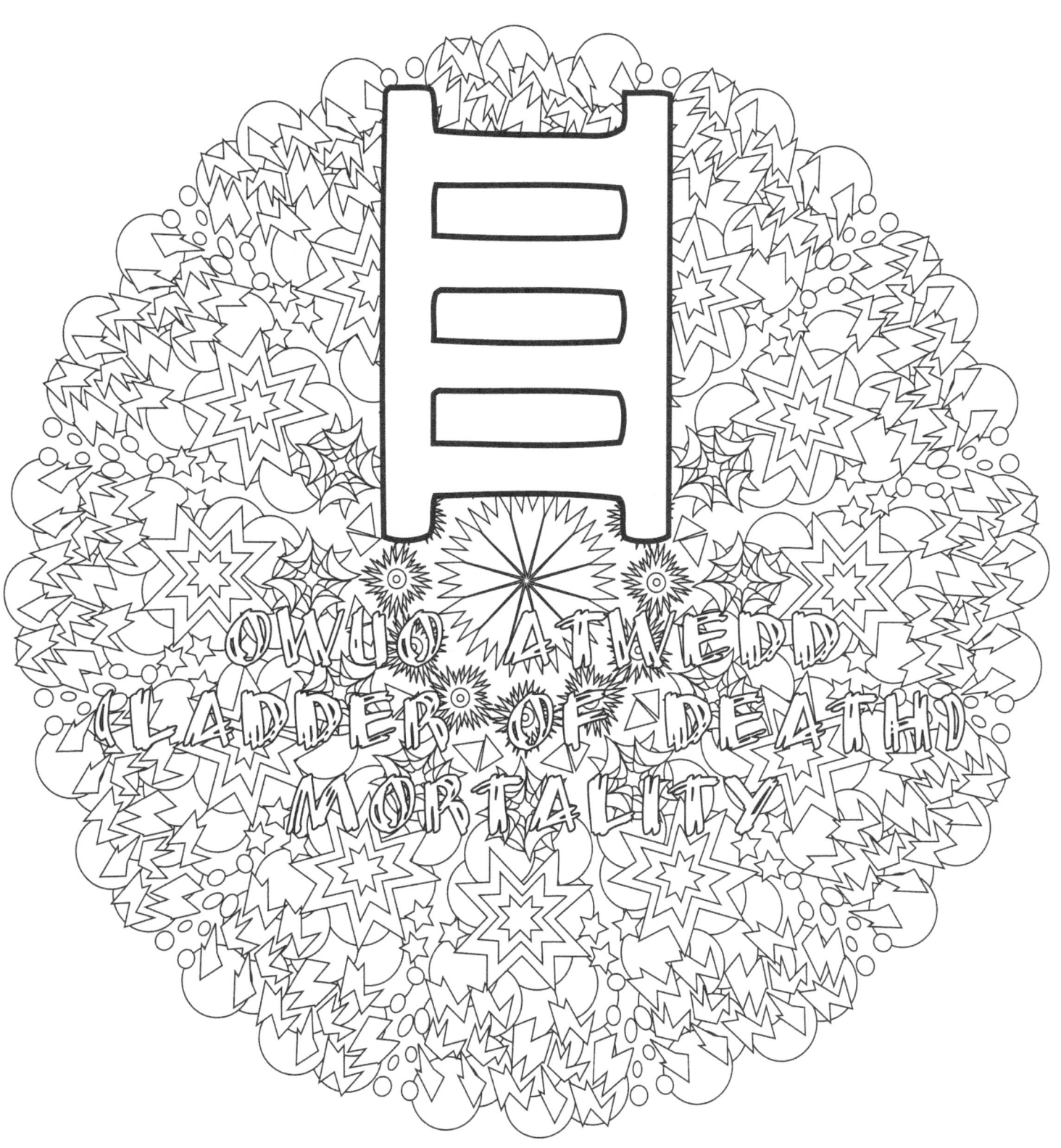

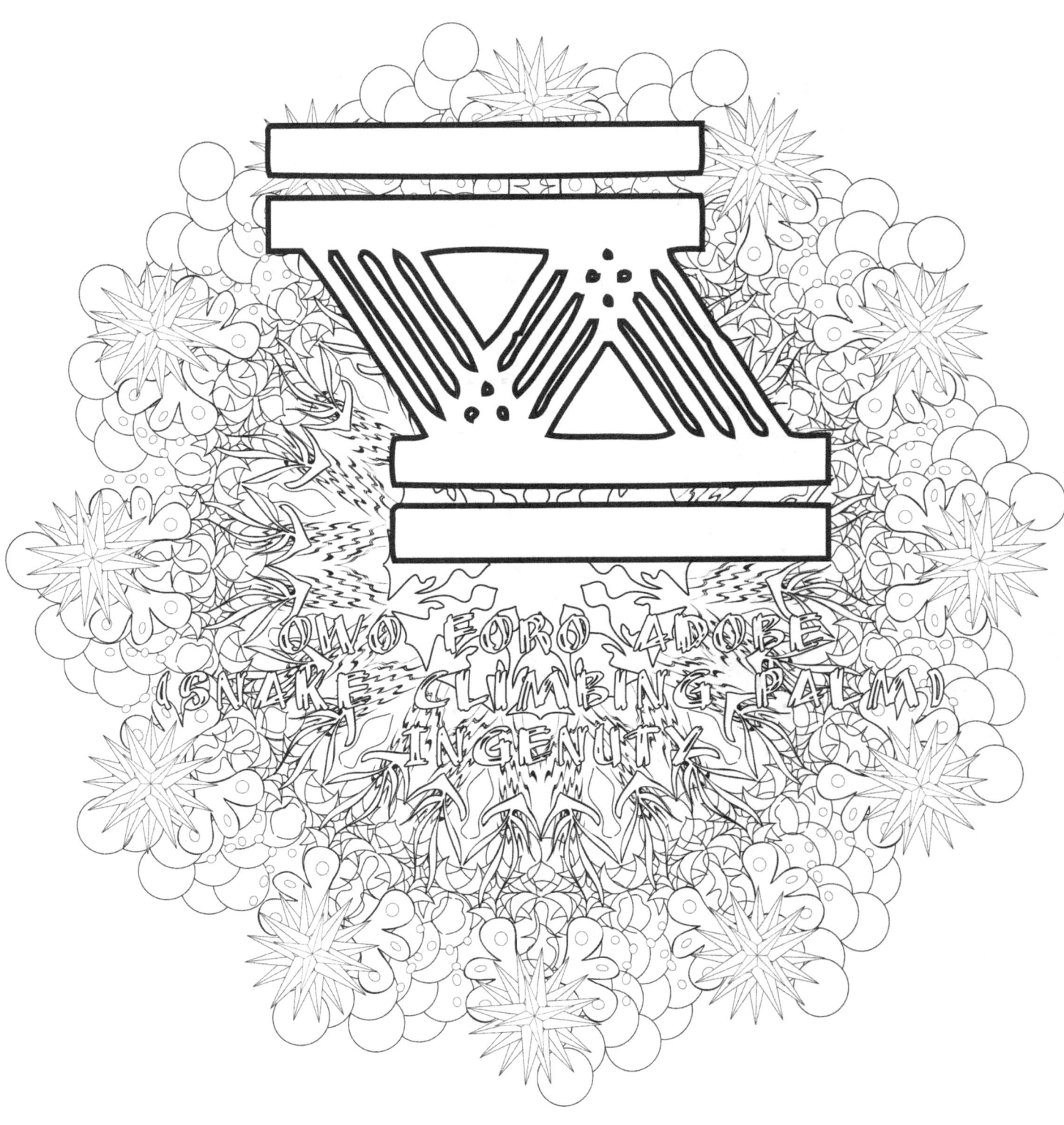

OWO EORO ADOBE
(SNAKE CLIMBING PALM)
INGENUITY

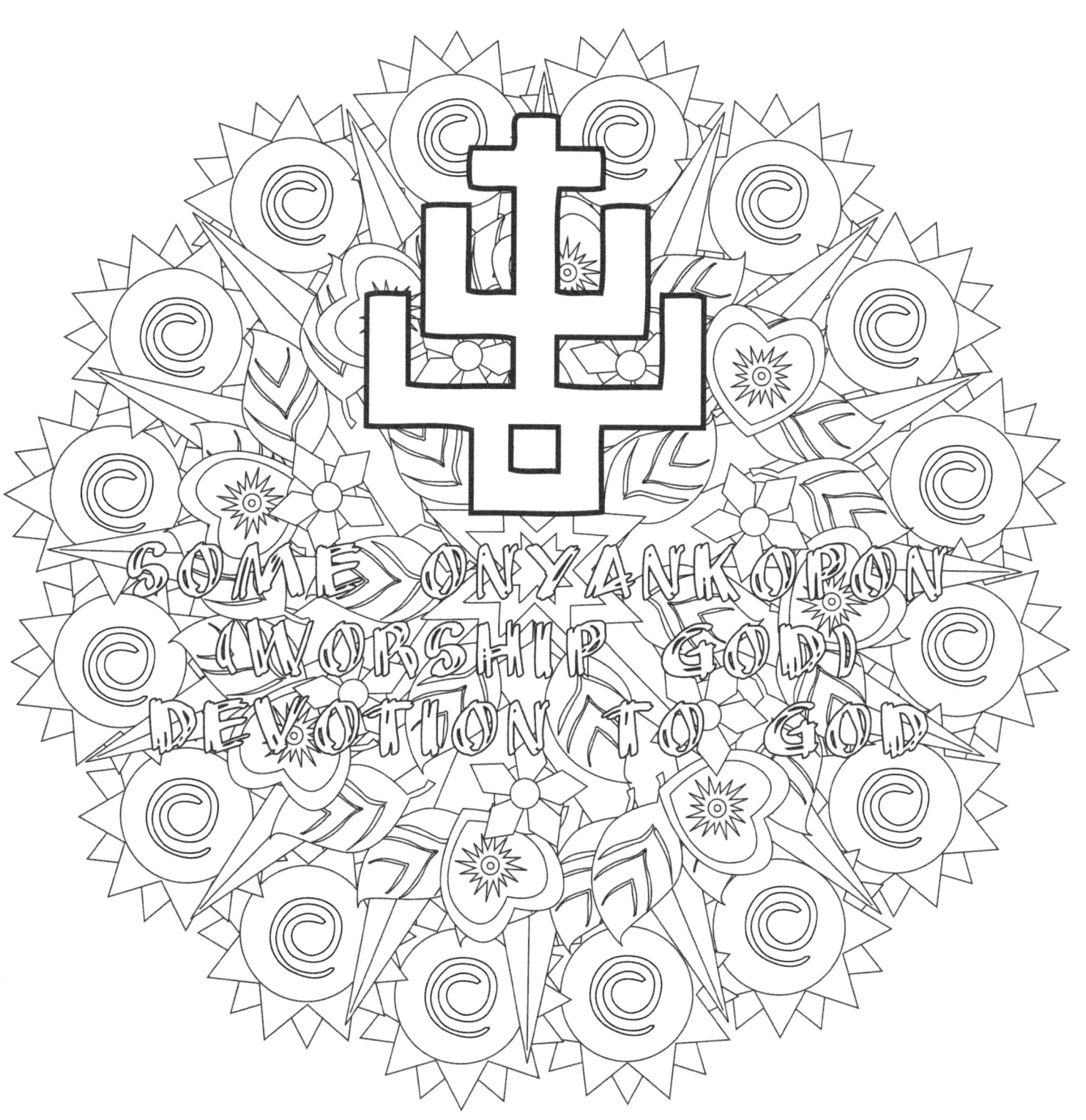

SOME ONYANKOPON
(WORSHIP GOD)
DEVOTION TO GOD

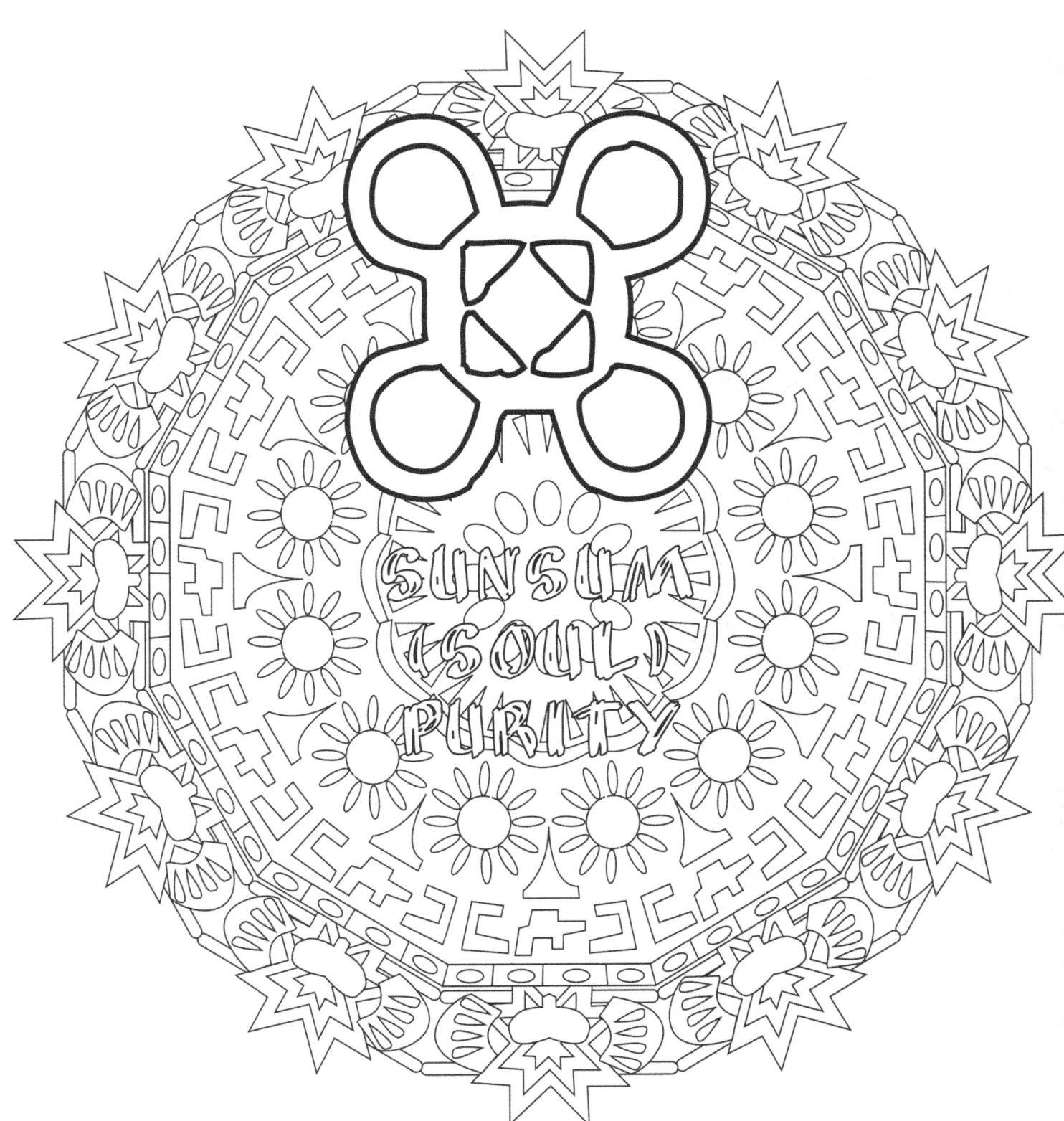

SUNSUM (SOUL) PURITY

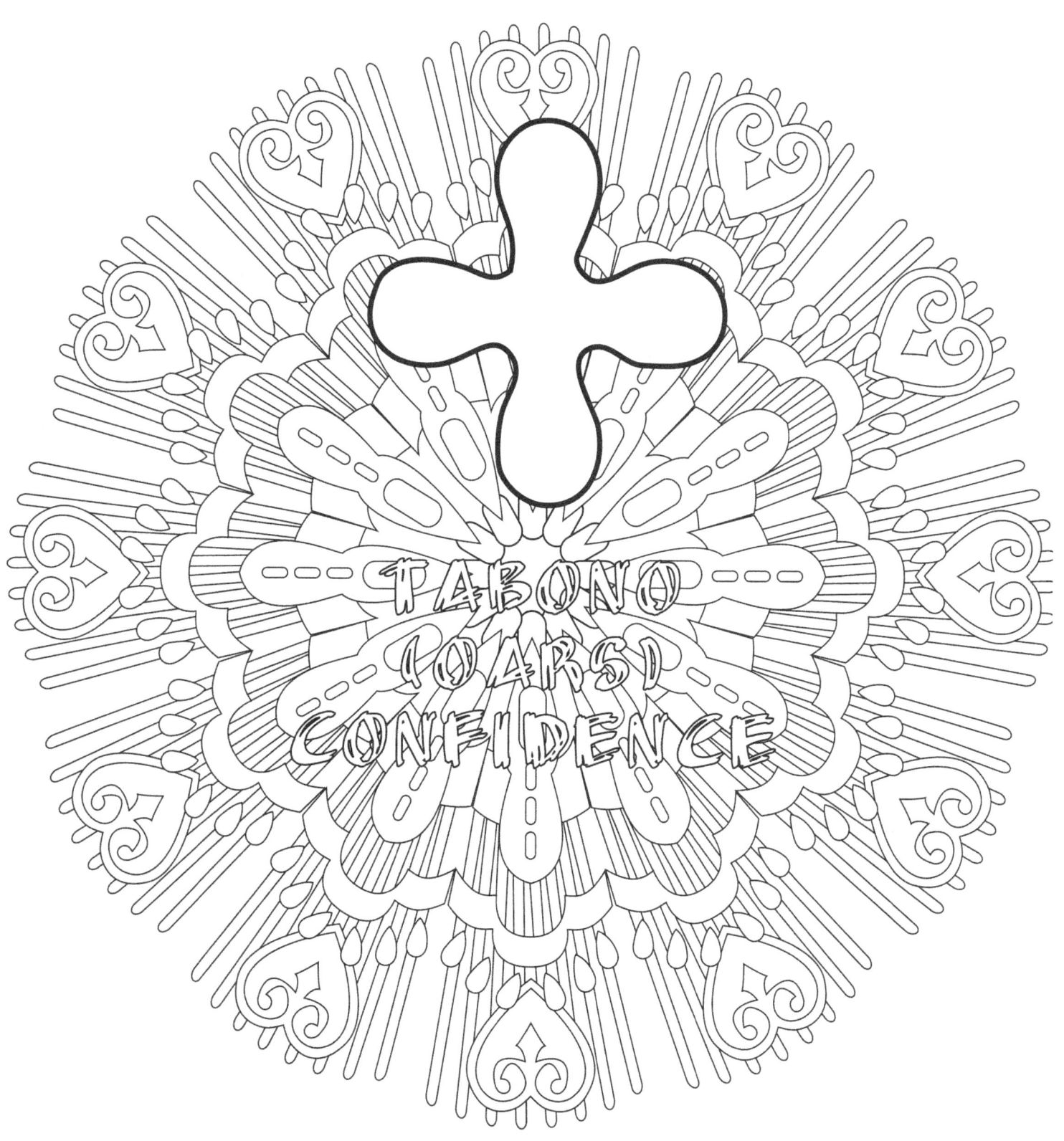

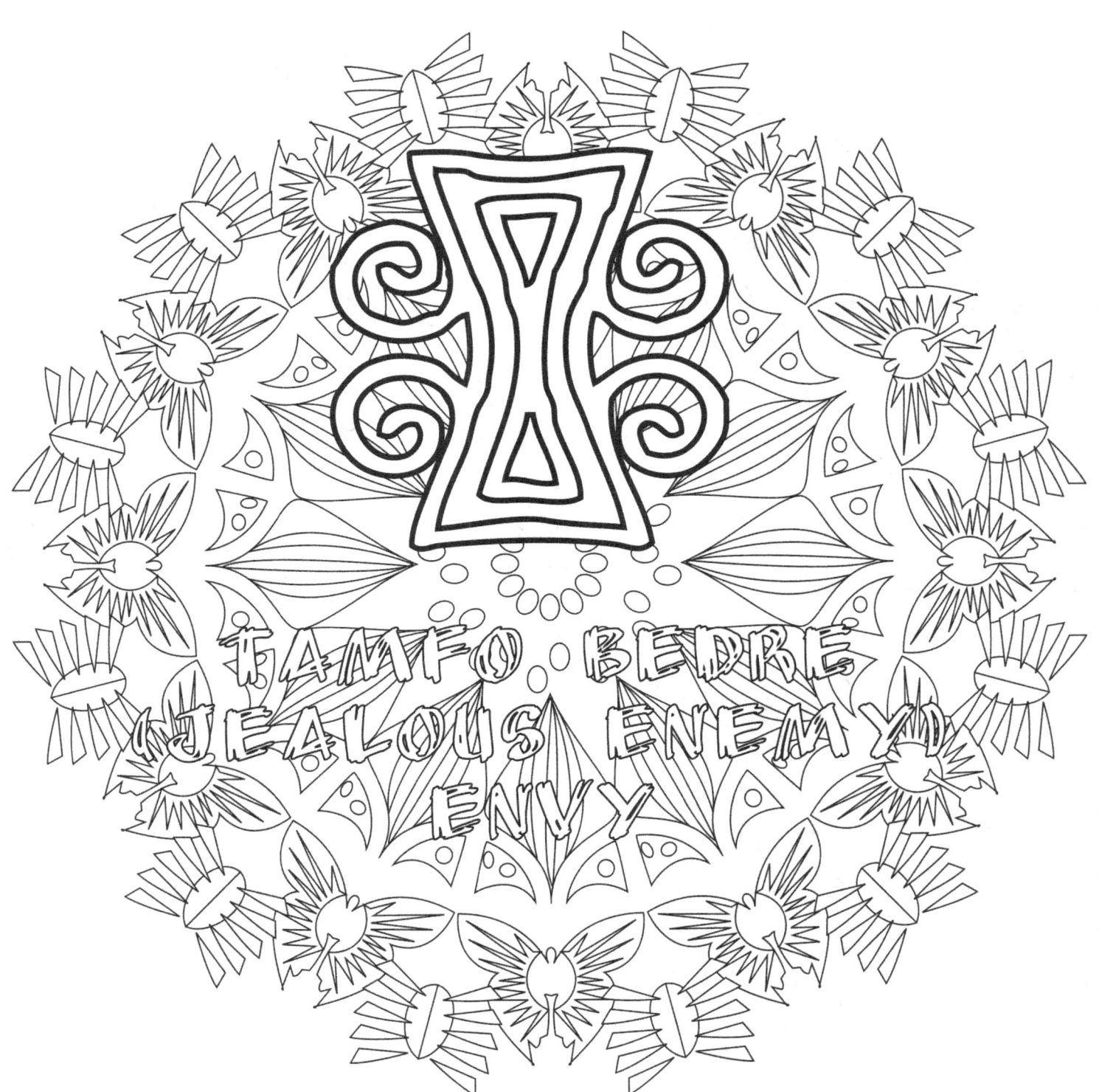

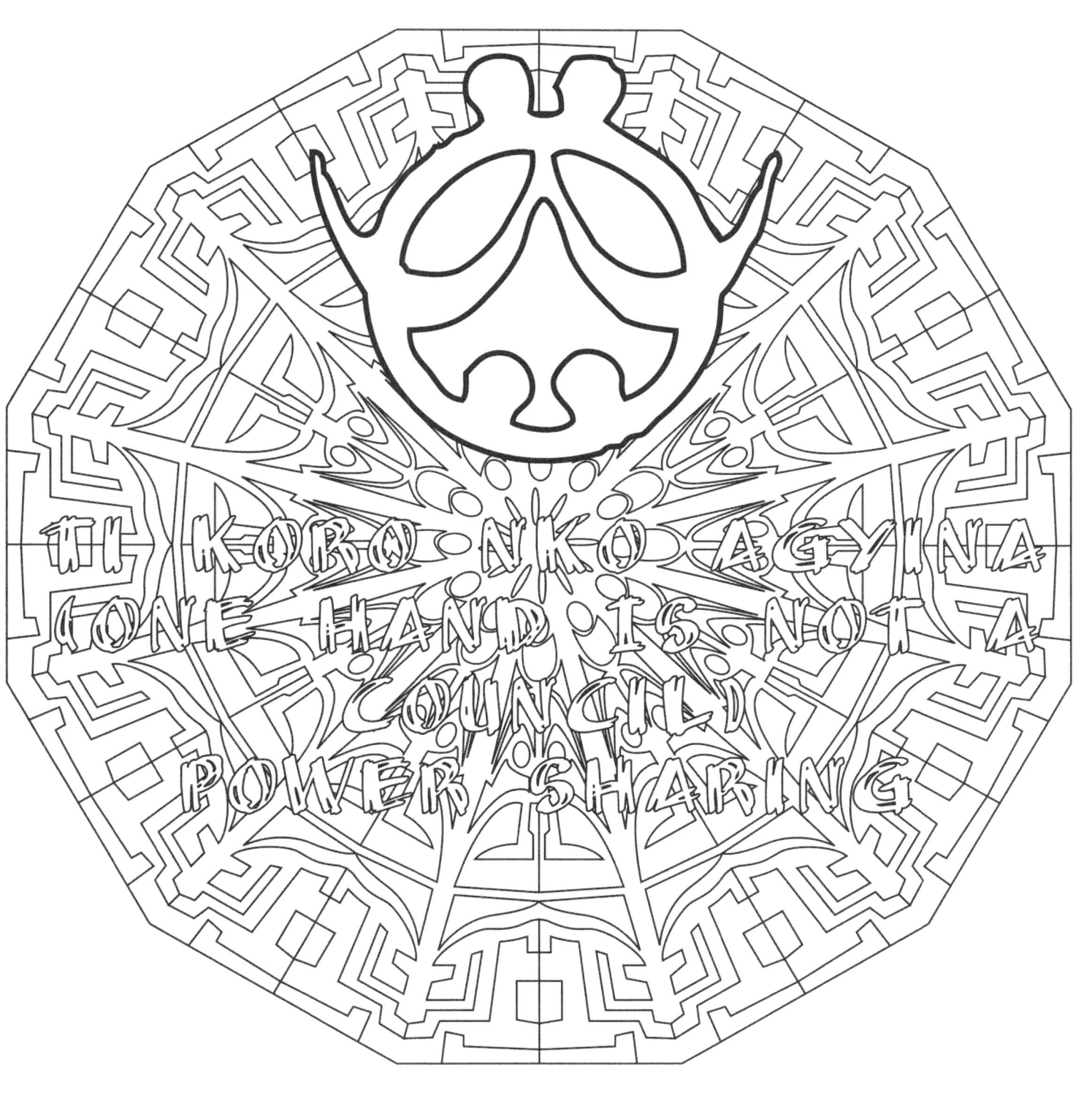